LITERATE ZEAL

PITTSBURGH SERIES
IN COMPOSITION, LITERACY, AND
CULTURE

David Bartholomae and
Jean Ferguson Carr, Editors

Janet Carey Eldred

LITERATE ZEAL

Gender and the Making of
a *New Yorker* Ethos

University of Pittsburgh Press

Published by the University of Pittsburgh Press, Pittsburgh, Pa., 15260
Copyright © 2012, University of Pittsburgh Press
All rights reserved
Manufactured in the United States of America
Printed on acid-free paper
10 9 8 7 6 5 4 3 2 1

Library of Congress Cataloging-in-Publication Data
Eldred, Janet Carey.
Literate zeal : gender, editing, and the making of a New Yorker ethos /
Janet Carey Eldred.
p. cm. — (Pittsburgh series in composition, literacy, and culture)
Includes bibliographical references and index.
ISBN 978-0-8229-4409-6 (hardcover : alk. paper)
1. Women's periodicals, American—History—20th century.   2.
Women periodical editors—United States.   3. American literature—
Periodicals—History—20th century.   4. American periodicals—
History—20th century.   5. Women—Books and reading—United
States—History—20th century.   6. Women and literature—United
States.   I. Title.
PN4879.E53 2012
070.5´10820973—dc23   2011048861

CONTENTS

PREFACE ᴄᴠ HAUTE LITERACY

"Nothing in our national life is more characteristic than our periodicals. They are as American as ice water."
Lady Editor, 1941

By its nature, editing is not highly visible work; in the case of women's work in the mid-twentieth-century United States, that work has been buried under layers of cultural history. To fully understand the symbiotic relationship between editing, high letters, and mass literacy, it is necessary to recover the work of women editors from the journalistic and literary histories that flit quickly past their editorial contributions. Editorial genius has been assigned largely to a few names: the book editor Maxwell Perkins and the *New Yorker* editors Harold Ross and William Shawn, for instance.[1] A look back at the editing profession during the mid-twentieth century reveals that more than a few highly literate women found their way into editing, and a number of them were influential. Women's publications, sometimes edited by men, likewise made important contributions to literary history and deserve study. That such a project takes us to the edge of belletrism (a term from rhetoric) and culture only underscores the deeply rhetorical nature of the work.

Let's open the critical story in 1889. In that year, Edward Bok, a young Dutch immigrant and a stenographer with few means and no higher education, transformed magazine history, creating in *Ladies' Home Journal* a middle of the road, middle-class magazine, a women's magazine with unprecedentedly large circulation numbers.[2] Some thirty-five years later, another young man, Harold Ross, a high school dropout but the son of a high school English teacher, returned from the service and together with his wife Jane Grant created the *New Yorker*, a magazine for urban, middle-class readers with upper-class aspirations.[3] A decade after Ross and Grant worked their magic, Betsy Talbot Blackwell, a young woman with no college education and the daughter of a department-store stylist, joined the staff of *Mademoiselle* and transformed it into a fashion magazine that promoted college educations for women and became a champion of serious fiction.[4]

One might believe that so-called smart magazines like the *New Yorker* appealed mostly to well-educated, upper-class men and that women's magazines appealed to middle-class women with limited educations or limited desire for intellectual stimulation.[5] Journalistic archives support a different story. Editors across a broad spectrum of large circulation magazines offered readers quality fiction and nonfiction alongside conspicuously leisured pleasures like the latest Paris fashions or the finest cigars or the sleekest automobiles. Gerald Clarke, the Capote biographer, characterized this time in the mid-twentieth-century United States as "that remarkable, but little-remembered, moment in American literary history, when fine fiction found a nest in a forest of lingerie ads" (81), as many writers of quality published in women's magazines as in publications like the *New Yorker*. The *Salon* columnist Kera Bolonik describes how many familiar names were printed between the covers of women's magazines: *Harper's Bazaar* won fifty-one O. Henry Awards and published McCullers, Wright, Steinbeck, and Welty, while *Cosmopolitan* was a well-known literary magazine, earning twelve O. Henry Awards. Magazines created a readership for a self-consciously modern "American" literature—one heavily targeted to and subscribed to by white, middle-class women.

In what appears to be a striking contradiction, an editor's long hours of mental labor enhanced another man's, or woman's, bodily leisure. But did it? Was leisure, in fact, what these publications were, to borrow a concept from Deborah Brandt, "sponsoring"?[6] Was leisure the social activity and value these editors believed they were furthering? Despite the distinctions between the accounts of editors such as Edward Bok, Harold Ross, and Betsy Talbot Blackwell—and there are many more—at the heart of these narratives are ideas about high literacy as something to be worked for, something of intrinsic value.[7]

A word about the term "literacy" is in order. Literacy is one of those value-laden terms that in theory we all agree on: who would be a proponent of *illiteracy*?[8] Yet in practice, literacy has proven a slippery term, and working definitions have ranged widely. Is it enough to be able to read a simple document and mark an "X" to serve as testament to that reading? Is the ability to read, say, the Bible sufficient, or must U.S. citizens be able to read and understand the Constitution to be considered literate? Does literacy mean only the ability to read? Must literacies be adaptive, able to travel across genres, cultures, subcultures, and media? Is a person literate if they can't use a personal computer or can't do basic math? These tussles over definitions have led scholars to conclude that literacy has as much to do with cultural expectations as it has to do with learned skills. *Literate Zeal* is concerned with a particularly narrow definition of literacy.

Throughout this book, I will use the term "haute literacy," by which I mean literature with high culture aspirations, marketed to a large reading public seeking intellectual affirmation. I use it only on certain occasions, for the purpose of invoking literature as leisured commodity and fashion. For those of us who love literature, the term might be jarring; maybe it even seems demeaning. The editors I study likewise would surely resist any notion of literature as a "raw material" that was styled, advertised, and consumed—despite textual evidence to the contrary.[9] They would also dismiss the idea that literature was merely ornamental. They saw in literature a core secular value, one with the power to bind social groups.[10] They advanced literacy by promoting it as classed leisure, a marker of refined learning and taste and conscience. One read the right material and was enriched, and at the very least an individual, at the most a culture, could be saved by the commitment to and experience of reading literature.[11]

Literate Zeal is a rhetorical book that examines the work that mid-twentieth-century editors in the United States did and the letters they sponsored. Drawing on histories of U.S. women's rhetoric and theories of literacy, I analyze archival sources to argue that editors, including many women editors, committed themselves with missionary zeal to a publishing culture in which high American letters became something to be consumed alongside haute couture. I look particularly at the expansive editorial correspondence of the longtime *New Yorker* editor Katharine S. White because the volume of work she left behind makes this story possible to tell.[12] I place her story alongside the documented work of other women editors such as Penelope Rowlands's biography of Carmel Snow, Jennifer Scanlon's biography of Helen Gurley Brown, Alexandra Subramanian's dissertation on the editorial relationship between Cyrilly Abels and Katherine Anne Porter, Michael Kreyling's examination of Eudora Welty's correspondence with her agent, Diarmuid Russell, or Sherrill Tippins's overview of the artist community February House, established by the editor George Davis.

I also examine the stories editors tell about that work through the literacy narratives they compose in biographies, memoirs, and letters. Editorial narratives invoke and reframe themes central to literacy narratives, fusing contradictory tales of domestic self-sacrifice (ennobling work for the good of society) with daring individual entrepreneurship (the American rags-to-riches story) and with the unfettered *Künstlerroman*, the story of the artist or untutored genius who leaps to the head of the most cultured class. As one might expect from a profession in which print is king—arguably, since many will claim that in this advertising-rich environment images surely ruled—literacy looms large, with self-education through literature often figuring as the magic carpet that transforms the journey from apprentice to editor. Editorial narratives feature heady stories about lives and generations transformed by literacy's promises. They play out for us the contentious, furious, and often pedantic debates over grammar and style (the subject itself might be dry, but the players who enter such debates are not). They investigate and critique our practices of consumption and underscore the link between what we consume and who we are. They elucidate the maxim "style makes the man" and make problematic that same maxim when applied to women, enumerating the many ways that style—in dress (or pants), in speech, in written sentences, in the cars we drive, the cigars we smoke, the appliances we use, the literature we enjoy—creates our image, perhaps even our very identity. Sometimes editorial narratives challenge our notions of "real identity" or "authentic experience," revealing it instead to be editorially enhanced, stylistically shaped.[13]

The form of this book has been dictated by the archives. The critical story dwells on those places where the archives are full and moves quickly, perhaps too quickly, when the archives are thin or silent. The structure of this book suggests that the archives support a full-length work on Katharine White. In fact, White's correspondence is so voluminous that Linda Davis wrote her excellent biography of White using only the record at Bryn Mawr College. The archive at the New York Public Library wasn't yet available, a collection that doubles what one could now say about White. It is tempting to focus solely on White, but I have chosen instead to present a portrait of Katharine White within a heavy, gilded frame, one so commanding it draws attention from its subject, demands to be seen and evaluated on its own terms. The last chapters, which build on the smaller vignettes in earlier chapters, will sharpen the image of Katharine White. By the end, I hope the reader will see both a specific "lady editor" (Katharine White) and the ornate frame (the gendered editorial culture in which she worked). A reader who expects an encyclopedic, comprehensive overview of the many women working in the editorial field will be disappointed; a reader who expects an uninterrupted analysis of Katharine White's editorial work will likewise be disappointed.

Why employ an organizational strategy that draws attention away from a subject as interesting as Katharine White and risk frustrating readers? The answer rests in a simple polemic. White, who worked at the *New Yorker* for almost half a century, whose work I draw on frequently in this book, and whose work I pay tribute to in the concluding two chapters, was not an exception, however much I want her to be. Feminist rhetorical histories are filled with exceptional women. We operate by venerating the unusual woman, the woman who has resisted or transcended cultural scripts and who led others to do so. The idea of "sisterhood," that politically powerful idea from radical feminism that stressed community, did not significantly trickle into an academy that privileges individual thought and accomplishment. Or so it would seem if we study rhetorical histories. To a great extent, archival recovery in rhetorical studies proceeds from an unstated obligation to prove a subject's striking worthiness for canonical inclusion. Although it is Gloria Steinem who captures our imagination as the feminist editor of the twentieth century, and for good reason, she followed in the steps of women earlier in the century. Some of these editors—and Katharine White was one of them—were college-educated women, growing into adulthood as the first generation with the right to vote, in a post-Victorian generation that created some space for women's professional aspirations. Still, even those who entered the profession without college degrees, via the fashion houses, retail work, or secretarial positions, even those who did not align themselves with feminist causes, understood at the very least the financial advantages of appealing to younger, more liberal-minded college women, and they found a college-educated workforce of women ready to advance the cause of high style.

Labels such as "exception" obscure this collective history and limit our understanding of early to mid-twentieth-century women rhetors, for whom ordinariness offered both a point of identification and the possibility of enriched lives. It is this latter point we have missed, overinvesting instead in the framework of repressive conformity that presumably defined the 1950s. Ordinariness by default becomes a kind of Stepford existence, rote roles in a patriarchal script. I am, of course, painting in broad strokes. I don't want to imply that all radical critiques of bourgeois conformity were without value. Those same late twentieth-century feminists who promoted sisterhood also celebrated, and justly so, those women who resisted oppressive conformity and changed oppressive work, home, and health environments.

This is all to the good. However, over the last decade or so, several feminist historians have made the case that scholars have overdrawn the mid-twentieth-century postwar mainstream, creating a bifurcation between women as social activists and women as domestic automatons. The "way we were," the June Cleaver in pearls, argues Stephanie Coontz, is perhaps more accurately the "way we never were," a proposition supported in her analysis of demographic and economic data. The result of this overformulation has been the erasure of another history, one that speaks to a large group of women who were, strictly speaking, neither activists nor conformists. Coontz and other feminist historians make a compelling case for us to revisit our commonplaces about mid-twentieth-century women.[14]

The archives that support such a full recording of Katharine White's life also offer the opportunity for a partial glimpse of other women editors and their work. Whenever possible, it is this glimpse I illuminate, shedding light not just on White, but on the women surrounding her. For example, one can look at White's schooling and early career in the context of other women students. Katharine graduated from Bryn Mawr in 1914 and joined the swelling ranks of women writing and editing for mass-circulation publications. She was part of the 20 percent of Bryn Mawr graduates who chose writing or editorial jobs in the 1920s when opportunities opened. She was like other women who transformed hourly or weekly editorial work into careers. She was a part of a group of women in the early to mid-twentieth century for whom it became normative, part and parcel of the "gendered imagination," to envision educated women as career citizens.[15] White came of age in a time period that was redefining the ideal female citizen. In this emerging paradigm, the ideal female citizen was psychologically and financially independent. She was educated and employed in a career; she had a civic duty to make a mark in the sciences, the humanities, or public service. She was not seen as extraordinary or exceptional in her aspirations, schooling, dress, speech, or manners; instead, she was part of a group who collectively formed an exception, one of a large number of women who, as Katherine Adams documents in *A Group of Their Own*, left private spaces and moved into classrooms and then into the workforce, a workforce greatly changed by the explosion of print culture.

The promotion of careers in writing and the sponsorship of high letters perhaps created, or perhaps only synchronized with nicely, a particular historical articulation of the career woman. Many of these women found themselves employed in the growing middlebrow publication industry, "aimed at making literature and other forms of 'high' culture available to a wide reading public" through book clubs, digests, anthologies, great book series, and book reviews (Rubin xi). This middlebrow culture formed an important part of twentieth-century U.S. literary history.

My purpose in studying editorial narratives is not to create a whitewashed cultural history based on the vagaries and selectivity of memoir or individual biographies. Rather, I look at these records of lived experience, alongside the remnants of work (memos, letters, markups), with the intent of explicating the role that class publications played in the making and sustaining of a certain kind of literacy, a vibrant American belles-lettres.[16] I use the term "belles-lettres" purposefully, to invoke its rhetorical history and mark it as a trope of literacy. I use it over objections that it is simply a fancy term for literature. The *Oxford English Dictionary* (OED) defines belles-lettres as a "vaguely-used term, for-

merly taken sometimes in the wide sense of 'the humanities,'
literæ humaniores; sometimes in the exact sense in which we now
use 'literature.'" In contemporary usage, the term is a synonym
for literature, although, as the OED describes "it is now generally
applied (when used at all) to the lighter branches of literature."
It is the critical story of this apotheosis of light periodical literature into literature to be marketed as haute literacy, and the degree to which class editors, particularly women, saw this as central to their mission that I narrate here. This historical revision is
useful, even necessary, because it counters a liberal elitism that
created an imaginary great divide between certain kinds of literature, devaluing women's editorial work and, by extension, rhetorical and literary achievements.[17]

LITERATE ZEAL

INTRODUCTION ∽ LITERACY, GENDER, AND THE RHETORICAL WORK OF EDITING

The following chapters endeavor to set forth the careers of some representative women now prominent in the editorial field, and tell not only their experiences, but their opinions and advice to young women wishing to follow similar courses today. It has been obviously impossible to list, much less to interview, all of even the topflight editors, but the following chapters aim at presenting an accurate and typical cross section of the magazine publishing field and its opportunities for women.

Lady Editor

Editorially, there was nothing Miss Cousins couldn't and didn't do. She could have been editor-in-chief of any magazine. When I had the opportunity to make her one, I didn't, convinced the political stresses she despised would depress her. She should have had the chance. I disappointed her. And, in the end, myself also.

Herbert R. Mayes, *The Magazine Maze*

Dueling Histories

In order to fully appreciate the work that women editors did in the mid-twentieth century, feminist researchers must reappraise the damning critique of women's magazines so forcefully argued in 1963 by the American feminist Betty Friedan in *The Feminine Mystique*. It is a daunting task. Friedan composes a formidable list of cultural agents who created an environment for women that denied them opportunities for forging individual identities.

The list includes Freudian psychotherapists and popularizers, educators, anthropologists (Mead in particular), and sexologists. Leading that pack, however, are those in the magazine trade who created and sustained the dream image of the suburban housewife. Friedan, who wrote for women's magazines, enacted tough indictments, including herself in the pool of criminals: "A geiger counter clicked in my own inner ear when I could not fit the quiet desperation of so many women into the picture of the modern American housewife that I myself was helping to create, writing for the women's magazines" (34). Friedan locates 1949 as the year that the "feminine mystique began to spread through the land" (43).

Friedan and other feminists of the 1970s, including Susan Brownmiller, acted on this powerful critique. In her memoir, *In Our Time*, Brownmiller recounts radical feminists' actions against such publications:

> I proposed that we target one of the big women's magazines that had remained immune to changing times.... [E]ditors warred over circulation and ad pages while they pushed a happy homemaker line from the 1950s that was white-bread formulaic. In a make-believe world of perfect casseroles and Jell-O delights, marriages failed because wives didn't try hard enough, single-parent households did not exist, and women worked outside the home not because they wanted to, or to make ends meet, but to "earn extra income in your spare time." The deceitful ideology discouraged the full range of women's ambitions. (83–84)

The rest, as they say, is herstory: the group "picked an invasion date" (Brownmiller, *In Our Time* 84), and in March of 1970, "representatives" of the Women's Liberation Movement "invaded" the offices of *Ladies' Home Journal* and asserted an impressive set of "nonnegotiable demands."[1] They executed their plan, defining for a time, *the* feminist position on women's magazines: real feminists didn't read *Ladies' Home Journal* or *Vogue*, magazines representing the "decidedly masculine preserve of feature journalism." By the 1970s, women's magazines were something to picket, in large part because they were being edited primarily by men: "From *Seventeen* to *Good Housekeeping* all the slick publications instructing their readers in feminine arts were run by men, except *McCall's* where Shana Alexander was new on the job, and *Cosmo*, the brainchild of Helen Gurley Brown" (Brownmiller, *In Our Time* 83).

It's difficult to reconcile this history with the enthusiasm expressed in *Lady Editor*,[2] a career guide written in 1941, but recovery work in feminist media studies provides the olive branch: *Lady Editor* is part of a tradition that evaluates and celebrates the fraught relationship between women and the publications they produce, ponder, and consume. In a little under one hundred pages, Knight offers her snapshot of women in editing history: "In 1828 when Sarah Josepha Hale left the 'keeping room' of her house in the little New England town of Newport to take over the editorship of the *Women's Magazine*, which later was to combine with *Godey's Lady's Book* and become the revered forerunner of scores of women's magazines, she probably never suspected, astute though she was, that she was inaugurating a field of activity for women which would offer employment to thousands" (*Lady Editor* 90–91).

Lady Editor is clearly a conscious attempt to create a feminist media history. In 1987, when Janice Winship published *Inside Women's Magazines*, a project similar to *Lady Editor*, she acknowledged her discomfort when "[a]dmitting within feminist circles that [she] was doing research on—of all things—women's magazines" (xiii). It is only recently that feminism has once again embraced, albeit tentatively, the world of women's periodicals. With the publication of Jennifer Scanlon's *Bad Women Go Everywhere: The Life of Helen Gurley Brown* (2009), one might even argue that feminist scholars no longer register tentativeness.

In *Understanding Women's Magazines*, Anna Gough-Yates provides a succinct overview of the trajectory of feminist media studies. Groundbreaking studies in the 1960s and 1970s largely "focused on women's magazines at a textual level, and analyzed them for their ideological content" (Gough-Yates 6). While such studies galvanized feminist criticism and institutionalized it in the academy—no small feat—they tended to present a monologic polemic: women's "magazines offered 'unreal', 'untruthful' or 'distorted images of women,'" period (Gough-Yates 8).[3] Later critics, following the influential work of reader-response pioneer Janice Radway, began to employ reader-response methodologies. Both of these approaches—textually based and reception oriented—complicated the earlier "women's magazines are sexist" polemic. Instead, these later studies scrutinized "the relationships between feminism, femininity and women's magazines, exploring the extent to which these texts foster dominant forms of femininity among their readers" (Gough-Yates 13). They came to conclusions various enough to offer only "the sheer unpredictability of the relationship between reader and text" (Gough-Yates 14). Readers skipped or embraced various features and, insofar as they were making conscious choices, used them for differing rhetorical purposes, varying from self-help to fantasy.

Subsequent studies work to further illuminate the dimensions of the relationships between women's magazines and their readership. Gough-Yates, for instance, positions herself with an emerging group of scholars interested in the conditions of production, an area only lightly explored. She is motivated in part by the work of Marjorie Ferguson, who once worked for a woman's weekly and whose work combines insider knowledge of the industry with academic analysis. Without a fuller narrative about production, Gough-Yates posits, we are left with only a partial, distant picture, including an incomplete understanding of the women who are industry insiders, women educated in feminist sexual politics, women who enjoy magazines but who have had university courses that taught critical analysis of media and feminist history. These women are in many cases self-identified feminists. In the almost two decades since Winship gingerly admitted her guilty research pleasures, the trajectory has become clear: feminist media critics now read nineteenth- and twentieth-century women's magazines as sites "where women's oppression was debated and negotiated, rather than merely reinforced" (Gough-Yates 10). As Rita Felski summarizes, radical feminists of the late 1970s (thankfully) sparked significant cultural and literary debates, but "to beat what is by now a very tired drum," all feminists do not "claim that literature either causes or simply reinforces the oppression of women" (11–12). Instead, feminist media criticism asks that "we rethink the dichotomy between women's magazines as mythmakers and feminists as unveilers" (Moskowitz 67).

While there are clearly differences between radical feminism of the 1970s and the latent, conflicted mainstream feminism of women's magazines, there are also surprising points of commonality, which are difficult to see when we look back in time rather than forward in time, when we start with Susan Brownmiller, rather than Sarah Josepha Hale or Ruth Adams Knight. Brownmiller's memoir, for instance, reframes another history, *American Story* (1968), a memoir written thirty years earlier by Bruce Gould and Beatrice Blackmar Gould about their tenure as coeditors of *Ladies' Home Journal*. The Goulds, as Brownmiller would later do in her memoir, placed women's sexual issues front and center. The feminist media scholars Alison Bashford and Carolyn Strange describe the work done by the Goulds' *Ladies' Home Journal* and other similar magazines: "During the first half of the twentieth century magazines played a leading role in the transmission of sexual knowledge, for they were much more accessible to working-class people than were expensive texts. Among the existing genres, it was the women's magazine, not the medical or specialized journal, that was most important. The advice column, a typical feature of the women's magazine, became the vehicle for mass sex education" (74).

As evidence, Bashford and Strange—and Mary Ellen Zuckerman before them—point to the *Ladies' Home Journal* survey in 1938 that queried readers about whether "they wanted to read more about such sensitive matters as divorce and birth control" (qtd. in Bashford and Strange 84–85). The readers apparently did.⁴ In other words, women reading the Ladies' Home Journal in 1938 understood that the quality of women's lives was deeply dependent on the ability to make informed decisions about relationships and reproduction.

In her preface to In Our Time, Brownmiller articulates her purpose: "I set out to write this memoir with a sense of urgency because I could see that much of the movement's story had already been lost or distorted" (10). Likely feeling the heat of growing radical feminism, the Goulds also write to set the record right. They proudly tell of the activist agenda they engaged over the course of their editorial partnership. Although they conceded that they were "not exactly crusaders," they enthusiastically explain how they indulged Beatrice's "bluestocking" tendencies (Gould 172): They changed the "absurd company rule that all secretaries and female clerks who married must quit their jobs immediately" (Gould 160); they worked to achieve editorial independence from their advertisers (Gould 170); they were early campaigners against the dangers of smoking (Gould 182–83); they used their growing power to introduce "distasteful" subjects such as "pregnancy and childbirth" (Gould 173); they rallied behind the cause of high maternal death rates; they continued Bok's policy of openly discussing venereal diseases (Gould 190); and they promoted the "hushed-up subject of birth control, expressing in print for the first that a majority of American women definitely approved family planning," angering both the Catholic church and advertisers in the process (Gould 195). They spoke as champions and as representatives of women's pursuit of full, happy citizenship. There is no mistaking Brownmiller for Beatrice Gould or vice-versa. Brownmiller might claim that she is articulating the "woman's point of view," but she would never write that she "found her true self in marriage rather than in the responsibilities and rewards of her position" (Gould 11), a sentiment Gould feels comfortable asserting. Gould considered herself a "bluestocking," but she did not sympathize with the newer generation of feminists. In her words: "Absolute equality was our view—with the male slightly more equal than the female, but both equally enjoying the unequal arrangement." Like many, she took cheap shots against what she perceived as radical feminists and saw her magazine as standing in defense against them: "We never let the hulking, overbearing, Amazon type get by" (Gould 201).

Gould and Brownmiller were not, literally or figuratively, on the same page. In pointing to their similarities, I am not claiming their sameness. Still, each woman uses memoir to write her *professional* history into a history of women's rights and privileges. Each insists on her place in a progressive history; each claims to be an authoritative narrator. Brownmiller explains on her website, "*In Our Time: Memoir of a Revolution* is not movement hagiography, nor is it 'a balanced history' written by someone with access to library archives but far removed from the actual events" (Brownmiller, "In Our Time"). In other words, *she was there.* The Goulds, too, authorize this insider view, insisting on the truth— and rhetorical stance—that memoir can contribute to institutional and cultural history. In the absence of memoirs, histories based on letters often make the same revelatory promise.

In one other central way, women graduating college in the 1920s and entering the work force were not so different from the radical women who would follow later in the century. Women in the mid-twentieth century exhibited the same tenuous intellectual, aesthetic, and gendered relationships to the publication material they consumed and produced. The central questions asked by researchers in feminist media studies can thus be mapped onto historical rhetorical studies: Can such periodicals lead to "the formation of fantasy and imagined 'new selves" (Gough-Yates 13), or must they necessarily participate in the process of patriarchal inscription? Could these magazines offer sites for women to realize their own rhetorical agency and to promote their own literate values, or were the women who chose this work over, say, teaching, forgoing any possibility of such work?[5]

To discover the answers to these questions, feminist media critics are using ethnography, firsthand accounts by those working in the publishing industry. Although rhetorical historians cannot elicit specific information through targeted questioning during interviews, cannot guide the process in the same way that ethnographers can their contemporary subjects and participants, rhetorical historians can use biographies, memoirs, autobiographies, and letters to provide accounts of production. When corroborated by multiple accounts and when coupled with textual analysis and reader responses through reception or through the filtered letters to the editors, we can begin to develop a nuanced, albeit incomplete history of mid-twentieth-century magazines and the literature contained therein.[6] In doing so, we can make visible the blue marks, the revisions, the editing, that went into the making of modern U.S. letters.

Surplus Literacy, or Women with Sheepskins

In the early twentieth-century United States, the typewriter changed writing practices, making demands for new kinds of literacy skills. As a technology, the typewriter was initially perceived as "sex neutral." By 1935, as Rosalyn Baxandall and Linda Gordon document, typing had become a thoroughly feminized skill. Still, once women were at the typewriter, they did more than merely imprint men's words; indeed, they entered print-related professions and careers (journalism, academia, publishing, agencies, and businesses) in record numbers. By 1930, women formed 23 percent of editors; "the highest percentage of participation occurred in the youngest age group, which included the early child-bearing years" (Adams, *Group* 154–55). The trend would continue through the 1940s.[7] In *Lady Editor*, Ruth Adams Knight sets out to advise these "career bent" young women who came "barging out of leading colleges with their sheepskins flying" (92). *Lady Editor* chronicles an industry peopled with women in high places. It trains its lens particularly on women in a range of publication types: "slicks," news magazines, digests, pulps, class publications, and traditional women's fare (fashion, home). It is an incredible snapshot of this "invisible" profession as it stood at the start of World War II. The tone of *Lady Editor* evinces the authors' enthusiasm for the opportunities that editing created for emancipated, enfranchised modern women: "It was only after the turn of the century [that] women really came into their own, until today they step right along with men in the publishing game. While there are still cases of ability which go improperly rewarded, there is no field where recognition of feminine ability is more universal" (91). Not surprisingly given these opportunities, many young women had set their sights on "getting on a magazine" (92).

With so many women graduating college, the issue was already hauntingly familiar to late twentieth- and early twenty-first-century academics. It was a problem of surplus English graduates, of greater supply than demand.[8] What would these women wielding sheepskins do? To what use would they put their newly found higher literacy? Some trained as teachers, careers they would likely be expected, perhaps even required, to drop upon marriage; others identified writing or editing as viable professions, suited for either activists or "ladies" or those, like Freda Kirchwey who edited the *Nation*, who found themselves betwixt and between the two labels.[9] Because it was low profile, editing particularly presented itself as suitable, meaningful work for women not wanting to be conspicuous. While my focus is on large-circulation magazines, it's worth noting that small-circulation, specialized magazines likewise provided many opportunities. For example, Noliwe M. Rooks argues in *Ladies' Pages: African American Women's Magazines and the Culture That Made Them* that African American women's magazines "allowed African American women to find work as journalists, printers, writers, and editors; to define personal, as well as group, identities; to create a sense of unity by establishing a communication network among women in different regions; to present and comment about world and local events from an African American female perspective; and to highlight achievement often overlooked and ignored by the dominant or African American male press" (3). What was true for African American women and smaller-circulation magazines—this opportunity for engaged work—was true in greater numbers for privileged, white women with growing access to college educations and to a bourgeoning mainstream publishing world.

These women were entering and graduating a curriculum that since the 1920s had experienced great changes, the result of "Progressive theories of education as well as ... the huge increase of career-minded students" (Adams, Group 30). In 1941 when Ruth Adams Knight published Lady Editor, universities were training not just "more literate mothers," "not just sensitive readers and community participants," but instead "creative writers who could influence and improve the populace through stories that described America's myths, moral imperatives, and visions for the future" (Adams, Group 49).[10] This progressive curriculum led to a professional class of women who "moved out of manners and childrearing into news and editorial writing, magazine feature writing, textbook writing, scholarship, historical studies, poetry, and fiction" (Adams, Group xvii). Still, not all critics have been persuaded that the change was so dramatic. Langdon Hammer in his "Plath's Lives: Poetry, Professionalism, and the Culture of School," acknowledges the shift in curriculum; however, he argues, using the case of Sylvia Plath, the "female professional" was not "a liberating alternative to the restrictions of the student's position" (66). Plath, Hammer continues, "conceived of the female professional as a kind of student, and vice versa" (66). In other words, once an apprentice, always an apprentice. As evidence, he points to Sylvia Plath's Mademoiselle feature from 1953, "Poets on Campus: 5 Talented Young Men Combine Poetry and the Classroom." Hammer argues that "Plath's role as a student journalist in a young women's popular magazine begins to suggest the difference gender makes. None of the 'Poets on Campus' has advanced his career by winning a guest-editorship at Mademoiselle. Their prestige is greater than Plath's, and it would only be weakened by the kind of commercial writing Plath was encouraged to do.... Nor are they really there in *Mademoiselle* to be emulated" (64). Rather, they are there as examples of "the young professional man for whom *Mademoiselle* is helping its reader to make herself desirable, because there is an equivocation in the future that *Mademoiselle*, like Smith, imagines for the college woman: a career, yes, but marriage too, and someday children, and when choices must be made, marriage will come first" (Hammer 64).

It is not within the scope of Hammer's argument to spend a great deal of time on the countervailing messages prevalent in *Mademoiselle*. Nor does he dwell on those originating from college campuses.[11] Consider the advice from M. Carey Thomas that "the Bryn Mawr woman" should "resist the temptation to marry" (qtd. in L. Davis 35). These students were taught that "the Bryn Mawr woman's place was not necessarily in the home, but rather in the world—as a person making a significant contribution to the sciences or the humanities" (qtd. in L. Davis 35). Hammer is correct that women did receive conflicting and diverging messages: these privileged college graduates had to choose the kind of woman that it was their duty to become—single career woman, single working woman who stops work upon marriage, married woman, or married woman with a career. Duty, of course, was more broadly defined than in the nineteenth century: while some were answering to church, others were answering to institutions, or elite society or political groups or international projects. The progressive career track certainly didn't broadcast itself as the easiest option. Women choosing it did so in an environment of unbridled optimism and unbridled criticism. As women entered the English major in record numbers, men such as Rollo Walter Brown, began to worry that women were driving men from this field of study, transforming "humane subjects" into "'ladylike' subjects" (qtd. in Adams, *Group* 38). Part of this transformation entailed a move from what was perceived as "hard" analysis that required "mental discipline," philology, for instance, to expressive and creative assignments "that required or allowed students to experiment with the genres being studied: poetry, drama, fiction, and the personal essays" (Adams, Group 42), assignments more conducive to "finishing" a young woman's education, perfecting a genteel style. Production (and appreciation) of literature was thus wedded to proper, gendered, classed behavior; to be a woman of style meant to be a woman who appreciated (or better yet composed) literature. Eventually, women entered the English major with other intentions, for instance, to become writers or journalists, the subjects of Adams's study, but they could not entirely escape the "natural" link between femininity and style. In some cases, this link served them well, opening doors into work as editors or literary agents. Katharine White's long tenure at the *New Yorker*, for instance, was secured by her image as a woman of taste. As I argue in chapter four, the opportunities that accrued from women's association with style and taste—with fashion—did not come without the attachment of heavy, binding strings.

Fine Flame, or Lady Editor: Choosing between Poisons

Second-wave feminists targeted *Ladies' Home Journal* not so much because of its content—although that was certainly part of the equation[12]—but because of its staffing: in 1970 the journal was once again edited by a man, John Mack Carter. *Ladies' Home Journal* was not unique. Friedan recalls, "I sat one night at a meeting of magazine writers, mostly men, who work for all kinds of magazines, including women's magazines" (36). One of these editors "outlined the needs of the large women's magazine he edited: 'Our readers are housewives, full time. They're not interested in broad public issues of the day. They are not interested in national or international affairs. They are only interested in the family and the home'" (Friedan 37). It was this attitude that Friedan and others sought to change: "The whole world lies open to American women. Why, then, does the image deny the world? Why does it limit women to 'one passion, one role, one occupation?'" (37). They started with *Ladies' Home Journal*. In 1970, at the *Ladies' Home Journal*, there was one woman "above middle management," and she, as Brownmiller explains, "belonged to a generation of tough lady editors who sat at their desks and wore flowered hats" (*In Our Time* 85). It is at this point in the critical history that scholars in feminist media studies raise their hands to interrupt. "Lady editors" is a fraught term whose implications are erased when we outlaw the term or when we mark certain women as exceptions.[13] Many of the women that Ruth Adams Knight profiles were using traditional venues—home or fashion magazines—to advance what they believed were forward, progressive, sometimes even self-proclaimed feminist or "feministic" ideas.[14]

In sum, not all backpedalled from feminism as quickly as Beatrice Gould,[15] although I would argue that with some frequency, feminism was subordinated to the goals of belletrism, the mission to disseminate high letters. Knight pitches this exalted mission to prospective female editors: "The modern magazine, with the pretty model photographed on the cover, and the name of the author of the most popular best seller listed in large type, is a comparatively recent concept. If you have ever taken the trouble to dig back into the origin of the periodical, you know that in the beginning it was concerned with the most solemn aspects of literature and of interest only to the erudite" (*Lady Editor* 90). Recounting the work of women like Irita Van Doren (*Herald Tribune Books*), Martha Foley (*Story*), Amy Loveman (*Saturday Review of Literature* and Book-of-the-Month Club), and Edith J. R. Isaacs (*Theatre Arts*)—the latter of whom was "confined to her bed for several years" (*Lady Editor* 151)—*Lady Editor* records how women, in the years preceding and following World War II, helped create a collective mass desire to consume literature, selling it as a commodity of women's magazines.[16] Some of these editors felt it almost an exalted mission to advance American literature by seeking out and publishing brilliant writers. Acting in their roles as editors, they were—or imagined themselves to be—purveyors of high culture and high art (visual and written). They were—or imagined themselves to be—what we might call emissaries of haute couture and haute literacy. This isn't the history we always see; it wasn't a history that sustained itself.

The career of Betsy Talbot Blackwell, the editor of *Mademoiselle* from 1939 to 1971, is emblematic. Though decidedly not a feminist,[17] Blackwell quadrupled the magazine's circulation by targeting college and young career women and by providing them with quality reading material. She also founded the New York guest editing program made famous by Sylvia Plath's *The Bell Jar*. Because Plath's particular perspective on her experience in 1953 has been written so firmly into American literary history, it's somewhat difficult to see what others might have perceived, a glimpse we catch at the class of 1953's fifty-year reunion captured by Alex Witchel's "After 'The Bell Jar,' Life Went On." Let me concede that I accept the reunion comments as just that—reunion comments, no doubt nostalgic, no doubt romanticized, perhaps even invented. Most of the comments participate in that most common of enterprises: mythologizing and re-mythologizing Plath. And yet these comments, together with other views gleaned from biographies or memoirs, show that there was another stance on the *Mademoiselle* guest editing program, one that signals pride— and tremendous interest and drive. The program began in 1939, its purpose as Alex Witchel writes "was twofold: the magazine's advertisers could get valuable feedback from the cream of its market, and the women whose writing and artwork were the best could travel to New York and work on the enormously popular August college issue." Those traveling to New York over the years included writers Joan Didion, Francine du Plessix Gray, and Ann Beattie. The program ended in 1979 (after becoming co-ed), but "in 1953 it was still in its heyday," and the guest editors were chosen from 1,500 applicants (Witchel). As Laurie Glazer Levy, an alumna from 1953, remembers, "Betsy Talbot Blackwell, the editor of *Mademoiselle*, put us against the wall and said, 'You are my writers and you will do great things'" (qtd. in Witchel).[18] Another of the group, Ruth Abramson Spear, recalls that a *Mademoiselle* ed-

itor really inspired her: "She told me, 'You're going to be successful in life. You have that fine flame'" (Witchel).[19]

"Fine flame" might seem like inflated language to apply to
young college women brought to New York to work on a fashion
magazine, but it represents the degree to which Blackwell and
others associated with the magazine prided themselves on doing
great things, for women yes, but mostly for American letters. Writing about the fiftieth reunion event, the journalist Alex Witchel
encapsulates a legacy that would surely have pleased Blackwell:
"*Mademoiselle* was known as a forum for exciting new fiction by
writers like Truman Capote; Dylan Thomas's *Under Milk Wood* was
published there in its entirety."[20] In 1935, when Blackwell joined
Mademoiselle, it was a magazine "aimed at young women (before
youth had any status)" and "contained fiction and poetry (not
a young woman's highest priority" (Rayner 42). It fell upon the
newly hired Blackwell to explain "to the businessmen a basic fact
of publishing: almost no one advertises in a magazine devoted ex-
clusively to fiction and poetry. If they hoped to attract advertisers
they would simply have to broaden their appeal ... that is, if they
were interested in making money" (Rayner 42). Blackwell succeeded in making her point, with the result of raising the profile
of the fashion and beauty sections and improving the *Mademoiselle*'s finances, a business success story that fits preconceptions
of women's fashion magazines. Yet it's what Blackwell does with
this financial success that makes the story interesting: "*Mademoiselle* was so awash in advertising it could afford William Faulkner,
Dylan Thomas, Joyce Carol Oates, and Robert Penn Warren. She
could afford to suggest that Truman Capote write about his childhood Christmas experiences in the South" (Rayner 43–44).

In contrast, the *New Yorker*, for all its aspirations, published
writers whose work was more palatable to a middle-class audience, work less stylistically experimental, not so regionally or racially or sexually charged: "It is something of a scandal," Brendan
Gill sheepishly observed to the Capote biographer Gerald Clarke,
"that [the *New Yorker*] didn't publish any of Truman's short sto-

ries. ... But it's also a scandal that we didn't publish anything by Hemingway or Faulkner and only one story by Fitzgerald" (qtd. in Clarke 75). The authors that Blackwell "published during her reign reveal the great sympathy she felt for the arts along with an understanding and ability to recognize talent. In the 1940s there were Ray Bradbury, Robert Penn Warren, W. H. Auden, and Colette. In the 1950s there were Elizabeth Hardwick, Carson McCullers, Lesley Blanch, Eudora Welty. In the 1960s there were Edward Albee, Gore Vidal, Isaac Bashevis Singer. In the seventies there were Rebecca West, Susan Brownmiller, Hortense Calisher, and Joyce Carol Oates" (Rayner 44). Others have written more convincingly that Blackwell hired people—George Davis, Leo Lerman, Mary Louise Atwell—who could recognize talent. Regardless, as editor in chief, Blackwell was able, through fashion, to work a kind of cultural magic, transforming a thirst for beauty products into an appetite for belles-lettres.

Ruth Adams Knight would have predicted this trajectory. Though magazines had modernized and expanded to accommodate "highly diversified tastes" (Lady Editor 89), many still retained the original literary quality. In fact, her very first chapter after the introduction presents "the class publications," or "fare for the intelligentsia," underscoring the relationship between high literacy and high-class culture, a formula that publishers such as Raoul Fleishmann (first publisher of the New Yorker) and Condé M. Nast had come to bank on. Such publications were not, Knight explains, off limits to women whose "interest in a periodical lies in its style and literary merit rather than in its popular appeal ... in quality above quantity" (Lady Editor 97). To be sure, such publications were smaller in circulation, although she believes that circulations are widening with "improving public taste," but they "are edited thoughtfully and fearlessly, with little consideration for mass approbation, and they frequently make literary history" (Lady Editor 97).

In Lady Editor, Ruth Adams Knight was particularly optimistic about women's roles on "class publications," the "fare for the intelligentsia": "Editorially this field is one where women have played an important part and where, when the world returns to normal again, they will doubtless continue to do so in the future. Such opportunities as the present offers to women are due largely to the draft, which, sweeping the field clean of the younger men in the publishing business, may provide openings which would not have existed in ordinary circumstances" (97). Knight was certainly aware of perceptions that women's literary presence was a soft and sentimental one; she recognized that editing opportunities for women might diminish if the critics weren't, in twenty-first-century parlance, "handled." The nineteenth-century editor Sarah Josepha Hale was her model rhetorician of choice: "Sarah was modest about her own talents, shy and shrewd about revealing too soon to a masculine world the threat of any feminine ability in the editorial field, or as a matter of fact, anywhere else" (*Lady Editor* 91). *Godey's Lady's Book* might look innocent enough, but only to those who didn't understand Hale's tactics: "Little by little *Godey's Lady's Book* expanded from a strictly fashion magazine to one of ever widening feminine interests" (*Lady Editor* 91). Hale thus made her mark—extended her rhetorical influence—not only by opening the editorial field to women, but also by changing the "vast proportion of the magazine market." In short, Hale made editing "a woman's game" (*Lady Editor* 91–92), one that the numerous examples in *Lady Editor* elucidate.[21]

While Knight does not include the *New Yorker* among the "thin ranks"—"*Atlantic Monthly* and *Harper's Magazine* carry the bulk of the old tradition" (*Lady Editor* 97)—by the 1960s, the time of its loudly lamented decline,[22] the *New Yorker* had achieved this status, and true to Knight's prediction, women had played a role, one that was decreasing as the United States recoiled not to prewar normalcy but to its distorted postwar twin. Numerous and varied cultural histories detail what happened in the postwar period, and it wasn't the sunny outlook that Knight predicted. When the postwar job market for women shrank, when public sentiment turned against women in the postwar workforce, that surplus of college-educated unemployed women transmogrified into an unprecedentedly large leisured consumer class. They read. They shopped. They aspired for more. The glossy women's magazines with their pages upon pages of advertising and domestic fiction designed to lull readers into complacency and conformity were an integral part of a bourgeois consumer culture that left women bored, dissatisfied, contained, and restless. When their restlessness grew too profound, they tranquilized themselves. This critical story works,[23] but there is for me one insurmountable difficulty: this is not the way lady editors working in the boom decades (the 1920s through the 1950s) told their own stories. If we accept the passionate renderings of their own letters and life stories—and I would argue that we should at least listen and represent these voices in our rhetorical histories—these women exercised their love of words, becoming missionaries in social and literary causes.

In 1941, Knight could point to the story of Martha Foley, who along with her husband White Burnett coedited Story and originated the celebrated annual collection of O'Brien short stories (Lady Editor 98). She is careful to note that Foley forged her own path. While Foley "is kind and encouraging to girls who long for the sort of editorial position she has held," she does not offer a training ground for them. "There are editorial secretaries, of course, proofreaders, copyreaders, girls who handle make-up and typography and absorb some of the editorial atmosphere. But there is no editorial staff and the cruel truth is that if you want to be an editor on a class magazine right this minute you may have to follow Martha Foley's example, and start your own" (Lady Editor 100). Freda Kirchwey did it with the Nation, Lila Acheson Wallace with her husband created the famous Reader's Digest (which, oddly enough, she categorizes as "Fare for the Intelligentsia"). Each was "launched tentatively as an experiment" (Lady Editor 101).

If reviews are an indication, Lady Editor likely did not receive the kind of commercial success its authors hoped for. The Spring-

field Republican devoted 180 words to it, the *Wisconsin Library Bulletin* about the same. Its fullest review, a mere 220 words, came in the *Journal of Home Economics*, which praised its scope: "Leaders in the various lines of work within each division were interviewed, often quoted, as to what personal qualifications, training, and experience are desirable, how to get started, and what the work includes" (Rev. of *Lady Editor* 746). Still the reviewers lamented its humanistic bent: "Journal readers may wish that in the section on magazines a paragraph or two had been devoted to the non-commercial, professional magazines that seem to offer limited but increasing opportunities for women trained in some branch of natural or social science who don't care for teaching or advanced research and who do like reading, writing, and human contact" (Rev. of *Lady Editor* 747). Why was *Lady Editor* such a flop? One possibility rests within this text, which simultaneously praises the accomplishments of "driven" women and doubts the motives of the majority of women who graduate college: "I want a job on your staff because I just love to write," explains Knight, "is an old and familiar chant in the ears of every editor who must interview aspiring applicants" (*Lady Editor* 92). Such applicants must be disabused, and frequently are, Knight indicates. "The demand, 'Write what?' is not the rebuff it sometimes seems, but an honest question to determine on what your ambition is based. For a vague and indefinite yen to 'write' considered alone is probably the greatest disqualification possible in the editorial field" (*Lady Editor* 92–93). This point is repeated several times in *Lady Editor*, such as in the "one bit of advice" Martha Foley of *Story* offers aspirants: "If you want to be a writer," she warns, "stay out of publishing. Don't try to combine the two activities.... If you are going to be a writer, be an honest one. Write out of your own convictions, believe in what you are doing. If you want to be an editor, forget the writing" (qtd. in *Lady Editor* 101). Women like Katharine White had learned this lesson well. In January 1959, Sheila Atkinson Fisher, a fellow Bryn Mawr College graduate, wrote to White to ask her to contribute to a collection of articles by prominent figures with connections to Bryn Mawr. Fisher specifically invited White to contribute a piece on the current state of the short story. White's reply evinced her professionalism:

> I am honored to be asked to contribute a piece to this anniversary issue of the Alumnae Bulletin, but I think I shall have to say no to this assignment. In a way it is tempting, for what I would write on if at all, would not be the trends in short-story writing with mention of young writers worth watching, for this would be impossible for a still active editor of The New Yorker. I could, though, perhaps write something on how to detect new talent and how to encourage young writers. (Oh no, this, too, would be too intramural!) But the fact is I simply do not have time to write a 2000 word article as an extra to my present work. Also I am not a writer; I'm an editor.[24]

While curricula in women's colleges, as Katherine H. Adams documents, grew to incorporate more creative writing both as separate class work and as an approach to studying literature, this belletristic work, Lady Editor warns, does not prepare women for the real work of editing. Rather, "experience in strange and seemingly remote fields results in important positions and that 'literary ability' of which you are so proud may count for little or nothing. Several outstanding magazines have a whole staff of editors who never write a line" (Adams, Group 93). For this reason, college graduates may not, in fact, find themselves in any better standing than those from vocational schools: "the girl who has only business school training and can act as a secretary is very likely to get the assistant editor's job you want so badly" (Adams, Group 93).

Young women looking for glamour and visibility were likely to be disappointed by a profession characterized by its invisibility: "The truth is, that along with one or two other creative fields, the stage, radio and the movies, the editorial field is almost universally misunderstood by those desiring to enter it. Because it has a certain allure, the assumption is ... that it is a fairyland of golden possibility" (Adams, Group 93). Far from being a fairyland, Knight makes clear, the editing profession is a place for hard work, much of which will go unrecognized. A good editor is like a good chorister or a good Rockette: she should not stand out. Such an ideal was easier to sustain in the collective environment of women's colleges than in the world of work where despite increasing numbers, they were still exceptions.

Loving Literacy

Women editing large-circulation magazines in the mid-twentieth-century United States did so at a time when women's schooling and expectations about women's ways of being in the nation were changing. It was also a time in the United States when literacy became a kind of secular faith. As a metaphor, Sylvia Scribner argues, literacy is politically, spiritually, and culturally freighted, as all metaphors are. Scribner identifies three metaphors identified with literacy (other critics have identified dozens more), including the formation of literacy as a "state of grace," "the tendency ... to endow the literate person with special values" (13).[25] This endowment accrues not just in the literate individual but in the texts that allow such an individual to come to be: "the literate individual's life derives its meaning and significance from intellectual, aesthetic, and spiritual participation in the accumulated creations and knowledge of humankind, made available through the written word" (Scribner 14).[26] In short, if literacy is a state of grace, it is made possible through introduction to shared, valued texts. Learning is sanctification.

Perhaps the best illustration of this trope—literacy as something holy, an act of reverence—appears in Harper Lee's *To Kill a Mockingbird*, published in 1960. Lee's particular use of the metaphor extends: literacy becomes a natural, powerful, sustaining form of love, both personal and civic. Scout's modern teacher would have preferred that children learn the science of reading at school, by parsing the words on the page, by memorizing an alphabet, by mastering phonics. In this scheme, skills can be isolated and tested. What such skills can accomplish is moot;

they simply advance one to the appropriate grade. Scout already knows how to read when she arrives at school, but she doesn't know the measurable science of it. She has learned to read at home by sitting on her father's lap, imbibing his love and commitment to letters and justice in a single repeated act: "I could not remember when the lines above Atticus's moving finger separated into words, but I had stared at them all the evenings in my memory, listening to the news of the day, Bills to Be Enacted into Laws, the diaries of Lorenzo Dow—anything Atticus happened to be reading when I crawled into his lap every night" (Lee 24). In Harper Lee's novel, this particular form of love—a love with the potential to bind families and cure the racially violent south—is under siege by new forms of education. In *To Kill a Mockingbird*, Atticus and Scout and Charles Baker Harris represent not the future but the past. Indeed, a great part of the culture of literate zeal is nostalgia, a fear that literate values are disappearing or that the sanctity of literacy is going unrecognized or that literacy is becoming soulless. It is this embattled feeling that produces the recognition of literacy's value. As Scout ruminates: "Until I feared I would lose it, I never loved to read. One does not love breathing" (Lee 24).[27] It's a common invocation in literature of the period, this idea that literacy is under siege; it both motivates and justifies efforts to proselytize a faith in letters and to create canons of literature worthy of preservation and worship.

Frances Gray Patton's *Good Morning, Miss Dove*—a bestselling novel adapted into movie and play versions—shares with *To Kill a Mockingbird* an appreciation for literacy so profound that it equates it to a natural form of love, a generous invitation to become part of a family of letters. As does Harper Lee, Patton draws on her own experiences in her fictional representations of literacy. In interviews, Patton reported that her parents read to her and her two brothers so much that they always felt most comfortable with a book in their hands.[28] *Good Morning, Miss Dove* is representative of a genre that Peter Mortensen and I labeled "literacy narratives" ("Reading Literacy Narratives"). Literacy narratives are not about reading and writing per se; rather their plots are motivated by and structured around schooling or the attainment of literacy and they make dramatic claims for a particular kind of literacy.[29] *Good Morning, Miss Dove* is an archetypal example of this kind of narrative, one of the reasons I will treat it in some detail here. Another reason is that the editorial correspondence—and the missing pieces of the editorial story—suggests the essayistic ground across which *Literate Zeal* traverses, the route through the correspondence of Katharine White, with side trips to other periodicals when possible.

If the number of late twentieth-century movies about teaching suggests—and the trend seemingly continues—that as a culture we find it hard to resist a movie in which teachers are portrayed as heroes or saints, then in *Good Morning, Miss Dove* the conceit is exploited with unabashed pleasure: Miss Dove is carried aloft reverently through the town by her ex-students in a Waspy variation of old-world celebrations in which the Virgin is similarly paraded. Over the course of Patton's novel, the imagined community grows to understand the sanctity of schooling and the right kind of teachers. Miss Dove is not the new kind of professional teacher that presides at Scout's school. She is not certified. She is a relic, an old-fashioned teacher, a trait that the community doesn't value, at least when the novel opens: "Occasionally a group of progressive mothers would contemplate organized revolt. 'She's been teaching too long,' they would cry. 'Her pedagogy hasn't changed since we were in Cedar Grove'" (Patton 11). Through the course of the novel, they will discover that Miss Dove's emphasis on self-discipline sustains, even saves, individuals in crisis. One of her students, Thomas Baker, writes from the war zone after his ship has been bombed: "For days he had floated on a raft with no food and only the water in his canteen. When they picked him up his tongue had protruded from his mouth, black and swollen with thirst. That was what got Miss Dove—he had run out of water" (Patton 133). When "Tommy" writes Miss Dove from the war zone, she has one of her current students read the letter aloud. It is a testament to Miss Dove: "when I was bobbing up and down like Crusoe on my raft, what do you guess I thought about? It wasn't any pin-up girl. It was Miss Dove." More specifically, it was Miss Dove's discipline that Thomas Baker remembers, "the fishy stare she used to give us when we needed a drink of water. So to make my supply hold out I played I was back in the geography room. And even after the water was gone I kept playing" (Patton 137). The message is literal: at sea, in a modern world, in battle, students could count on stability, if they paid homage, venerated the "Terrible," awe-inspiring Miss Dove and adhered to the gospel she taught. After reading the letter aloud to the class, the child comes forward to receive a kiss, one formal and ritualized. It as if, Patton writes, Miss Dove has pinned a medal on him.

Miss Dove has powers beyond offering stability to unstable modern psyches. She, or more accurately the kind of learning she stands for, can create a better, more just, more unified society. She is a teacher who binds young and old, rich and poor with her "impartial justice, adamantine regulations, and gray, calm, neutral eyes" (Patton 1). Her world is one in which wayward women marry and become respectable, in which poor children from illiterate and drunken families become police officers, in which children perform well on scientific standardized tests (veneration of learning insures science, not vice-versa), in which all citizens aspire to gentility, a value instilled in Miss Dove's class by the requirement of a clean handkerchief pinned to the shirt or blouse of each child. It is an American educational system unburdened by progressive theories of education and uncomplicated by race. There are no rich Paris Hilton types here, no rich girls born to shop, no co-eds gone wild (they hover in the background of other Patton stories); instead genteel values and humble work manage unruly excess across classes (risky investments, conspicuous consumption, overinvestment in fashion, alcoholism, filth). In this pristine world, old-fashioned education and modern liberal values work. Miss Dove delivers in her classroom something sacred, almost liturgical in its rhythms: She "liked making and keeping rules. And just as a teacher with a genuine love for poetry will awaken that passion in her pupils, so Miss Dove imbued her charges with her philosophy. By her insistence upon even margins and correct posture and punctuality and industriousness, she told them, in effect, that though life was not easy, neither was it puzzling. You learned its unalterable laws. You respected them. You became equal to your task. Thus, you controlled your destiny" (Patton 34). And thus one followed his duty to society.

Frances Gray Patton is not a well-known writer today, but she was a writer of some renown in the 1950s and the 1960s, largely as a result of "The Terrible Miss Dove" in *Ladies' Home Journal*, its evolution in 1954 into a *New York Times* best-selling novel and Book-of-the-Month Club selection, and the movie starring Jennifer Jones released in 1955. Thus, Patton achieved popular success, but by the time she wrote *Good Morning, Miss Dove*, she had already earned her credentials as a writer of serious literature. She was deeply connected to the academy, initially by marriage. Her husband was Lewis Patton, a Duke University English professor and romanticist who in 1958 published "A New Approach to Freshman Composition at Duke" in *College Composition and Communication*. Patton published her first short story, an O. Henry prize-winning story in 1944, at his urging. Her reputation grew steadily after the *New Yorker* editors spied her work in *Harper's* and wooed her to their publication. Patton eventually moved in MFA circles, teaching university creative writing courses and summer fiction writing workshops.

Patton's correspondence with her editors, particularly Katharine White, gives us some insight into the growing space in the academy for creative writing.[30] Publishing in venues as varied as small literary magazines, the *Ladies' Home Journal*, and the *New Yorker*, Patton enjoyed a highly successful and varied writing career, one emblematic of the literate zeal that came to mark the mid-twentieth century, a time of explosive growth in attempts to make literature and high culture available to a greater number of people.[31]

Editorial Archives and Rhetorical Criticism: Katharine White's Correspondence

Frances Gray Patton and Katharine White's correspondence spanned eleven years. Like Patton, Katharine White frequently wrote long, impassioned letters, and this trait makes their editorial correspondence particularly rich. Their relationship began in May of 1946, when Katharine White first queried Frances Gray Patton in care of Harper's, one of the competing magazines that the New Yorker tracked: "This is just a note to say that The New Yorker would be very glad to have you contribute short stories and humor sketches. We have read your work in other magazines and would be glad to have a chance at it. It's possible that you have sent us some in the past but if we could not take it then that doesn't mean we might not like any you cared to send us in the future."[32] When this message received no response, White sent another similar message in June. Patton was receptive to the offer. By later that summer, Patton had submitted two stories, and one, "And Hearts in Heaven," was accepted with only minor revisions. By 1947, Patton had an agreement with the New Yorker, whereby all her stories would first be submitted there.

The book jackets for her short story collections boasted her connection to the magazine, so much so that some came to the mistaken conclusion that "The Terrible Miss Dove" first appeared in its pages. But it didn't—Ladies' Home Journal had the honor. Common wisdom would have that the New Yorker likely rejected the story because it was too sentimental or too lowbrow. A review of the early magazine and the editorial correspondence reveals that logic to be faulty. In topic and literary treatment, Miss Dove is not unlike New Yorker fiction. It is, for instance, no more or less sentimental than Clarence Day's "Life with Father" series, which had been serially published in the New Yorker before being made into a movie in 1947. The likeness to Day's work and to other popular texts was noted by at least one reviewer. Charles Poore describes Miss Dove as a "cheerful mixure of 'Goodbye Mr. Chips' and 'Mary Poppins,' with touches of the rigorous way of salvation from 'Life With Father.'" Indeed, Patton and others were sometimes rejected because they were too close in type to Sally Benson's wildly popular "Junior Miss" pieces, which the *New Yorker* published. There were other reasons Patton's manuscripts had been or would be rejected: the *New Yorker* rejected Patton's submissions because they were too contrived (the situation or characters seemed fabricated), too literary (Patton liked words like "adamantine"), too coarse (a boy pees in a maid's shoe), too incendiary (they chronicled racial tension), and too suggestive (hints of homoeroticism). In sum, in the late 1940s and early 1950s, sentiment was rarely the cause for an outright rejection from the *New Yorker*. And in some cases, authors were encouraged to write sentimental recollections, rather than fiction, as evidenced by the editorial correspondence surrounding Patton's "And Hearts in Heaven." When the *New Yorker* contracted to publish the story, they did so with the usual proviso: revisions needed. Patton expressed some concerns about these revisions but agreed to them in advance because of the magazine's literary reputation and a friend's experience with Katharine as an editor. Patton responded to the recommended changes and also suggested a few of her own, including cutting what she now believed were unnecessarily gendered phrases or constructs: "I have also cut my own original statement that 'I often whispered with other girls etc.' I always disliked that and its only purpose was to establish my sex. Now that I am known from the first paragraph to be a girl I think it is unnecessary. I hope you can indulge my whim there—I think it has a girly-girly, prissy sound that spoils the tone of the story."[33] And it was Patton who was determined to move the piece from sentimental reminiscence to fiction. To that end she changed her character's name from Fanny to Dolly to place the story more clearly in the realm of fiction. This seemingly small change in name prompted Katharine White to ex-

plain the connections between fiction and first-person reminiscence—and also to reveal something about the *New Yorker's* readers and its literary sophistication:

> We took it to be reminiscence—very likely considerably
> heightened and fictionalized reminiscence, but anyway a first-
> person childhood memory.... Almost all reminiscences are
> fictionalized anyway—we've run dozens that have been. For
> instance, the famous Thurber series about his childhood in
> Columbus that we published and that later became the book
> he called "My Life and Hard Times" must be 50% fiction and
> Ruth McKenney's "My Sister Eileen" stories even more than
> that. Even Clarence Day's "Life With Father" was fictionalized
> to some extent though accurate in background and essential
> facts of character, and in many episodes. But all these writers
> used real names and wrote their stories as actual memories.[34]

In light of recent debates over the veracity of first-person memoirs, White's letter makes an interesting claim, namely, that everyone expects such work to be fictionalized to a great extent.
(It's also interesting note to that Joseph Mitchell's *Up From the Old
Hotel* pieces made use of characters represented as real but constructed as composites, the kind of move that has since led journalists at other publications to be fired.)

Katharine White's correspondence to Patton also underscored
a point made with some frequency in the editorial archives: *New
Yorker* readers were not particularly sophisticated readers and thus
must be guided by simple generic cues (I look at more explicit examples of this in chapter one). *New Yorker* readers, it seems, were
easily confused:

> Here is our difficulty: if you had wanted to make this story
> read like fiction, and be understood by a reader to be fiction,
> it would have been better to have put the whole story into the
> third person.... *The New Yorker* has a peculiar problem in that
> it runs so many reminiscences alongside its short stories. Mr.
> Ross, our editor-in-chief, feels quite strongly that fiction told
> in the first person is therefore confusing to our readers, un-

less it is the sort of "I" story that reader can quickly understand to be fiction. This would hardly be true of a story that
started, as yours does, with the words "When I was eleven."
We believe that the story will lose some of its effectiveness
if your little girl is named "Dolly" since careful readers, who
have been charmed by what they think is a real childhood
memory, when they get to your signature may say "Why it's
nothing but a story—a fake," and be let down.... Therefore I
hope you'll write us that we may keep "Fanny" and place the
story in North Carolina. This will allow our readers to think
they are reading a real reminiscence of your childhood.... The
problem is a rather peculiar one and I'm not at all sure I've explained it clearly. First person fiction that sounds like reminiscence is often written—we ourselves have published some. But
it has never worked out too well and only leads to difficulties
and confusions, if used in The New Yorker which publishes such
a peculiar mix of faction and fiction.[35]

Patton found the arguments convincing, noting that when
she read a recent New Yorker reminiscence piece, she herself did
not like when the narrator's name did not match the author's.[36]
A few years later, she wrote White a letter that indicated that she
had received fan mail and so now understood the kinds of readers her work reached:

Thanks for the fan-letter. That sort of mail fascinates me.
I've begun to receive it in fair quantity now. Some of it is very
charming, and some of it very strange. An old judge in Georgia sends me camellias from his garden (they are rather battered by the time they arrive), and a gentleman from Kansas—
a graduate of Princeton, class of 1890b—wrote to me that I
had a "wonderfully nice mind." Then there are the surprising
number of people who remark upon my vocabulary and sentence construction and style in the spirit of a teacher about to
mark my paper with an A, or at least an A minus.[37]

There is reason to believe that "The Terrible Miss Dove"
would have appealed to New Yorker readers. Before and after the

serial publication of her Miss Dove stories in *Ladies' Home Journal*, Patton published her Professor Potter stories in the magazine, taking up similar issues of teaching and families. "The Terrible Miss Dove" likely didn't find a home in the *New Yorker* for one reason: competition from other large-circulation magazines and from the growing novel-to-movie phenomenon. The *New Yorker* had long been competing with large-circulation magazines for fiction writers, but the novel, and particularly film, raised the financial bar for authors, holding the promise of much more money than could be had publishing short stories. The *New Yorker* was not the highest paying serial publication; it had initiated the first-reading agreements in combination with quantity bonuses to make the magazine more attractive to writers. These arrangements enabled Katharine to query authors with reminders like "you need only one more story to reach your percentage bonus." Still, without the first-reading agreement, the *New Yorker* was somewhat hobbled: other publications could pay more and sometimes promised larger circulations.

Perhaps sensing the possibilities for a Hollywood movie—or simply recognizing the potentially larger circulation and higher pay off—Patton's agent, Diarmuid Russell, first broached the issue of the *Ladies' Home Journal* contract for *Good Morning, Miss Dove*, suggesting that the author ask the *New Yorker* for an exception to the first-reading agreement. Patton was rightfully nervous about breaking the agreement: "When Diarmuid first broached the subject of asking such a favor I was not inclined to let him do so because I was afraid that you would feel that I was trying to weasel out of something. But he assured me that you wouldn't and, as events have proved, he was right." Patton also noted that there is something different in writing a story suitable for the *New Yorker*, not necessarily more challenging, but something more time consuming, something that required a certain frame of mind: "I certainly hope that I'll be able to write more stories—and many more—that will be acceptable to *The New Yorker*. My connection with that magazine is a source of the greatest possible pride, satisfaction and pleasure to me (all quite apart from the financial rewards it has brought me which I consider extremely generous) and I should be wretched indeed if I thought my usefulness to it had come to an end. Believe me, when I don't turn out those stories it isn't because I don't want to!"[38]

For her part, Katharine wrote to congratulate Patton on the financial success of *Good Morning, Miss Dove* and, in doing so, signaled the growing competition from the movie industry. She urged the author to spend more time on work of literary quality. She even suggests that Patton find a playwright who might rework some of the Professor Potter stories, which had been published in the *New Yorker*, for the stage:

> Dear Fanny:
>
> This is just to congratulate you on the sale of the Miss Dove book to the motion pictures. I am happy for you that you have had this bonanza—at least I hope it was that, and hope they paid well—and in your case I have the reassuring feeling that the sale of a book to the movies will not have the horrid result, as it does with some writers, of making you write hereafter with the cinema rights in mind. The people who sell their books to best advantage for plays or movies are the ones who do not do this, it seems to me. What I wish now is that some experienced playwright would make a good stage play around the characters in your stories of the southern professor and his wife and children. And I bet this will happen eventually. I don't mean that I hope you yourself will try to do this, since the dramatic life is so hazardous and the dramatic technique so special a thing, and I feel that if you should set out to master it, it would deflect you from writing the short stories that are your natural element. Or the novels. I think the background of your stories would be something new for the stage though—a different sort of picture of the South.
>
> Don't you think that Peter Taylor' book is splendid? I have been so happy over his good reviews. But he, and you, seem to have stopped writing short stories and this is a terrible loss to us.[39]

The *Miss Dove* correspondence presents a vivid picture of the market conditions in which editors worked and the degree to which the appetite for fiction curtailed their efforts to produce literature for large-circulation magazines. The documents reveal other institutional secrets. They show the work behind the ease of privilege. Global concerns, for instance, were unabashedly expressed as leisured concerns: where to buy the best (e.g., Paris fashions) or where to find the best travel resorts. Race was mostly erased, even though, as Mary Corey documents in her study of the post–World War II *New Yorker*, the "readers and contributors … saw themselves as liberal exemplars of American conscience" (76). Unpublished documents show the degree to which editors were aware of creating a crust that was elite, cultured, and white. As an example, Corey offers up Frances Gray Patton, the *New Yorker*'s "spy-emissary into the enemy camp of the American South," a writer "particularly adept at offering the magazine's readers a narrator who was in but was not of Southern culture—someone who could take them inside the polite racism of high bourgeois Southern life but who was not entirely tainted by its values" (92–93). What the unpublished correspondence between Patton and Katharine White shows is just how much White (along with other fiction editors) was furthering the *New Yorker*'s editorial vision, orchestrating it, supporting her "Dear Fanny," a well-known and valued contributor, but trying simultaneously to create literary fiction that would, from their perspective, rise above the fray of racial unrest and sustain, unfettered, the *New Yorker*'s reputation. Here, for example, is White's editorial response to Patton's short story, "A Piece of Luck," which later became the title story for a volume of short stories. White's advice stitched together the concerns raised in many an editorial session with Harold Ross and other *New Yorker* editors:

> Whenever we run a story involving Negroes, we get hopped on tremendously with floods of letters of protest for the slightest suggestion of patronage, the slightest indication that col-

ored people are not exactly like white people. . . . In this [story] there are just a few places that we felt would jar Northerners, especially the hyper-sensitive, or Negroes, places that might bring us floods of Society for the Advancement of Colored People mail. . . . These are hyper-sensitive days for anyone who lives north of Baltimore. Magazines are particularly vulnerable.[40]

Again and again in the White and Patton correspondence, White repeated this advice (the words are mine, but the gist comes straight from the editors): do not write about race. As compromising as this advice appears now, it was then, literarily and commercially speaking, sadly prescient. Patton achieved her highest success as an author when she accepted this advice. Miss Dove is a feared and beloved spinster schoolteacher in a small, all-white town. Reminiscent of the "vanishing Indian," the lone black character (the butler in the Dove household) appears only as a remnant of lost nineteenth-century culture. By the time of the story's present, he is disappeared.

Editorial materials are important because they help us understand what happens behind the scenes or, to use a more apt metaphor, between the sheets. The stories these materials tell is not a guarded one, not a carefully crafted, censored, edited history. For archival correspondence and memoirs to be useful, however, one must glean observations and analyze them apart from the workaday filter through which they are presented. One must imagine, in other words, what another narrative voice might make of the same potential facts. In the course of studying this material, I have refracted the archival facts, turning them into first one narrative pattern and then another. Sometimes, the facts fell together in just the way archival voices might have wished, and that critical story looks something like this: Lady editors like Katharine White took with fervor to the promising fields of American letters and high culture, becoming zealots for belletrism, placing their faith in aesthetics that promised to transcend messy social ills and conflicts. Good literature was good literature, period. They helped create an audience educated to value contemporary U.S. letters. They created and sustained not just a market but an American literature that otherwise would not have existed. They witnessed as universities began to offer courses in American literature and creative writing and took credit for changing higher education, particularly for American women.

This is the history progressive editors advanced. This is how they would have us remember them. If their claims seem silly or exaggerated to early twenty-first-century readers—and they likely do—it is, I would argue, because of the literary and rhetorical histories constructed for and consumed by us, histories in which we succumb to a kind of reasoned arrogance that excises personal, sentimental, gendered stories.[41] Still, I can't quite narrate the story just as progressive editors would have it. One can't simply make autobiography, memoir, and personal letters stand in for critical histories, although one can see the way in which facts and misstatements first published in memoir *have*, over time, folded seamlessly into histories. To see the work of these editors for what it was—pioneering, remarkable, limited, flawed—we must simultaneously revisit several facets of rhetorical and literary history: a late twentieth-century feminism that led to the innovation of the broadly circulated *Ms. Magazine* but, in the process, branded all women's magazines irredeemably sexist; the strict division of periodicals into two camps, literary (or "smart") versus popular (or the unspoken correlative "dumb"), with overtly tagged "women's magazines" falling unambiguously into the latter category; and a continuing emphasis on individual authorial genius, with a corresponding deemphasis on the rhetorical work of editors and agents and popular markets in building literary careers. Each of these facets or themes has developed into its own intriguing academic (sometimes popularized) story.

My goal in this research is not to simply reverse these narrative trajectories, to create three new monologic narratives that

overwrite the old. Such an enterprise would result in an unintu-
itive, extreme rhetorical history that looks something like this:
the feminism of the late 1960s and early 1970s created ex nihilo
the fiction of Stepford wives, programmed to shop and cook and
clean and copulate; there is no difference between the *Paris Review* and *People Magazine*; there are no brilliant authors, just brilliant editors—all women. In this study, I tread the vast middle
waters that fill these opposite shores, navigating between academic histories and the lived experience of letters and memoirs.
I accept both forms of evidence as revelatory but neither as gospel truth. My purpose in studying this editorial work is to expli-
cate the zeal that women brought to the project of making and
sustaining what I call American haute literacy, a literary movement characterized by a belief in an accessible, transcendent aesthetic that could rise above troubling social issues. Doing so allows us to reenvision a time in U.S. letters when women's literate
labor was in surplus, when there was a strong faith in the powers of literacy, when haute literacy became something to be consumed, enjoyed, and proselytized through large-circulation periodicals as seemingly varied as *Mademoiselle* and the *New Yorker*—
publications whose missions, I will argue, aren't so far apart.
What becomes apparent when one studies the place of literature
in large-circulation magazines is a pattern, in our literary and
cultural and popular histories, of apotheosis and degradation,
the tendency to venerate the *New Yorker* as a literary shrine and
denigrate the women's magazines that published the very same
caliber of authors, sometimes the very same authors, sometimes
the very stories the *New Yorker* might have published had they gotten first rights. This historical revision is useful, even necessary,
because it counters a liberal elitism—even more pronounced in
the opening years of the twenty-first century—that assumes that
women's magazines and literature are antithetical and thus ignores decades of women's editorial and literary achievements.
The promotion of belles-lettres was a project undertaken with
zeal by highly literate women (and men) who used their language

skills not just to access elite spaces in elite culture but also to en-rich the popular women's publications that had long been their domain. Women editors working for mass-circulation publica-tions, including women's magazines, played a larger role in cre-ating U.S. literature than has previously been recognized.

ONE ⁓ BETWEEN THE SHEETS

Editing and the Making of a *New Yorker* Ethos

> It was not the printed word that was its chief power: scores of editors who have tried to study and diagnose the appeal of the magazine from the printed page, have remained baffled at the remarkable confidence elicited from its readers. They never looked back of the magazine, and therefore failed to discover its secret.
>
> Edward Bok, *The Americanization of Edward Bok*

Frequently placed on coffee tables as a shrine of literate sophistication, the *New Yorker* magazine enjoys an iconic status perhaps unparalleled in U.S. periodical history. In the introduction to his *About Town: The New Yorker and the World It Made*, Ben Yagoda recounts the overwhelming subscriber response ("nearly seven hundred cards and letters") he receives to his reader survey: "You couldn't imagine," he surmises, "a survey about *Mademoiselle*, *Popular Mechanics*, or *U.S. News and World Report* eliciting this kind of response" (12). Today, mugs, calendars, framed calendars, joke books, and Christmas-themed collector's editions are all indications that the *New Yorker* still captures loyal followers, eager to align themselves with or define themselves by its iconic image. I, for instance, am the proud owner of a framed cover by Helen Hokinson, a calendar, and my very own digital copy of the entire *New Yorker*, which faithfully renders each page so that it appears just as it did in the original.

Yagoda's claim certainly holds insofar as it describes the *New Yorker*, but the speculation about other publications shouldn't follow so easily. In fact, other magazines have claimed to inspire similar intense devotion, or so those connected to these large-circulation magazines have boasted. Flashback eight decades and witness, for example, this characterization by Edward Bok, who served thirty years as editor of the *Ladies' Home Journal*: "Thousands of women had been directly helped by the magazine; it had not remained an inanimate printed thing, but had become a vital need in the personal lives of its readers. So intimate had become this relation, so efficient was the service rendered, that its readers could not be pried loose from it.... They explained to their husbands or fathers that *The Ladies' Home Journal* was a necessity—they did not feel that they could do without it" (179).

This relationship, Bok explains, did not develop automatically; he purposefully designed and nurtured it by assuming an audience of "intelligent" women, rather than "intellectual type[s]" (374–75). He aimed, in other words, to attract an audience of curious bright readers but to exclude the nineteenth-century specter of the female pedant, the woman who carried intellectual curiosity to quixotic extremes. *Ladies' Home Journal* was and always has been a mixed bag in terms of literary variety and quality, but Bok did publish, among other genres, personally inflected, groundbreaking social memoirs by women including Jane Addams and Helen Keller.[1] It is this intellectual and political content that Bok highlights in his autobiography. He tells how he "encouraged and cajoled his readers to form the habit of looking upon his magazine as a great clearing-house of information" (Bok 174), as a textbook of sorts. He supplied a thirty-five-member editorial staff who immediately supplied answers to readers' questions. According to Bok, the subscribers came to rely on this information service and wrote letters that "streamed in by the tens of thousands" and eventually into the "hundreds of thousands, until during the last year, before the service was finally stopped by the Great War of 1917–1918, the yearly correspondence totaled nearly a million letters" (174). Even after the discontinuation of the service, letter-writing readers did not disappear but, instead, hovered in reserve. On several occasions, Bok mobilized his literate subscribers, rousing them to write letters lobbying for civic causes. For instance, when he saw that power companies surrounding Niagara Falls were threatening "America's greatest scenic asset," he urged *Ladies' Home Journal* readers to campaign: "Very soon after the magazine reached its subscribers' hands, the letters began to reach the White House; not by dozens, as the President's secretary wrote to Bok, but by the hundreds and then by the thousands. 'Is there any way to turn this spigot off?' telegraphed the President's secretary" (Bok 353).

As different as the *New Yorker* and *Ladies' Home Journal* seem, they—and several other mid-twentieth-century large-circulation magazines—shared a similar social goal: to provide edifying material that improved minds and material lives. These publications sponsored literacy and were an integral part of a thriving mid-century, middle-class devotion to literacy and education.[2] This chapter underscores the *New Yorker*'s similarities with other large-circulation publications and argues that its ethos had as much in common with middlebrow as with elite culture. As Joan Shelley Rubin carefully documents in *The Making of Middlebrow Culture*, "in the three decades following the First World War, Americans created an unprecedented range of activities aimed at making literature and other forms of 'high' culture available to a wide reading public" (xi). Not all literary critics were happy, however, with what Van Wyck Brooks called a "genial middle ground" (qtd. in Rubin xii). Dwight Macdonald in particular articulated the critique: "It pretends to respect the standards of High Culture while in fact it waters them down and vulgarizes them" (qtd. in Rubin xiv). While Rubin respects the impulse for self-education, "the legitimate needs and aspirations of millions of 'average intelligent readers'" (xix), she ultimately laments that "worthwhile aesthetic commitments" were subordinated to "consumer priorities" (xix). My own impulse, as someone invested in the scholarship of new literacy studies, is to reverse this logic—to grant that consumer pressures, and social values, did inevitably affect decisions about what to print. Sometimes the concessions do indeed seem too great; the editorial letters can be disturbing from this historical distance. Nonetheless, I applaud the impulse and the effort to offer literature to a wider reading public.

Put differently, the literature published in many large-circulation magazines emerged as the result of an ethos that wed editors and subscribers in a joint literate effort. I will be drawing on an older definition of ethos, one that shifts our metaphoric understanding from the traditional figure of the "good man speaking" to "dwelling places" that "define the grounds, abodes or habitats, where a person's ethics and moral character take form and develop" (Hyde xiii). Thus envisioned, ethos is the practice of designing and arranging a space into which audience members are made not only to feel welcome but also to feel as if they belong.[3] As part of their jobs, midcentury editors massaged the strictures of institutional authority, established genres, language conventions, and individual authors, while at the same time they created a recognizable institutional "personality" and place of identification. Trade accounts of editors frequently produce an uncomplicated story, depicting saints (or geniuses) who overcome institutional obstacles to promote originality and excellence and enrich culture. Academic studies tend to veer in the opposite direction, depicting villains (or merely patsies) who compose not-so-little white lies and employ wholesale deception to sell a commercial gospel.[4] As the above brief definition of ethos suggests, I will not be studying editors as either saints or geniuses or villains or patsies. Rather, I look at the textual evidence of their work to examine the rhetoric editors practiced. As the examples in this chapter illustrate, mid-twentieth-century editors struggled with these varying representations in their attempt to work from or with or through an effective ethos. Much of the work of forging this ethos occurred "between the sheets," in the editorial meetings and correspondence and proof. Some occurred outside the pages of the magazine, in trade journals certainly but even in odd places like memoirs. Thus, I pay considerable attention to these sources too.

Edward Bok's Golden Rule

Philanthropist, conservationist, and editor, Edward Bok believed his own story fantastic enough to pen his memoir, *The Americanization of Edward Bok*. This memoir earned him the Pulitzer Prize for autobiography in 1920 and royalties from more than sixty editions, including three geared to inspire elementary school students—*Go To It, You Dutchman!*; *America, Give Me a Chance!*; and *Edward Bok: Young Editor*. Edward Bok published his memoir before magazine circulations boomed yet again, before behind-the-scenes accounts of mass-circulated magazines proliferated into a genre.[5] As the popular success of Lauren Weisberger's *The Devil Wears Prada* attests,[6] we continue as a culture to be fascinated by what we see when we lift the sheets. Bok simply figured this angle early on. According to Edward Bok and the press surrounding him, his prescience shouldn't surprise. He was a wonder. Bok used the platform of *Ladies' Home Journal* to campaign for sex education at a time when sex was everywhere, except in respectable publications.[7] He used part of the multimillions he earned as editor of the *Ladies' Home Journal* to solicit and reward ideas for world peace.[8]

Not everyone concurred with his high self-appraisal, but Bok felt that no man was without his detractors. Still, one claim particularly nagged him. Bok was hired by Cyrus H. K. Curtis to replace Louisa Knapp, known socially as Mrs. Cyrus H. K. Curtis. Some suggested it was Bok's "womanliness" that qualified him to step into the shoes of the boss's wife. Bok felt that his autobiography had to set the record—and his manhood—straight. In 1889, when he, a single man, assumed the editorship of *Ladies' Home Journal*, he knew nothing about women, or so runs his account. He locates an ethos he frequently constructs and inhabits—a characterization of *Ladies' Home Journal* as a commercial site for women who worried more about improving their minds than their bodies. He was successful, he maintains, because he ignored the physical and material details of women's lives:

> When Edward Bok succeeded Mrs. Curtis, he immediately
> encountered another popular misconception of a woman's
> magazine—the conviction that if a man is the editor of a peri-
> odical with a distinctly feminine appeal, he must, as the term
> goes, "understand women." ... No man, perhaps, could have
> been chosen for the position who had a less intimate knowl-
> edge of women. Bok had no sister, no women confidantes: he
> had lived with and for his mother. She was the only woman he
> really knew or who really knew him. His boyhood days had
> been too full of poverty and struggle to permit him to min-
> gle with the opposite sex. And it is a curious fact that Edward
> Bok's instinctive attitude toward women was that of avoid-
> ance. He did not dislike women, but it could not be said that
> he liked them. They had never interested him. Of women,
> therefore, he knew little; of their needs less. Nor had he the
> slightest desire, even as an editor, to know them better, or to
> understand them. (Bok 167–68)

Bok bragged that he saw *Ladies' Home Journal* as a purely speculative venture. Granted, women's magazines had traditionally
been the site of public hilarity, but he saw them as possible sites
of significant learning and, more importantly, of huge profits.
He recounts the Wall Street baron Jay Gould's warning: "I always
felt you had it in you to make a successful man. But not in that
business" (Reneham). The joke, of course, is on Wall Street: Bok
turned down more than one entry position on Wall Street and
then laughed all the way to the bank and through the pages of
his memoir.

Critics expecting to find a forgotten gem in this Pulitzer
Prize–winning memoir are likely to be disappointed. By twenty-
first-century literary standards, it is a self-congratulatory exercise. Despite cues that might lead twenty-first-century readers to
train a queer eye in hopes of a more interesting persona, there is
no such persona in this narrative. Sure, he replaces a woman as
editor of a woman's magazine, but even this radical act is simply a
result of his own clear and clever thinking. He finds fault with the
"popular notion that the editor of a woman's magazine should be

a woman" (Bok 160). Instead, he confidently asserts his countervailing truth, namely, that women worked "infinitely better under the direction of a man than of a woman," that they weren't capable to perform the required executive functions, and, moreover, they weren't inclined to such work (160–61). Rather than the self-deprecating humorous "I" of twenty-first-century essayists, readers find a self-aggrandizing "he" with impeccable mainstream social credentials. He does not remain immigrant, but becomes American. He not only marries, but he marries the boss's daughter. There are no soul-baring confessions in Bok's memoir. He lists the famous people he's encountered, but this is no kiss-and-tell: he simply recounts how he collects famous people's autographs, soliciting them by letter or by enlisting the help of acquaintances. "Look at this tremendous boy!" is the underlying message to his would-be signatories, "he has dared to approach you. Such bravery should be rewarded." (Today, such persistence might suggest a potential stalker.) According to Bok, his bravery was rewarded, as it should have been. He feels impressed; the reader should feel impressed. His is the perfect (white) immigrant story: young Dutch boy arrives on American soil and through ingenuity and initiative, through learning not schooling, he strikes it rich, becomes influential and charitable, a role model for American boys.[9] The Americanization of Edward Bok on the whole is a memoir that creates an ideal American world of unbounded opportunity, a world in which work doesn't interfere with the time needed for leisured learning, in which literacy is acquired through sweat and taste, in which an American boy can grow up to be successful, if he is just determined and brave and savvy enough. In this world, a young man with no college education can trump elite institutions, working until he could endow, say, the Woodrow Wilson Professorship of Literature at Princeton, as Bok did. Just as impressively, such a man could sponsor literacy for millions.

It's difficult to tell whether egotism or sexism motivated Bok more because ultimately he implies that it's not just women who couldn't do his job—men couldn't either. He believed his fantastic accomplishments a "rare" phenomenon: despite "the enormous growth of the modern magazine," Bok boasts, "few successful editors" have emerged (163). In 1920, Bok could sell himself as a child prodigy destined to stand apart and above. Still, Bok's pride in his rare accomplishments might be excused. He bragged that he was the beginning of something big, and he was. By the mid-twentieth century, the world of magazine editing had grown wide and deep, with many editors and publishers profiting from the *Ladies' Home Journal* editor's greatest career tip: "The average editor is obsessed with the idea of 'giving the public what it wants,' whereas, in fact, the public, while it knows what it wants when it sees it, cannot clearly express its wants. The American public always wants something a little better than it asks for, and the successful man, in catering to it, is he who follows this golden rule" (163–64). It is subscription to this golden rule—that the reading public aspired for more and thus wanted to be "improved" materially and intellectually—that resulted in a periodical culture that produced and sustained reverence for literacy and a vibrant, consciously crafted, modern national literature.

This thesis holds particularly for the work of a particular subset of periodical editors, those engaged in producing the "class publications," defined in the first few decades of the twentieth century and reaching unprecedented success in the post–World War II years. In his article "Class Publications," which appeared in *Merchants' and Manufacturers' Journal* in 1913, Condé Nast wrote:

> Among the 90,000,000 inhabitants of the United States . . . there is lack of "equality"—a range and variety of man and woman kind—that simply staggers the imagination; every degree of learning from the man who prefers to read his Testament in the original Greek to the man who can't read anything in any language. . . . A "class publication" is nothing more nor less than a publication that looks for its circulation *only* to those having in common a certain characteristic marked enough to group them into a class. . . . The publisher, the editor, the advertising manager and circulation man must con-

spire not only to get all their readers from one particular class to which the magazine is dedicated, but rigorously to exclude all others. (Nast qtd. in Seebohm 79–80)

While Nast articulated that the "common characteristic might be almost anything," he clearly was using literacy as a delineating factor (qtd. in Seebohm 80). He also employed "class" in a more popular sense, as evidenced by his acquisition of *Vogue*, which, at the time of acquisition, was a provincial society newsletter. In 1923, Nast copyrighted *Vogue's Book of Etiquette*. The preface to the book makes clear its appeal: "These pages have been written not by people who have *learned* the practice of polite society, but have grown up *knowing them*" (Eds. of *Vogue* preface). Nast had discovered that the market potential rested not with those who were already "society" but rather with those wishing to belong to a national elite. He could invoke the problem of lack of taste and solve it simultaneously by offering instruction "to those who know and those who want to know" (Eds. of *Vogue* preface). Such knowledge, the editors of *Vogue* moan, is difficult to acquire, particularly in the media-noisy modern times. *Vogue*, the editors stake, even in "the circle of constant change ... has long been a central mirror reflecting the best standards, tastes, and traditions of the revolving throng. So people, inside and outside, have to rely upon its presentments ... and to regard its authority as the authority of Truth" (Eds. of *Vogue* preface). Part of that "Truth" involved mastery of language standards. Commercial culture had regrettably affected "that large class whose speech is uncultivated or cultivated in all the wrong ways" (Eds. of *Vogue* preface). Usage is primarily a problem for those who do not "inherit" language: "Persons who have an inherited language would not speak of a 'matching hat' when they meant a hat that matched a certain costume" (Eds. of *Vogue* preface). Commercial speak isn't the only vice: overly refined speech is as offensive as "unpleasant" diction. Not quite as comprehensive as Fowler's *Modern English Usage*, another book inspired by the fear of class identification, the language section of *Vogue's Book of Etiquette* is filled with examples that underscore a kind of fussy precision.[10] Such distinctions, the magazine assures us, still matter, even if some may scoff at them as highbrow or affected.

Of course, where speech is so corrupted, writing is likely also to be. Letter writing, we learn, is threatened by postcard culture, but the well bred are holding the line. The literacy crisis invoked is familiar enough to twenty-first-century readers: "standards have been so lowered that any attempt to show differences between the customs of classes may cause the majority to scoff" (Eds. of *Vogue* preface). Yet learning, the editors warn, is essential to acceptance, to belonging:

> "Well-bred English" has no better title to distinction than that it is the English well-bred people speak. There are often no whys and wherefores. They just do say some things, and they just do not say others. They are rather like a great world family who have used the same kind of slang, selecting what pleased them and rejecting what did not, played the same kind of game, grown to know each other's tastes in jokes, and admitted only what members they choose to their inner circle. They know of their own kind from a stranger by a thousand little sayings and doings. The stranger may look like them, may dress like them (or better), may live like them (though more sumptuously in the wrong places), but, if he neither feels nor behaves nor speaks like them, he will be known for a stranger and, no matter how politely treated, may never grow into a comrade. (Eds. of *Vogue* preface)

Vogue invited its middle-class readers to imagine themselves as subscribers who could find a rightful place in high culture. The editors provided lessons in assimilation.

Like other editors of class publications, Nast would sell "cultural improvement," in manners and in letters, by recasting readers as learners whose class advancement depended on a kind of instruction that schools couldn't supply. Likewise, Edward Bok enjoyed his tremendous success with the *Ladies' Home Journal* by creating an institutional dwelling place in which women, with some instruction and improvement, could enter and feel a sense of belonging. *Vogue* and *Ladies' Home Journal* crafted entirely different abodes, but the key to entry for both was an appreciation for high literacy standards. It was literacy that gave the feeling that these spaces—and those who occupied them—were simultaneously accessible and secure from infiltration.

Forging a *New Yorker* Ethos

Most accounts of the early *New Yorker* point to an ethos decidedly different from the one composed for either the high-life *Vogue* or the middle-class domestic *Ladies' Home Journal*. George Douglas perhaps best articulates the ethos of the *New Yorker* and other "smart" magazines, at least in the 1920s and 1930s: "These were magazines for people who believed themselves witty and clever (a group that is never in short supply), for people who didn't want to be bombarded with sermons about the state of the nation, who didn't want to have their days spoiled by the obligations of 'thoughtful essays,' or dignified fiction, who didn't want their minds 'improved.' Their minds were already sufficiently improved, thank you! They wanted to be entertained and enlightened by others who shared their more expansive and uninhibited tastes" (11).

In 1925, when Harold Ross began editing the *New Yorker*, he imagined mostly the kind of magazine that George Douglas describes—a commercial magazine geared toward the night life, light witticisms, and stylish living. It hinged on sophistication; it was "knowing, a trifle world-weary, prone to self-consciousness and irony, scornful of conventional wisdom or morality, resistant to enthusiasm or wholehearted commitment of any kind, and incapable of being shocked" (Yagoda 57). Such characterizations have solidified the reputation of the *New Yorker* in U.S. cultural and literary history. However, there is plenty of editorial evidence that shows that the *New Yorker*, well into the 1960s, was solidly middlebrow.

With some frequency, editors of the *New Yorker* rejected submissions not because they didn't meet high literary standards but because they were too literary. As part of her duties at the magazine, Katharine White frequently had to explain that a piece was too "special," the euphemism for any piece that narrowly restricted the audience for a piece—too academic, too strangely particular, too literary (K. White letter to M. Callaghan, qtd. in Yagoda 55). In April of 1928, Katharine wrote to reject a piece by William Rose Benet on the grounds of its inaccessibility to a middlebrow audience: "As I told you, we have puzzled a good deal over 'Work in Progress,' and now our regretful decision is that the satire seems to be rather too much a good thing for us. We feel that it is probably more a 'Bookman' piece than a *New Yorker* one and that the 'Transition' poets are perhaps too esoteric for our public."[11] Two years later, Harold Ross returned William Rose Benet's "Danseuse" with this rationale. While the sentiment is more pointed and less apologetic, the gist remains:

> Dear Bill:
> We like your stuff, God knows, but this verse, damn it, is obscure. I read it three or four times and then wasn't quite certain what you were getting at. We have been getting kidded for using obscure verse, and I don't think we should. I showed it to two or three other people and they were slightly baffled too. There are too many lines to throw you off.[12]

Women as well as men who contributed to the magazine found themselves judged too literary or too intellectual. Not surprisingly, Djuna Barnes's high modernist style provoked such a response from Katharine in 1928:

> Dear Miss Barnes:
> We have been frightfully dilatory in our reply on your three articles about women because frankly they have puzzled us and all of us have read and reread them several times. They are so witty in details that we should love to use them all but we find the second and third articles unavailable for us because their dizziness, if you know what I mean, seems to put them out of bounds for us. We are afraid that almost none of our readers would understand what you were getting at and it

really is impossible for so simple-minded a magazine as The
New Yorker to publish a manuscript that is so subtle as to be
ambiguous.[13]

Katharine (then still Mrs. Angell) was able to make room for one
of Barnes's "dizzy" submissions, but only after the New Yorker editors exercised significant revisions. Katharine writes Barnes that
these "somewhat drastic changes" have made it possible for "The
Woman Who Goes Abroad to Forget" to be published: "your material was the sort that aroused a good deal of discussion as to
whether it was New Yorker material after all. I am glad to say that it
very much is in the case of this one story and that we are now very
enthusiastic about the piece. The changes were made for clarity
because, as you must realize, your piece was pretty 'dizzy' for our
rather straight forward and not esoteric public."[14] In the pages of
the magazine, the editorial "we" frequently alluded to the sophistication of its discerning audience. Between the sheets, the editors frequently drew a picture of a different audience, one "not
esoteric," one impatient with lengthy or difficult or challenging
pieces, one that would not countenance the avant-garde.

Such an audience was presumably comforted by the familiar,
one of the reasons the editors urged New Yorker contributors to
develop series. In this same letter to Barnes, Katharine encour-
ages the author to create stock characters and stick to them: "we
do very much hope you will send us others on women but suggest that you make the type as clear and definite a one as 'The
Woman Who Goes Abroad to Forget.' She is just the kind of person that The New Yorker wants to satirize and I think there must be
a lot of others like her. We should like to use this story separately
but even more we would like to see it a part of a series which we
think would lend great distinction to the magazine."[15] Other authors received similar advice on potential series based on formulas and recognizable social figures or stereotypes.

Louise Bogan perhaps most dramatically pushed the boundaries of what was acceptable for fiction as well as poetry in the
magazine. In 1934, Katharine White, who was an enthusiastic

fan of Bogan's work, composes a string of painful rejection letters, a few of which I present here in excerpted form:

> Dear Louise: June 1, 1934
>   I am awfully sorry for the delay on the story, a delay that
> was caused, as usual, by differences of opinion and general
> puzzlement on the part of the office as to whether this story
> of yours belonged in The New Yorker. Alas, alas, Mr. Ross's final
> decision is that it doesn't. He thinks that for a light magazine
> it is too abstract and psychological, or something. I am desperately sorry because it is beautifully done for its kind and it
> was just a question as to whether it is our kind. It has aroused
> great admiration here, in spite of our sending it back to you—
> a small satisfaction to you, I fear.[16]

> Dear Louise: November 16, 1934
>   Alas, "Half a Letter", interesting as it is, just doesn't seem
> to us to be New Yorker material. It would be too difficult going for our readers we feel, this literary psychology. It is one of
> those pieces of writing that is perfectly fascinating to people
> who have concentration enough to read it, the people who Mr.
> Gibbs calls the "articulate minority," but it really is not in our
> field. . . . I think you admit yourself it is pretty special. I like
> it, but I have to admit it takes a lot of concentration to understand it, and maybe it's right that such attention is more than
> we can ask of our readers.[17]

As was common practice for most New Yorker editors when they encountered a piece judged "too special" for the New Yorker, Katharine suggests other places where the piece might more easily fit. She is, as always, part agent and part pragmatist in her thinking, keeping in mind both literary reputation and pay: "If I were you I should certainly send this piece to the Atlantic or Harper's, and if they don't take it, to The Mercury. The Mercury pays so little, I suggest the others first, or maybe Scribner's would be good."[18]

Poetry by its very nature created special problems for what was essentially defined as a light magazine. Witty limericks and verse fit in easily, but despite Katharine White's efforts to print more serious verse, serious poets often met resistance and rejection. In 1936, *New Yorker* editors continued to avoid material that they deemed better suited for the "articulate minority," who were reading highbrow publications like *Harper's* or *Scribner's* or the *Atlantic* or small literary magazines. For instance, despite Katharine White's energetic sponsorship, Bogan's poem "Four Quarters" did not garner the necessary editorial vote. "Four Quarters" is somewhat unusual in that the editorial notes have survived—such notes appear randomly in the *New Yorker* archives. They provide a snapshot of the kinds of responses Bogan's work sparked and reveal the editors' deliberative process and guiding principles. These notes evidence the day-to-day workings of the magazine and, thus, the kind of informal prose one would never expect to be preserved. They are candid. For example, Wolcott Gibbs writes to Mrs. White, "I guess I like (and understand) this one. Some nice lines. As usual she trips me up now and then (I don't get much out of 'stricken to a device' for instance) but not enough to bother me seriously."[19] In her note to Ross, White not surprisingly argues for the piece and explicates the difficult line: "I think *yes*: Gibbs' puzzling line makes sense because it uses the word 'device' in the sense, to quote the dictionary 'anything fancifully devised for dramatic presentation; a masque or show' & *stricken* in the sense 'impress' as of a die or coin—i.e., these men? Or houses in the north gleam like a dramatic scene on a coin."[20] As it turns out, quoting the dictionary might not have been the most effective means of persuading Ross, who reacts to the necessity of scholarship. He fires back a harangue, one that makes Bogan stand for a class of high literary affect that the *New Yorker* would not accommodate:

> Gibbs may guess he likes it but I don't like it and no guessing at all. Oh I loathe it. I am about to make an issue of this gals stuff, I'm afraid, after reading this and that prose piece (which I'm holding to reread). I suspect it all. I don't understand this and there's a kind of objectionable and, I think intentional fuzziness and obscurity about [it that] annoys me greatly. Whedon is with me in this, in not liking this piece. As he says,

you've got to read her with a dictionary. I suspect she writes it with a dictionary, to gain superiority. Think she writes for poets, and the arty poets at that.[21]

It falls again upon Katharine White to explain the source of the controversy to Bogan, to delineate the magazine's ethos, arguing why Bogan's work falls outside the boundaries.

> Dear Louise: April 13, 1936
> The delay on your story ["Whatever It Is"] and poem ["Four Quarters"] has been because they have aroused controversy. Mr. Ross wanted to be absolutely sure he was right, in his own mind at least, in saying that he has to say "no" on them both. He seems to feel that the story covers a very special circle and that it is hard for him to identify and keep track of the emotions, and that the story is not very clear. I am awfully sorry. Of course, I think that the real point is that it is a very literary story and there is always a question in his mind whether literary stories of this sort belong in The New Yorker.
> The poem, too, he finds obscure and thinks that we "oughtn't to buy poetry that you have to read with a dictionary." This particular reference I think is to the line "Stricken to a device"…. It is a great disappointment to me and I know it will be even more so to you, but I am absolutely sure that other magazines will jump for these.[22]

It's easy to read into this editorial correspondence a quick judgment of Ross as a philistine who finds no room for any art he does not understand. Such a judgment has been frequently circulated, perhaps most notably in Thurber's The Years with Ross and Brendan Gill's Here at The New Yorker, but it is, as Thomas Kunkel's biography Genius in Disguise argues, superficial. Ross had particular ideas of what made literature and art good and, just as importantly, what would make the magazine a commercial success,[23] and those ideas turned on the truthful and clear presentation of facts. As a former reporter, Ross envisioned the New Yorker as a real news magazine, a source trusted for its careful checking and rechecking of facts and surface details, even in its fiction, poetry, and art. If, as in the case of Frances Gray Patton's "And Hearts In Heaven," the author mentions the Smoky Mountains, then the story must take place in either North Carolina or Tennessee. Further, that precise locale needs to be fixed in the story with the same precision that one would fix it on a map.[24] In short, Ross subscribed fully to the tenets for journalistic clarity and simplicity that E. B. White encountered in 1919 in his Cornell English class taught by Professor Strunk. Ross the high school dropout might easily have written: "Avoid the elaborate, the pretentious, the coy, and the cute. Do not be tempted by a twenty-dollar word when there is a ten-center handy" (Strunk and White 76). (The Elements of Style, with its roots in a Cornell classroom, is the quintessential midcentury middlebrow book.) Elaborate diction deserved to be stricken, in the most common editorial sense of the word. No devices necessary.

Bogan's generous response indicates why she was able to enjoy a long-standing relationship with the New Yorker, eventually signing on as a regular contributor of poetry reviews. Bogan sensed Katharine White's frustration and did the one thing that would further endear the poet to the New Yorker's fiction editor: she praised and defended Ross's judgment. "Dear Katharine: Will you tell Mr. Ross from me that he is right, in both cases: his criticism of the poem was particularly good, because it went off just exactly at the device line, and got steadily worse thereafter. —I mean this, Katharine."[25] What the editorial correspondence shows, I would argue, is not the limitations of Ross's literary imagination, but the restricted capacity of the "smart" magazine ethos.

Katharine White Plays Dueling Ethos

From its inception, the New Yorker held together two potentially contradictory genres: humor and realistic fiction or news.[26] The editors saw their magazine as a place for apolitical limericks and other light literature; they also saw it as a place for civic-minded profiles, reminiscences and stories, and serious fact reporting. While some "smart" readers might not have looked to the magazine for improvement, others—that inarticulate majority—quite seriously did. Still others found appeal in its middlebrow offerings. At different points in the magazine's histories, the various genres—and the ethos they inhabited—were more or less commodious. Most chroniclers of the magazine's history, for instance, argue that World War II forced a profound shift from a preponderance of light entertainment to a prevalence of grim reporting.[27] Corey Ford's *The Time of Laughter*, published in 1967, grants World War II's dour influence, but Ford suggests another reason for the shift in tone—the magazine had become too august for its own good: the "high standard of excellence discouraged young writers, and the lengthy articles and stories and departments left less space for experimenting with unknowns, as Ross had done" (219). In this retrospective, Ross's antiliterary stance, his refusal to be bowled over by famous names and claims to "serious" art, left ample room for newcomers who experimented and brought the kind of fresh perspectives necessary for humor to thrive.

Upon receiving a copy of Ford's *The Time of Laughter*, White writes Ford a somewhat lengthy personal review, a genre she frequently practiced when she admired either the content or the style of a book. White shared Ford's worries about the demise of humor, but she hoped that there would be a resurgence of humor to balance the grim realism of the mid-twentieth century:

> Even to this day, the magazine averages one or two unknown names to each issue, so I can't agree that new young writers and humorists have no place to turn to now or that the stories in *The New Yorker* crowded out the humor. That fact is that in the forties, fifties, and sixties the best humorous writers moved from writing "casuals" into writing humorous short stories. Cheever, J. F. Powers, Updike, Peter De Vries, Frank O'Connor et al., more of whom also wrote grim ones. I do agree that humor in *The New Yorker* reached its peak in the '30s both in text and art, but new funny men are turning up weekly. . . . As for parody, I don't despair of it. Beerbohm and Gibbs were the masters so far in English in my opinion, but it

goes right on in *The New Yorker* and elsewhere and always will, I'm sure.[28]

The *New Yorker* survived because it moved with the times, sometimes matching the abruptness of world events. Given a particular moment in cultural time (the gay atmosphere of prohibition, the inescapable realities of the depression), one or another mood characterized an issue or a series of issues or a stretch of time. The magazine thus teetered between two types of ethos, both held together by Professor Strunk's dictum that good writing demonstrated the qualities of a direct, clear, precise, accessible style. This twin ethos became a problem that accompanied success, as loyal readers, critics, and *New Yorker* contributors began to create an iconic image. Some readers noticed and were irked by the gap between the constructed audience and the pieces offered, by anything that looked like "dumbing down":

> Dear Sir: June 21, 1943
> I am a constant reader of your magazine, *The New Yorker*. I have been greatly disappointed lately in the standard of some of your selections.
> It would interest me to know which one of your editors accepted to publish "Love Letter" in your issue of June 12th, by a certain Karl J. Shapiro.
> One cannot prevent people from writing such nonsensical and pretentious lucubrations, as sordid as they are degenerate, but you could ask your staff not to insert them in your magazines.[29]

As early as the mid-1930s and early 1940s, there was increasing pressure to name the magazine's signature type, to figure out its principles of inclusion and exclusion, to reveal its formulas. These accounts would increasingly focus on genre. Writers like Corey Ford believed strongly that the magazine's earlier offerings were its strength. His emblematic *The Time of Laughter* locates the 1930s as the magazine's magic years, characterized by light but highly crafted humorous sketches, short stories, verse,

and cartoons (always referred to as "art"), coupled with reminiscence pieces and profiles. *The Time of Laughter* works from the
premise, articulated in the introduction by Frank Sullivan, that
the turn toward realism, "the output of the solemn, humorless emancipators of the four-letter words," marked the end of a
golden age: "Our spirits would have tobogganed if we had had
to reckon with the Sword of Damocles that has hung over the
world since Hiroshima. In these days an old man tries to remember this when tempted to impatience with the odd behavior of
the young generation" (Ford xiii).[30] However, for others, the turn
toward realism, which Shawn advocated and accelerated, consti-
tuted its literary apex. In his *Here at* The New Yorker, published
in 1975, Brendan Gill celebrated the move away from a kind of
metropolitan provincialism that marred even the early magazine and that in the postwar era was simply and sadly dated.[31] He
praised Shawn's editorship and argued strongly that the quality
of literature had improved under Shawn's tenure or influence. As
proof, Gill cited extended pieces that tackled serious social is-

sues, pieces such as John Hersey's "Hiroshima" and Rachel Carson's *Silent Spring*. In this view, Shawn's *New Yorker*, unlike Ross's,
demonstrated an ability to change with and engage the seriousness of the time. Reviews were quick to pick up on the representation. In the *New York Times*, reviewer John Leonard summarized
the narrative trope structuring Gill's account: "the fear of being
thought a philistine haunted Ross" (2); such fear dissipated under Shawn, who knew he was not one.

Over her long career, White found herself at the fault line of
the two competing brands of *New Yorker* ethos. She was proud of
the work produced under the editorial direction of both Ross and
Shawn and was extremely frustrated by published accounts that
valorized one form of literature over the other. Finally, for White,
the *New Yorker* was a place that literate readers who valued quality
could come to be entertained *and* educated or uplifted; they could
expect exacting standards across genres. She saw the *New Yorker*
as a publication that held a range of good literature—humor or

realism, sketch or story, fact or fiction, limerick or poem—and did justice to all these genres. It was for her only a question of presentation; the layout of the magazine, when done correctly, could do each genre justice. For this reason, she watched the layout of the magazine carefully and registered her outrage when printers destroyed the careful divisions between serious and light pieces. In October of 1935, White was bothered by a printer's decision to place one of Louise Bogan's poems next to frivolous content. She writes to Bogan to apologize but also to the copydesk in order to "take up for the poets," a role she would vocally play on a number of occasions when she felt as if the magazine, with its commercial interests that saw poetry as just so many lines of text, had "sinned" against poets or poetry.

> Dear Louise: October 23, 1935
> I should have told you over the telephone today how distressed I was by this week's issue when I saw your very beautiful and sad poem placed in the particular position that it was in the magazine. It never should have been put in there opposite a page of crazy poems and surrounded by the irregularity of Mr. Brubaker's paragraph. Everybody says it was very bad judgment, but apparently it was one of those things that happens because of time and space problems. Do please forgive us since we recognize our sins.[32]

> Dear Mr. Whedon and Copy Room: October 28, 1935
> Mr. Ross says "somebody ought to raise hell, but nobody will" about this boner on the Bogan poem. Well I will for the sake of the poets. It is a most unfortunate error and we must find a way to prevent the printer putting over errors like this on us, even when there is a slight explanation of the mistake in a similarity of the two lines in the third and fourth stanzas. It's enough to make a good poet stop contributing at all.[33]

> Use of *Newsbreaks*—To harp again on point I made an issue or two ago about there not being enough bofb [back of book] verse. I definitely think it is bad practice to follow a poem with a newsbreak, wind up a column that way.... It's unattractive

makeup and is hard on the poets, very.... Both Holms' and McGinley's verses in this case deserve a better fate than to become little islands in the midst of hodgepodge of type and subject matter.[34]

Katharine White's ethos, her idea of a print space that could hold all genres together under an umbrella of literary excellence, finally proved untenable. She came to accept, albeit with deep regret, Ross's premise that haute literature was out of bounds for the publication. Ten years before her death at age eighty-four, a disturbed White notes the persistence of the "fashionable ... attacks and digs at The New Yorker and even at Ross."[35] This tug-of-war over the New Yorker's worth and reputation, which continues today, played out in news and magazine articles and in memoirs. Some, like Renata Adler's Gone: The Last Days of The New Yorker, loudly decried that the New Yorker was dead (or at best dying), that it had changed too much:

> As I write this, The New Yorker is dead. It still comes out every week, or almost every week.... The magazine was already, at least arguably, declining under Mr. Shawn. This change goes beyond decline. It may be that a magazine has a natural life span and then sputters out. I don't think so. Or it may be that, from the remains of what was once a living enterprise, something else ... will grow. Apart perhaps from its logo, that would not be The New Yorker. The format, the look, the content, the humor, the level of seriousness; the ambition, at the top; the standards in the middle, the limits beneath which it would not sink; the relationship between editorial and advertising considerations; the balance between prose and pictures; the signature; certain notions of excellence; certain understandings with readers; the institutional memory—these are not qualities that can be set aside and then taken up again. (11)

Others offered the equally damning account: the magazine hadn't changed at all; it remained snobbish, artificial, cliquish, thoroughly and ironically provincial. Yagoda best summarizes this argument: "the aesthetic that eventually came to inform the *New Yorker* had its shortcomings. It was rarely receptive to elliptical, experimental, gritty, or subversive artists, or to work that came from the margins of society. And it provided a home to writing that was precious, smug, tiresomely literal, too long, or just plain dull" (21). Still others promoted its iconic image as a unique place for the "articulate minority," a place where the value of the literary enterprise is revered and sustained even under the onslaught of commercial culture. Katharine White's frustration rested in her belief that all these characterizations failed to capture the magazine's history or its middlebrow mission—to provide literature to a wide audience who believed in the social and cultural value of literacy and letters.

Juggling Ethos and the *New Yorker* Type

As fiction editor of the *New Yorker* for a good many years, Katharine White had reason to take personally the critiques of the magazine's literary offerings. White joined the staff as Katharine Angell in 1925, the magazine's first year, and worked in the New York City offices or from the Whites' Maine farmhouse until her official retirement on the first of January 1961. Though clearly biased, E. B. White sang his wife's editorial praises in 1969 when interviewed by George Plimpton and Frank Crowther of the *Paris Review* if it were true that his wife was the "intellectual soul" of the *New Yorker*:

I have never seen an adequate account of Katharine's role with The *New Yorker*. Then Mrs. Ernest Angell, she was one of the first editors to be hired, and I can't imagine what would have happened to the magazine if she hadn't turned up. . . . She quickly discovered, in this fumbling and impoverished new weekly, something that fascinated her: its quest for humor, its search for excellence, its involvement with young writers and artists. . . . Katharine was soon sitting in on art sessions and planning sessions, editing fiction and poetry, cheering and steering authors and artists along the paths they were eager to follow, learning makeup, learning pencil editing, heading

the Fiction Department, sharing the personal woes and dilemmas of innumerable contributors and staff people who were in
trouble or despair, and, in short, accepting the whole unruly
business of a tottering magazine with the warmth and dedication of a broody hen.

I had a bird's-eye view of all this because, in the midst of
it, I became her husband. (83)[36]

E. B. White's account is largely personal and homey: the Manhattan offices sound surprisingly like the barnyard he composed
for *Charlotte's Web* (a comparison perhaps made incomplete mostly
by the absence of a literate spider named Charlotte). Katharine
White's obituary in 1977 makes, as obituaries tend to do, the
strongest and most succinct case for her professional influence,
reporting that she was widely "credited with having transformed
The New Yorker from a humor magazine into the purveyor of much
of the best writing in the country. She 'discovered' such authors
as ... Vladimir Nabokov, and sponsored the work of ... writers
such as Mary McCarthy, John Cheever, John Updike [and oth-
ers].... With her husband, E. B. White [whom she hired before
they married], she was long regarded as the major literary force
on *The New Yorker*, wholly dedicated to elegance and precision in
language" (Hess 15).[37] Five years after Katharine White's death,
Brian Nerney in 1982 was the first to proffer a full accounting
with his dissertation. Linda H. Davis followed in 1987 in a research project that began as a master's thesis and ended in the
only published biography of Katharine White.

Such tributes, such attention, would have first embarrassed
and ultimately pleased Katharine, but during her lifetime, she
was mostly upset by references to her in *New Yorker* memoirs. Over
her working years, White was apt to encounter indirect criticism
of her work in the form of the persistent and nagging claim that
the *New Yorker* published a certain type of fiction. Two years before
E. B. White's *Paris Review* interview, in 1967, Corey Ford published
his *The Time of Laughter*, the book that points nostalgically to the
magazine's humorous, early golden years. The book locates pre-

cisely the awful moment when this humor was supposedly supplanted by a new short story type. According to Ford, the end of humor was foreshadowed quite early, in 1931, when Kay Boyle "pioneered the school of introspective fiction ... with a short story called 'Kroy Wen,'" a work that marked the beginning of the "self-analytic and pastel stories-without-plots which have become a *New Yorker* standby" (132). Ford also located a prime mover: "Mrs. White guided their writers, with sensitivity and tact" (132).

Katharine White remained on good terms with Ford, but his critical rendition struck more than one of her steely nerves, as evidenced by the letter she wrote him:

> Of course I don't always agree with your opinions or even your facts.... I winced over the sentence in *The New Yorker* chapter about "the self-analytic pastel-stories-without-plots" as a *New Yorker* "standby," which is the fashionable cliché to my mind, but is a matter of opinion, not fact. We *did* make the break from the then artificially plotted or overplotted S.E.P. [*Saturday Evening Post*] and *Ladies' Home Journal* short story but if you will reread the three collections of *New Yorker* short stories (now in paperback), I think you will find mighty few that are pastel and only a few that are without plots.[38]

Ford's *The Time of Laughter* was finally a celebration rather than a lament; the reference to the interloping new short story type was a detail, not the story. Katharine could live with it.

It was another book—Brendan Gill's *Here at The New Yorker* —that emerged as the proverbial straw to break Katharine White's back. Only after his wife's death did E. B. White reveal to friend and coeditor Bill Maxwell exactly how deeply the book had affected her: "Her loathing of the book was so intense that she was beginning to lose her sense of proportion, her steadiness as a critic. I watched her, day by day, as she sat picking Gill to pieces, and realized that she was becoming obsessed by the thing she was doing. It worried me, and I finally got up my courage and advised her to knock it off. She did knock it off and soon regained her poise."[39]

Katharine White filled a thick folder with notes articulating her grievances with the book. Certainly Gill's book, among its other sins, added catastrophic force to the idea that *New Yorker* literature had devolved into formula fiction. With the giddiness of an exposé writer, Gill identified the darlings of *New Yorker* anthologies—John O'Hara, Dorothy Parker, Robert M. Coates, Sally Benson, "and one or two other writers"—and credited them with the creation of "what the world came to call the 'New Yorker short story'" (264). Of course, he needles, "nobody who has written a short story for *The New Yorker* would ever admit that there was such a thing" (B. Gill 264). Loyal readers also resented (and still resent) the suggestion that the *New Yorker* published formula fiction. One *New York Times* reviewer decried: "There is no discernible 'type' to the taste in fiction of a periodical that regularly publishes Cheever, Welty, Singer, Barthelme, Borges, Updike and Wolwode, unless excellence is a 'type.'" (Leonard BR1).

Still, by the 1960s, the familiar critique had gathered quiet steam, fed even from writers aligned with the *New Yorker*, like Corey Ford. Unlike the others who kept secret such practice, Gill cheerfully confessed, defending writing to type as part of the commercial writing life. He records how he willingly accepts his agent's suggestions "to make stories salable" (B. Gill 157) because he likes, for instance, the rate that the *Saturday Evening Post* pays. Such concessions, he claims, didn't diminish his work: "The *Saturday Evening Post* was then still in its glory, and to have one's stories published in the magazine that had published Fitzgerald and Lardner and was currently publishing Faulkner, Marquand, and Thomas Beer was considered no small thing" (B. Gill 157). Gill located only one problem, that of stylistic preference: the "*Post* liked longish stories, with elaborate plots, and it turned out that I wasn't especially interested in making up plots" (157). Eventually, he determines, the task became tiresome. He was willing to leave the elaborate plotting—what he implied was commercially inspired overplotting—to Faulkner. What made Gill so gleeful in these paragraphs is the knowledge that he was laying his finger on a very hot button. The issue of type—and of writing to a type—was a touchy subject for most editors and authors, particularly as MFA programs gained in popularity, and critics began to decry that fiction, as well as poetry and drama, were becoming a craft to be taught and edited into existence; fiction in particular seemed to some critics increasingly manufactured.

Over the years spanning her career (1925–1960) and her retirement (1961–1977), White had numerous occasions to formulate and practice responses to allegations that the New Yorker published a type of fiction. Indeed, well before Ford's book or Gill's, the editors of the New Yorker had battled such accusations. Such criticism began the minute the magazine's success became the subject of features in trade journals. The idea of a New Yorker type was also no doubt fueled by various anthology projects edited by White, collections popular enough to be reprinted in paperback editions.[40] Anthology work by its very nature was a double-edged sword. It both rendered necessary visibility and market share to New Yorker fiction and made easier the kind of collective criticism that, having achieved some traction, accelerated.

Perhaps even more upsetting to Katharine White was this: accounts of a New Yorker type invoked the already popular caricature of Ross—his literary shortfalls, his simple consumption of humor, and his purported inability to see literary value in realism. Ford recounted that "Ross was never quite comfortable about running what he called 'grim stuff'" (132). Katharine White retorted that "Ross would rail in public at grim or sordid stories but his public rantings seldom represented his literary feelings. Take Robert Coates—his best short stories were grim and violent indeed and Ross rejoiced in them, as he did in O'Hara's early grim stories and many others" (qtd. in L. Davis 113). Realism was not new to the magazine—a point Ford concedes when he locates the above mentioned "Kroy Wen" date in 1931, a year early in Ross's tenure. Indeed, Katharine had been soliciting and arguing for serious fiction beginning in 1928, three years after the magazine was founded. By 1929, White was querying poets for serious pieces as well, taking at least William Carlos Williams by surprise: "Really I didn't know that *The New Yorker* was interested in poetry as poetry" (qtd. in Yagoda 54). Still, serious fiction, realism, simply was not as prevalent in the early years. *New Yorker* readers, even through the Depression years, valued humor.

By the early 1940s, the balance between humor and realism shifted, and almost immediately, the *New Yorker's* high literary mission became the object of scrutiny. In 1943, Irwin Shaw complained about the critical response, "the patronizing sniffing" to pieces published there (qtd. in Yagoda 22). The *New Yorker* story had come to signify "something pallid and cold that is inexplicably used to pad out the space between cartoons and the Talk of the Town" (qtd. in Yagoda 22). Shaw believed he had identified the editorial impulse that was creating this impression: "you're overworking your famous urbanity and objectivity to a point where too much of your stuff has a high, even gloss, whether it's on the subject of death, disaster, love, anything" (qtd. in Yagoda 22). Just a year later, the *New Yorker* editors again found themselves on the defensive. This time a *New Republic* review by Delmore Schwartz prompted Ross to query Katharine about the validity of the criticism. She replied:

> I would take with several grains of salt the digs at *New Yorker* fiction made by this reviewer, Delmore Schwartz. He is a . . . poet and I have tried without any pleasure to read his poetry. He is impatient of writing which is not very modern in approach and the stylized sort of thing we are apt to find distressing. However, he makes a point when he says "the anecdotal idiom of *The New Yorker*." (This is our idiom in half of our fiction anyway and with reason, since it suits our sort of magazine.)[41]

In internal memos and letters, White does not reject the idea of a prevailing "idiom." Her work acquiring pieces for the magazine and compiling the anthologies demonstrate her awareness that the magazine needed to secure a market share in the middlebrow publishing niche that marketed "best of" literature. Although committed to the promotion of high letters and quality literature, the New Yorker editors never confused their mission with those of the small literary magazines. Healthy circulation figures depended on participation in the mass book sector. White objects not to Schwartz's characterization of an idiom but to his ungenerous characterization of it, his reducing of haute letters to a kind of effete posturing, one perceived as callously out of place as the war claimed more lives. In the 1940s, talk needed to be serious, sophistication needed substance. White believed the magazine had changed with the times; the Whites had been lured back to the city from their Maine farm in part because they felt they needed to help the magazine write seriously about world governments: "I think [Schwartz] is talking through his hat when he mentions our 'insignificant patter' and our 'bogus sophistication.'"[42] According to Katharine White, what Schwartz could rightly complain about was the magazine's war fiction, heavy in naturalism, not always artistically rendered. But here, the war itself and a new generation of writers were the sources to blame: "[Schwartz] is sound in saying we sometimes use too much 'flat naturalism.' Seems to me this is especially true of our war fiction except where a really good writer takes naturalism and adds art, as Irwin Shaw usually does, Newhouse occasionally but by no means always, McLaughlin very seldom. O'Hara does add art when he's at his best—not that he has done much war fiction. But we have a whole crew of young fry who imitate the 'flat naturalism' of the better known boys."[43]

Editorially, the war was too big a subject, too serious a subject, to avoid, and yet, Katharine White felt that few authors could raise the raw details of war to the level of art, particularly when the New Yorker ethos demanded that such details be factually verifiable but not graphically upsetting. This balance the magazine accomplished: the New Yorker's war fiction was sufficiently "flat" to lend itself to production as a coffee-table anthology.

Despite all her protestations to Ford, Katharine White at some level had to acknowledge that there was a *New Yorker* type. It was her job, after all, to vet manuscripts and determine whether, in either current or edited form, they were or were not right for the magazine. In rejecting manuscripts, Katharine suggested that there was a type, usually by invoking the familiar editorial trope that "this is not quite right for us" and pointing to an elusive mark the writer had missed. However, White would have insisted that the mark was not a contained thread on a vast fabric but rather a collection of threads, knit together by the transcendent criteria of literary excellence. Most often, White succeeded with this persuasive maneuver; it was flattering to writers to be judged both an original artist *and* a part of an elite *New Yorker* cadre of writers. But occasionally, White failed to persuade, as she did in her comments when rejecting Frances Gray Patton's story "The Second Grade Mind." The problem manifested when White sent the rejection notice, complete with her candid judgments, to Diarmuid Russell, Patton's agent, not realizing that he intended to convey the editor's exact, no-punches-pulled wording to the author. Patton, "disturbed by its implications," writes a detailed, angry letter to White, which I quote here almost in its entirety:

> You suggest, it seems to me that I was either writing with a "different kind of magazine" in mind—that is, pandering to the slicks and doing only lip service to my agreement [to submit all stories first to the *New Yorker*]—or, which is almost worse, that I was so fatuous as to consider your very polite "appeal" for fiction as a sort of cry of desperation that I could answer by beating out any old kind of stuff and tossing it in your direction. One way I am something less than perfectly ingenuous; the other way I am a fool.
>
> As a matter of fact, I did think the story acceptable material for *The New Yorker*. I thought the character real, the dialogue fairly amusing and the situation true though I was prepared to consider certain cuts and changes of emphasis and to welcome, as always, your shrewd editorial advice. But the fact that you did not like the story is neither here nor there at the moment. (You could turn down a dozen of my pieces on the

score of the broadness of their strokes, the clumsiness of their expression, the sentimentality of them, or just the general insipidity of their tone, and though I might bleed, I would not be stung to anything approaching resentment!) What I must explain to you is my literary ethics.

I do not "slant." Sometimes I deal with subject matter that is obviously not for The New Yorker (witness the Dove stories that the [Ladies' Home] Journal likes); oftener—and perhaps with more pleasure—I write things that could not conceivably find a resting place outside The New Yorker. But in writing, itself—in the treatment of my subjects—I try very hard to be "my own man." I do not pore over magazines in an effort to discover the secret formulae of their fiction, or their favorite adjectives, or even their tabus. I do not do this for two reasons: first, if I did I should feel dishonest—as if I were stealing someone's thunder; second, I don't believe it would help me sell anything as I have never been able to compose with my tongue in my cheek.[44]

Patton characterizes any kind of discourse and audience analysis as antithetical to art and to an artist's ethical process. Art is divorced from rhetorical purpose; its origins are organic, not planned. Only slick writers write to type, only slick writers pander. Katharine's words made Patton especially sensitive because, as she explains, "Especially have I been careful not to try to copy what is vaguely known as 'a typical New Yorker story'. I think that story is mythical. It is my conviction that The New Yorker is impressed only by freshness and the kind of urbanity that derives from real wit and that it can smell imitation a mile away. The best fiction you have printed seems to me to have been the result of the happiest sort of accident—the natural talents of the writer have been in tune with the sensitive taste of the editors."[45]

Not surprisingly given the heat of Patton's letter, White responds, expressing at length, in four single-spaced pages, her astonishment that Russell had passed along the letter without permission and delineating the misunderstanding. White's appeals to Patton are many and varied—appeals to friendship, to the harried state of affairs in the wake of Ross's death, to her admiration of Patton's art and integrity. Although it is a model of how an editor might quiet an outraged author, I quote here only from the parts of the letter that shed light on the contentious issue of the New Yorker type.

White begins by placing blame on the magazine's first-reading agreement, the contract whereby the author would automatically submit all work to the magazine, which held the right of first refusal. The agreement, which came with a cash incentive for contributors, helped ensure that the magazine wouldn't be scooped, an increasingly common phenomenon as the periodical market for short stories grew more competitive beginning in the 1940s and extending through the 1960s. The agreement also meant that the magazine regularly received material that was "not quite right":

> It is a common happening that contributors who have agreements with us occasionally conceive and write pieces which they think will fit better into other magazines. Any versatile writer is bound to do this, since we are, after all, a fairly special magazine and there are many types of subject matter or treatment that we do not use. If having an agreement with The New Yorker prevented a writer from doing this, I think we would have much to answer for in a literary sense. We have never wanted a writer to feel restricted or hampered by his New Yorker agreement and we feel that no good writer should be prevented from trying his hand at any type of material. All we ask, if they do this, is that we see the manuscript first, before submitting it elsewhere, since they are often mistaken in thinking we will not want it.[46]

Patton has only acted professionally, White praises, by sending in the "not quite right" piece. White also tries to redirect Patton from a vision of the author as artist, who works in the unfettered region of the mind, to the model of the professional writer, who negotiates his artistry in the marketplace. E. B. White ("Andy") stands as his wife's model:

> You seem to think that writing with a certain magazine in
> mind is a cardinal literary sin. We don't think so at all; we
> think it is a natural and inevitable and sensible thing for a
> professional writer to do. I can take an example from what is
> happening in my own home at this moment. Andy is in the
> midst of writing a long leisurely discursive essay about our old
> dachshund, Fred. Now Fred is a good subject for a *New Yorker*
> "casual" if Andy should write about him in a certain way. But
> he is, in this case, writing about him a way that he thinks
> would fit *The Atlantic* better than *The New Yorker*. He may well be
> wrong about that but it is what he feels. We wouldn't dream
> of thinking him unethical or think that he was "slanting"—a
> word I detest—but only that the form he conceived this piece
> in just doesn't happen to be right, in his mind, for *The New
> Yorker*. He did not arrive at this decision by studying *The Atlantic*
> or by studying *The New Yorker*, but he happens to have read both
> magazines enough to know their differences.[47]

Andy is not catering to the magazine's whims, he is not "slant-
ing"; rather, he is locating his piece within a hospitable and recognizable ethos. Of course, Katharine believes her husband is
not correct in his assumption that the *New Yorker* would not welcome Fred. Or rather, she feels that he is articulating this reason rather than another, one that underscores that he is a professional as well as an artist. Katharine White suspects that he
is submitting to the *Atlantic* "for career reasons," which are not
commercially inspired, "I suspect, though he hasn't said so, that
he likes to appear in *The Atlantic* occasionally even though he
knows he would get far more money from *The New Yorker*."[48]

Writers also, Katharine White continues, make logical decisions based on choice of genre, which along with quality and
ethos determine the proper venue for a piece:

> The same sort of thing could happen to a short story writer
> who might, let us say, suddenly get an inspiration for and
> write an out and out sentimental story or a melodrama or a
> crime story or a period story or a historical background story.

Every one of these different types of story, although some of them sound merely "popular," can have real literary merit if well done. If he didn't write this story, he would be untrue to himself. If he didn't write it because he felt *The New Yorker* would not like its type, *The New Yorker* system would be at fault.[49]

The *New Yorker*, Katharine White argues, is not the best home for every piece of writing. Its parameters, its ethos, was staked by Ross and, in January of 1952, in the wake of Ross's death, seemed destined to change: "We have our personal tastes, whims, idiosyncrasies, and our contemporary scene limitations and we have our personality and character as a publication which was, I suppose, based chiefly on Ross's own predilections.... But Ross himself was always reaching out for new things. So are we all."[50]

Katharine White would have agreed with the biographer Thomas Kunkel's assessment that Harold Ross was a genius. It seems clear that Ross was successful because he exercised patience as the magazine settled into its identity. He recognized talent and skill and encouraged both. He invited contributors' identification with the magazine and its literate enterprise. He urged them to see themselves as part of an educated and cultured elite. To this list, I would add another distinguishing feature: Ross understood that class publications would succeed to the extent that they could *exclude* or seem to exclude a readership. The official line was that his publication was not for the Lady in Dubuque, even as editors kept her very much in mind, whittling and cutting and revising "special" pieces to fit the broader contours of middle-class U.S. suburbia. Ross absorbed and practiced Bok's golden rule, giving *New Yorker* readers something better than they expected. More accurately, Ross went one better: he presented them with middlebrow goods but convinced his readers that they were getting material much more sophisticated, much more innovative and artistic, much more rare. Perhaps most importantly for the magazine's success, he understood the importance of branding and type. Faced with the choice of becoming a literary hothouse or a magazine for the "inarticulate majority," he consciously chose the latter, preserving the very type readers had come to expect. Shawn took more risks, but by nature and by *New Yorker* affiliation, he too was cautious. Under both editors, *New Yorker* readers were shocked only on occasion, yet they felt that what they were reading was cutting edge and edgy. They were simultaneously troubled by the rendering of social ills and comforted by the idea that knowledge alone could cure or at least rise above the thorniest of problems. Readers expected to find in the magazine's pages a comforting, familiar literacy that promised to still any social chaos, and they found it.

The *New Yorker* survived because it never strayed too far from its middlebrow ethos. Its readership would not allow it. This is the lesson Tina Brown learned when she tried to widen the readership and include the previously excluded when, for example, in 1996 she transformed Eustace Tilley into a woman for the cover of a special women's issue. The *New Yorker* survived not by broadening its ethos, not by creating a larger space to house more and different readers but instead by replicating (in anthologies and calendars and even shower curtains) the familiar contours, the recognizable type that editors and aficionados claimed did not exist.

TWO ∾ "THE PRECISION OF KNIVES," OR MORE THAN JUST COMMAS

Ross had done [Capote] a favor, an unintentional kindness, in firing him. Indeed, if the reverse had happened, if by some bureaucratic aberration he had been made a writer at *The New Yorker*, the result might well have been disastrous for both his writing and his career. He was only just beginning to find his true voice, his distinctive style as a writer, and if he had stayed and moved up, he might have been tempted, perhaps without even knowing it, to trim his increasingly luxuriant prose to a more muted, understated pattern favored by the magazine. Such a mutation, a kind of protective coloration, had been the fate of other spirited young talents, certainly, at *The New Yorker* and elsewhere.

Gerald Clarke, *Capote*

In 1925, when Ross started the magazine, Jane Grant delineated the *New Yorker*'s competition, stating its intentions to vie for market share with periodicals like *Harper's Weekly*, *Life*, the *Smart Set*, and *American Mercury*.[1] By the 1940s, that market, at least in terms of literary contributions, had expanded, with stiff competition from middlebrow magazines like the *Saturday Evening Post*, *Collier's*, and from women's magazines like *Mademoiselle* and *Harper's Bazaar*. Harold Ross believed that careful editing, including new, heightened levels of fact checking, was one way for the *New Yorker* to distance itself from the pack. In his *Genius in Disguise*, Thomas Kunkel documents Ross's obsession with discovering the perfect, efficient system to handle manuscripts, an impulse that resulted in the "magazine's aggressive approach to grammar and punctuation" (259). Editors at the New Yorker, Kunkel explains, "took their cues ... from a man who could hold forth for hours on the application of the serial comma" (259). While Ross's affection for Fowler's *Modern English Usage* is legendary, he was willing to depart from it when a rule seemed to defy fact or obscure a realistic portrait. It was a quirk James Thurber had some fun with. "A British professor once asked Thurber why New Yorker editors placed a comma in the sentence, 'After dinner, the men went into the living room.'" Thurber was quick with an explanation, "this particular comma was Ross's way of giving the men time to push back their chairs and stand up" (qtd. in Kunkel 259).

From the beginning—perhaps because of Ross's background as a military journalist and his exacting temperament—the New Yorker promoted rigorous editorial standards, with factual accuracy occupying the top of the blue-pencil hierarchy. This commitment to journalistic and particular (some might say "fussy") grammatical principles, rather than to literary license, both furthered and hindered the magazine's reputation for belles-lettres. Fifteen years after the New Yorker's founding, critics began to complain that the magazine's editorial rigor discouraged promising writers from submitting their work and, more damning still, that the demanding journalistic standards resulted in inferior literature. Authors with real genius, the critics insisted, were taking their work to magazines that allowed creative license, even to the women's magazines *Mademoiselle* and *Harper's Bazaar*. New Yorker editors struggled with this criticism, as evidenced by this snippet from a six-page memo from Katharine White to Harold Ross: "[Diarmuid] Russell keeps saying that *Harper's Bazaar* fiction is better than ours because there is more stylistic individuality allowed in it and more experiment. *Harper's Bazaar* and *Town and Country* do not, I believe, edit at all. I do not agree with Russell and I don't suggest no editing, for heaven's sake—just more casualness and less fanaticism on it."[2]

This counternarrative is one that surfaces with some consistency. It raises a provocative question: was the New Yorker, as a result of its aggressive editorial practices, being eclipsed by other magazines, by women's magazines that attracted unrestrained genius and thus published higher quality fiction? This question became dramatically public in the 1940s, 1950s, and 1960s. To fully appreciate this drama, we must remember that the *New Yorker* was not then the magazine we know it as today, a point underscored in the previous chapter and explored further here. In the early 1940s, the *New Yorker* had not ossified into a well-recognized, literary powerhouse with wide circulation (*Lady Editor*, for instance, still characterized it as a quirky, very small-circulation magazine), but it was well on its way to making good on a formula of high journalistic standards coupled with excellent literature. Its reputation as a highbrow literary publisher was beginning to emerge. Truman Capote recounts how he and fellow aspiring writer Phoebe Pierce spoke of the *New Yorker* in the "hushed tones of worshipers at a shrine" (Clarke 70). Even allowing for sentimental reconstruction, it's clear that in 1943, Capote was inspired enough by a vision of the magazine that he acted on his goal of publishing in the *New Yorker* and sought employment there as a copyboy, the only position he could acquire. He wanted to be noticed or, better yet, *discovered*. A decade later, in the postwar period when the magazine's circulation swelled, Sylvia Plath likewise dreamed "of seeing her own writing in the trademark typeface of 'the blessed glossy *New Yorker*.'" (Hammer 78). Plath eventually published with the *New Yorker* and recorded her pleasure in her journal: "Felt radiant, a New Yorker glow lighting my face" (Plath qtd. in Hammer 78).[3] Capote's choice of jobs was unfortunate. Not an insider by any measure, Capote did not realize that "*New Yorker* copyboys had never been looked upon as potential writers or reporters, as they often were at other publications" (Clarke 70). Although at work he tried to let it be known to anyone who would listen (and even those who wouldn't) that he was a writer, when he submitted his fiction he was "politely rebuffed" (Clarke 81) both before and after his employment there. The *New Yorker* eventually published Capote's nonfiction pieces (*The Muses*

Are Heard [1956] and *In Cold Blood* [1965]), but his early experience with the magazine was rejection, guaranteed by the route he took. Even so, Capote referred to the *New Yorker* as "probably the best magazine in the world," at least "at that time," and working there was certainly, in his judgment, "a hell of a lot better than going to college" (Clarke 75).

Capote might have gotten the broader literary world to agree with him that "real-world" experience was better than academic training in creative writing, a subject that in the idealized imagination exists outside of institutional structures. Still, not all shared this idealized aesthetic view. From early in the 1940s well through the 1960s, persistent claims about over-editing publicly nagged *New Yorker* editors, even as its reputation as a literary institution grew. By the early 1940s, this insistent critique and the increasing competition for prize-winning short fiction prompted some institutional soul searching. Were *New Yorker* editors ripping the literary out of submissions? Were they oblivious to real genius? For a publication that placed its faith in language rules to produce quality prose and in the power of literature to transcend social ills, such a suggestion was profound.

The Incredible Miss Gould

It wouldn't have done for E. B. White to locate a problem with the magazine's editorial team. Perhaps to ensure marital happiness, he retrospectively located the problem of aggressive editing with the copyediting department: "If sometimes there seems to be a sort of sameness of sound in *The New Yorker*, it probably can be traced to the magazine's copy desk, which is a marvelous fortress of grammatical exactitude and stylish convention. Commas in *The New Yorker* fall with the precision of knives in a circus act, outlining the victim. This may sometimes have slight tendency to make one writer sound a bit like another" (Plimpton and Crowther 79). It proved an easy target but, as examples in this chapter will show, the magazine's heavy-handed editing extended far beyond punctuation and usage and was exercised on fiction as well as nonfiction. The *New Yorker*'s meticulous line editing, its adherence to Fowler's *Modern English Usage* on matters of diction and punctuation, and its detailed house glossary of usage (developed after World War II) contributed to a polished surface. The magazine wasn't error free; readers wrote in with their corrections. One Oberlin graduate, an English major who wanted to "do something along literary lines or succeed in becoming a French professor" wrote this letter to William Shawn on July 23, 1945:

> Dear Mr. Shawn:
>
> In looking over the last two issues of the magazine, with what cannot help being a professional eye, I found six mistakes—about which I am sure you have already heard in no restrained terms from your public. But the two grammatical errors in one paragraph of the Christine Weston story ("different . . . than" and "flowers smelled differently") make me believe that I am not taking too great a liberty in writing to you.
>
> Five years as copy editor and proofreader with Appleton-Century and shorter terms with Duell, Sloan and Pearce and Creative Age Press would have served me badly if they had not given me something of a nose for this sort of thing, and I wondered if you would care to let me have a talk with you. . . .
>
> Sincerely yours,
>
> (Miss) Eleanor Gould[4]

Eleanor Gould's letter inspired an interview, this although the magazine was reserving editorial positions for men returning from war and thus actively discouraging applicants.[5] On October 3, 1945, her twenty-eighth birthday, William Shawn hired Gould. Most accounts record that she had no official title. However, in his "postscript" for her, David Remnick, who took over as editor in 1998, tagged her as the Grammarian, "a title invented for her" and "retired with her." As the magazine's Grammarian, she was integral to *New Yorker* authorship: "If it's true *The New Yorker* is known for the clarity of its prose, then Miss Gould had as much to do with establishing that as its more famous editors and writers" (qtd. in Wade).

Remnick hasn't been the only writer or editor to apotheosize Gould. Her fifty-four-year tenure at the *New Yorker* evolved into the stuff of legend: "She has been called the Orwell of copy editors, the Kasparov of syntax. Her name has become adjective, gerund and verb" (Scott). Her admirers are effusive: "'It's like having Newton help you with your physics homework,' Hendrick Hertzberg, the writer and editor, said in 1995 in a toast to Miss Gould. 'Or more precisely—and precision is the key here—it's like having Beethoven give you some pointers on composition'" (Scott). A few anecdotes about Gould circulate and recirculate among the *New Yorker* faithful, including the originating myth "that she flyspecked an entire issue and enclosed it with her application" (Wade). Miss Gould remembered only that she "noted two mistakes in recent issues, including, good Lord, a 'different than'" (Wade). Her memory demonstrates a modesty not displayed by the subdued "smart" tone of her application letter.[6] While she didn't "flyspeck" an issue—a task that Katharine White assumed when she first worked long distance from Maine—Gould did scan two issues and locate six errors. The *New Yorker* editorial staff took lapses in proofreading almost as seriously as misstatements of fact or Ross's own personal nightmare, undetected innuendo.

Gould struck the right note, one bolstered by a faith in the purity of language. She knew the magazine's creed; she was the copy editor of Ross's dreams. Remnick describes how Gould strived for "a kind of Euclidean clarity—transparent, precise, muscular." He posits that this "ideal ... seemed to have not only syntactical but moral dimensions" (Remnick). That this moral dimension is gendered seems obvious, but it also carried aesthetic dimensions, the stylistic affinity for directness perhaps the most striking and consequential. The *Oberlin Alumni Magazine* provides a list of Miss Gould's most distressing writing issues. Some are widely accepted (e.g., number four on her list, improper tense sequence); others are contested rules adhered to by traditional prescriptivists (e.g., number two on her list, commas in restrictive and nonrestrictive phrases, or number three, "who" vs. "whom"). Number one on her list is simply "indirection." As Henry Finder illustrates, a sentence marred by indirection might read, "Her two Afghan hounds have the run of her 24-room apartment." A potential fix? "She lives in a 24-room apartment and has two Afghan hounds that have the run of the place" (qtd. in Scott). This dedication to rooting out indirection certainly produced a different rhythm and voice, a kind of casual ease—an urban, estate, country club ease—"a deliberate shucking of sophistication" that another New Yorker editor characterized as the magazine's voice (Daniel Menaker qtd. in Scott). It is presumed to be an assuring rather than off-putting voice. The reader must be carefully led and this voice will guide. In this light, this direct style represents perhaps the cardinal middlebrow principle: offer the readers more but don't strain them.

Clearly Eleanor Gould knew that some of her Euclidean geometry was at odds with literary aims; the Oberlin Alumni Magazine feature notes that "fiction editors and some of the fiction writers, including John Updike, whose book reviews and other fact pieces she still works on, felt that her precision was out of key with their personal style" (M. Clark). She and others document that copyediting changes were mere suggestions; other editors could accept or ignore them. Still, the marks on the page pricked the egos of some authors, and thus, Eleanor Gould was not just well-known and well-respected, she was also infamous and denigrated. As Janny Scott wrote in the New York Times, "Miss Gould is not everyone's cup of tea." Yet no matter how loud the authors cried that their artistry had been violated, Gould had Ross's support and later William Shawn's; she remained an integral part of the system. The New Yorker would be known for its editing.

The New Yorker's "Whichy Thicket"

The New Yorker's vexed reputation for editing literature into or out of existence—the perspective changes with the source—is perhaps most clearly represented in the press the magazine received in the *New York Herald Tribune*. In 1963, the *Herald Tribune* skirted over the magazine's detractors and triumphantly promoted the *New Yorker*'s literary excellence, pointing to the magazine as a place that offered a home to writers who might elsewhere have been rejected. "Despite the Chronic Snipers," the jump head read, "*The New Yorker*: Flourishing Fountain": "No modern American magazine has launched so many new writers of importance, or published so many established ones who might not have been made to feel at home elsewhere" (Hutchens 8). The book critic John K. Hutchens attributed this success to fiction editors Katharine White, Gus Lobrano, and William Maxwell—"all three sympathetic but firm, hospitable to new forms and skills, uncanny in their ability to spot a structural weakness, an overlooked possibility" (8). It is team praise that would have pleased Katharine White, whose job it was to keep up with the trade trends.

Two years later, for the *New Yorker*'s fortieth anniversary in 1965, Tom Wolfe used the *Herald Tribune* to "pop the balloon," to expose the façade of the magazine's "illustrious traditions" (250).[7] He raised the fear that many loyal *New Yorker* readers harbored: their magazine, once the darling signature of sophisticated, highbrow, high-class, supremely literate culture, had on the occasion of its fortieth anniversary become outdated, passé, or to use Wolfe's striking image, mummified. Wolfe presented this critique as satiric gothic: living in the tall shadow cast by his rough predecessor, William Shawn—an elegant, venerable, soft-spoken man with a shocking resemblance to the classic mortician—cast a pall over the publication, killed its vibrancy, and thereby transformed the literature during his editorial term into perfect mausoleum specimens. This narrative drew just the kind of embattled response that fuels an iconoclast's pen. Many cried that the *New Yorker* was still very much alive, but Wolfe's barb had driven straight to the magazine's heart.

In particular, Wolfe singled out the editorial team, providing an account of how the magazine's "thises and its thats be-

gan effusing in print, like gas inflating a balloon" (250). Wolfe
focused on a perceived signature style, one that was anything but
direct and, yet still, formulaically journalistic rather than inno-
vatively literary. For him, *New Yorker* prose was characterized by
what he called the Lillian Ross-inspired "formula lead," (273) a
"fact gorged sentence" (272) with "all those clauses, appositions,
amplifications, qualifications, asides, God knows what else,
hanging inside the poor old skeleton of one sentence like some
kind of Spanish moss" (273). In writing about *New Yorker* excess,
Wolfe couldn't contain his own. The "formula lead" was "just
the warm-up" to the full-blown "*New Yorker* style specialty known
as the 'whichy thicket'" (273). Wolfe had his own image of how
such prose—"piles of whichy whuh words—*which, when, where,
who, whether, whuggheeee*" (274)—came to be manufactured:

> The system is Shawn's refinement of Harold Ross's query
> theory and operates something like this: Once an article is
> accepted, some girl retypes it on maize-yellow paper and a
> couple of other colors, and Shawn sends the maize copy to a
> chief editor. The other two copies go to the research depart-
> ment ("Checking") and the copy style department. The copy
> style department's task is seeing to it that the grammar, punc-
> tuation, spelling, and word usage in the piece correspond to
> *The New Yorker*'s rules on the subject.... Meanwhile, the re-
> searchers down in the checking department are making
> changes. The researchers' additions often take the form of
> filling in blanks some writer has left in the story. He may
> write something like 'Miss Hall appeared in Sean O'Casey's
> (t.k.) in 19(oo) ... ' and the researcher is supposed to fill in the
> blanks, t.k. standing for 'words to come' and (oo) for 'digits
> to come.' This is precisely the way the news magazines oper-
> ate. (274–75)

Wolfe continues over the course of a page to offer his rendition
of the process, which ends, according to him, when "the ho-
mogenized production is disgorged to the printers" (276). One
would imagine that writers would complain, but according to

Wolfe, they are too eager to join "The System! *We* Ambrosial org-lit!" (277). Wolfe grants that the magazine occasionally manages to produce something good, but he highlights the magazine's omissions. In contrast, he praises the genuine literariness of *Esquire* and underscores that even that most middling of middle-class magazines, the *Saturday Evening Post*, has a more prestigious roster of writers.

Wolfe wrote this parody of a profile, the very form the *New Yorker* claimed to invent, in part because Shawn's private nature foiled an exposé. As Wolfe recounts: "Despite the fact that he was one of the most prominent figures in American journalism, he never showed his face to outside journalists" (251). To learn more about his subject, Wolfe telephoned Shawn, only to be lectured by his subject on journalistic ethics: "Here at *The New Yorker*, if we tell someone we want to do a profile and that person doesn't want to cooperate, we don't do the profile. We would expect you to extend us the same courtesy" (251). Wolfe is not known for being courteous, and he certainly wasn't in this instance. In his letter to the *Herald Tribune*, E. B. White charged, "Mr. Wolfe's piece on William Shawn violated every rule of conduct I know anything about. It is sly, cruel and to a large extent undocumented, and it has, I think, shocked everyone" (qtd. in Yagoda 340). Moreover, White continues, "The piece is not merely brutal, it sets some sort of record for journalistic delinquency" (qtd. in Yagoda 340). J. D. Salinger concurred, labeling it "inaccurate and sub-collegiate and gleeful and unrelievedly poisonous" (qtd. in Yagoda 339–40).[8]

Wolfe's parody worked in part because it was a familiar, even over-worn trope; he provided style and volume to the "chronic snipers" who had for two decades been launching the same claims. I will not be asking whether Wolfe's article was effective—at the very least it evoked the kind of turmoil among the *New Yorker* staff that would have made Wolfe gleeful.[9] Instead, I will focus on the *accuracy* of Wolfe's argument. Because Wolfe's piece is clearly a lampoon, such a question might seem un-

founded. Yet looking into the accuracy of Wolfe's descriptions—
and characterizations—of the *New Yorker's* editing practices
takes us to the edge of a central issue in rhetorical studies, the
degree to which composition is (or should be) a product of individual genius or collaboration.[10]

E. B. White argued in his *Herald Tribune* letter to the editor,
that "Wolfe's violent attack on [Shawn] is not only below the
belt, it is essentially wide of the mark, in point of fact" (qtd. in
Yagoda 340). Of all the magazine's defenders, Renata Adler and
fellow writer Gerald Jonas were perhaps its most forensic. In
Gone: The Last Days of The New Yorker, Adler describes Jonas's outrage when he discovers that "a lot of the piece was demonstra-
bly false" (86), outrage that led to a determination to fact check
the *Herald Tribune* piece. Adler and Jonas attempt to have the fact
sheet published in the *New Yorker,* only to find that a vague editorial "they" didn't judge it "a good idea" (Adler 88). Eventually,
William Shawn consented to having the fact sheet published in
the *Columbia Journalism Review,* but fact checking and publication took four months. "By then," Adler comments, "not even
we cared" (88–89). As Jonas and Adler took pains to show, Wolfe
clearly didn't have all his facts straight. Still, even with his invention of detail, Wolfe was largely correct in his assessment of
the degree of intervention editors exercised on submitted manuscripts—and he was equally as wrong about how writers reacted
to such substantial editing. While some found comfort in the
New Yorker "we" and praised the editors for improving the quality
of their work, others vociferously protested.

"Up Our Street": A "Serious Showdown" between Katharine White and Isabel Bolton

In 1946 Mary Britton Miller published her breakout novel,
Do I Wake or Sleep under the pseudonym of Isabel Bolton. She
was sixty-three years old, working with failing eyesight. Before
then, Miller had written five volumes of poetry and a novel about
twins,[11] none of which were successful commercially or criti-

cally. *Do I Wake or Sleep*, a novel written, according to *Time* magazine, "in a new, free style,"[12] captured the attention of influential critics Diana Trilling and Edmund Wilson. Miller, or rather "Isabel Bolton," found with *Do I Wake or Sleep* what was essentially a new career, or a much more visible phase of an older one. In the pages of the *New Yorker*, Wilson enthusiastically praised Bolton's surprising "first novel," comparing the writer to Henry James and, in passing, to Fitzgerald and Hemingway. He praises her "poetic impression," similar enough to Woolf to invite comparison and yet "so unlike the original" (Wilson 113). He explicates the difference: Bolton's "writing rarely shapes and paints; it either makes people talk or talks itself, but it does have its own personal tone, a voice that combines, in a peculiar way, the lyric with the dry; and it is exquisitely perfect in accent: every syllable falls as it should" (Wilson 113). Bolton's work, Wilson concludes, resists blurbs and summarizes; she has "remarkable technical skill" (Wilson 113). Bolton is a largely unremembered figure in American literature, although there have been attempts, both inside and outside the academy, to bring her work back into the light. Inspired by Diana Trilling's short book reviews, in 1993 Doris Grumbach champions Bolton's literary reputation in her *Extra Innings*: "It is hard to see how it is possible for such distinguished work to fall into total oblivion" (291). In 1997, Steerforth Press printed *New York Mosaic: Three Novels*, with an introduction by Grumbach. In 1999, Virago Press reprinted the edition. Because some of Bolton's fiction portrays lesbian and gay characters, she is a significant figure in recovery work by queer theorists, where her work is praised for its style as well as subject matter. Robert L. Caserio, for example, describes *The Christmas Tree* (1949) as a work "utterly and undeservedly forgotten" (170).[13]

Bolton made her *New Yorker* debut in July 1947 with her story "Ruth and Irma," a Hemingway-inspired story of an American lesbian couple, "little Lady Bretts," (Bolton 21) in St. Tropez in 1928. Bolton's experience publishing the story with the *New Yorker* does not seem atypical: she is followed on Wilson's lead, she submits the story, and it's accepted and moves through a comparatively light editing process. She receives the galleys from Katharine White, which contain one big editorial query concerning potential libel but otherwise small sentence-level changes. Bolton's eyesight is failing, so making changes on the galley is difficult for her; arrangements are made for her to visit the *New Yorker* offices to work with White on the galleys, again not an unusual practice for writers generally. Before she visits the office, she writes Katharine a letter, responding to the galleys. On the issue of libel, Bolton is able to assure the publishers that this is a fiction piece, only loosely based on fact:

> Dear Mrs. White:
> I'm *sure* I can say that these girls would not recognize themselves! To be sure they looked like that, talked like that and wore the costumes as described. We used to sit around with them in the evenings. We speculated. The Lesbian characteristics I never discussed with anyone—just knew they belonged to that particular sisterhood. Every bit of the plot is embroidery on this sense I had of them. No young men came in on a yacht; they did not leave in a hurry. As far as I know neither girl was in love with a young man of the town. They came in at all hours of the dawn and certainly mummed and batted it about that town in the good old Hemingway manner. I didn't have a room next to them. I merely watched them attentively—two girls carrying off their difficult little secret as best they could—so that question is settled.[14]

The rest of the letter, however, is a warning shot. Bolton makes it clear that she is "here and there disturbed at the changes … made in sentence structure." "Disturbed" is the operative word, it is perhaps an understatement; as the correspondence demonstrates, Bolton hasn't the temperament to be simply miffed. Her disturbance escalates rapidly over a series of letters. Initially, it seemed that the changes to sentence structure only offend Bolton's ear. The changes "seem to me often to throw out the rhythm." Bolton reminds White of the favorable review Wilson

wrote for the *New Yorker*: "Of many pleasant things that the reviewers said about my novel I liked the best what Edmund Wilson
said—'every accent falls in the right place.'" She argues that she
has "something of an ear" for her prose and that it's her understanding of grammar that allows her to create her particular style:
"I think the present participles (even some of the queer ands) do
good service in bringing everything together, giving one the scene
or the flow of various thoughts and ideas all in a kind of flash—the
way certain paintings give you everything, sea, cloud, sail, head-
land all coming together in one blink—it's what I try for." At this
point, she is still rather conciliatory. She concedes that she "wasn't
so sure of having pulled it off." Yet more than once in this relatively
pleasant letter she lets her editor know that this is one author who
does not intend to go gently into *New Yorker* style: "when I *really* feel
I've got it I don't like to see it tampered with.... I want to say this
before signing that contract so that you will realize that if you do
become genuinely interested in my work we may get into contro-
versies."[15]

There is no record of the meeting between editor and author,
but it's clear that some changes were negotiated. In a letter following publication, Bolton writes White: "Yes I saw and liked
the final version of Ruth and Irma." The published story receives
little of Bolton's attention, however, because now she has other
concerns, her "anguish" over her new novel—her feeling that
the "tongue and the pen always falls short of conveying the truth
that lies within one's heart"—and her disappointment over the
rejection of two of her stories, one of which Bolton is convinced
is "the best story I've written."[16] White has apparently written to
Bolton using an editing cliché, something like, "Thank you for
letting us see these; they're not up our street." This cliché pro-
vokes Bolton; she unpacks the trite metaphor, questioning just
what the *New Yorker* street is—and if she even wants to walk on it:

> Now please don't think I'm being impertinent. But do you oc-
> casionally feel that your street has become a little bit too stan-
> dardized a street—like some of the streets in which one dis-

covers always the same stores—the same architecture—The
Main Streets—let us say—Strictly American—and with all the
A and Ps—all the Woolworth signs etc. etc. So familiar to the
eye, that to find on it a different variety of building—a lawn,
a street—perhaps an antelope grazing on the green grass,
would not only surprise the reader but perhaps give him a moment of delight?[17]

From here, Bolton moves to the familiar argument about the
New Yorker type, aligning herself with critics who judged the magazine's fiction to be overly formulaic. As an author, and even as
a reader, Bolton charges that she is looking for more, something
original and literary:

Personally I happen to be so weary of this street that I find
myself unable to read the *New Yorker* stories—I try, indeed I do
try—but before I'm a page along in them I turn them down.
It's the only thing about the *New Yorker* I don't like. The stories—in every other department are superb. But it doesn't
seem to me that fiction can be subjected to so rule of thumb a
standard—an attempt to wrench its neck and say damn you—
get into pattern—be a *New Yorker* story—give off the essence
of all this sophistication . . . this *New Yorker* style. Be at all costs
up our street.[18]

Isabel Bolton was aware of her inability to restrain her opin-
ions. This letter stands as Exhibit A. It's not enough for her to
point out the bourgeois character of the *New Yorker*'s fiction,
not enough to show its formulaic tendencies. She has to point
out that she is not alone in her feelings. Reviewers and readers
congratulate her for her individual style; they celebrate her as a
maverick, untamed by the *New Yorker*: "I've had, I can't tell you
how many congratulations on having done something quite my
own—stuck a new note—got away from the *New Yorker*—now
dear Mrs. White how *am* I to be expected to be as you say up your
street if it's been my whim and desire to live on my own street?"
Bolton ends by conceding that there are commercial reasons she
would like to be associated with the magazine, but that she is

not willing to trade her artistic integrity: "I'd love to write for the *New Yorker*—I'd like nothing better. You have an enormous audience—You pay most generously. But I begin more and more to be afraid that I'm not likely to write the kind of stories that comply with your editorial standards."[19] Katharine White does not immediately reply to the letter.

A month after "Ruth and Irma" is published in the *New Yorker*, Bolton reconsiders her stance. The story receives a good deal of attention, in part a credit to Bolton's unusual style, in part the happy coincidence of the profound nostalgia for a St. Tropez that no longer existed after World War II, and in part a result of the magazine's growing postwar circulation. In the *New Yorker* archive held at the New York Public Library, it's somewhat rare to find letters from readers to authors, but several exist in the Bolton file:

> "Ruth and Irma" were made specifically for me—and beautifully made. That's a lovely piece of work. I was greatly moved. My most sincere congratulations. You are very wise. The descriptive passages are wonderful and they come and go just where when they should. I know the time and the place and you have evoked them as I have not seen them brought back before. I can't tell you how much I admire the story.

> I want to tell you what a pleasure it was to read "Ruth and Irma" in last week's *New Yorker*. I read the *New Yorker* faithfully from week to week but I am, I must confess, often disappointed. I persist, however because every so often I find something good, viz Rebecca West's article on the Greenville lynching trials; viz, again, "Ruth and Irma."
> Like most semi-literate people, I fancy myself a writer, and as a quasi-writer, I pay a good deal of attention to style. Yours is fluid and even haunting. It is a real pleasure to light on a first-rate craftsman. There, are, I need not tell you this, so few left in the world.

> I have just finished reading your "Ruth and Irma" in the July 26 issue of the *New Yorker* and, for the first time in my life, am writing what might be termed a "fan letter" to an author.

I am assuming that since you write of St. Tropez you have been there—pre-war, of course. Since St. Tropez, next to the isle of Capri, is my idea of heaven on earth, I thought that perhaps you might be interested in hearing something about St. Tropez as I knew it—just after the invasion and for several months thereafter.... I guess you would like to hear about what happened to the village and its environs.

First, St. Tropez was roughly about one-quarter destroyed.... Life in St. Tropez was not at all "arty" and the celebrated Well of Radcliffe Hall was completely dried up. But from what I learned from a local "character," St. Tropez must have rivaled Capri before the war in its gaiety.[20]

The happy reception of "Ruth and Irma" sparked Bolton to apologize to White. She begins her letter with "something of a capitulation": "I had had a feeling that 'Ruth and Irma' was not one of my best stories—but one in which I'd conceded something to the *New Yorker*—But the more I think about it, the franker I must be, both with myself and with you. The story has been improved by the corrections and eliminations that you all imposed upon ~~me~~ it."[21] This apologetic tone, however, is difficult for Bolton to sustain; the editorial marks have scored not just the page but Bolton's ego. The "me" that she strikes conveys a different mood swing, forewarning of the tone of the rest of the letter. Bolton ponders again the two rejected stories. She is no longer drawing the "you vs. me" lines, no longer writing as one who stands alone, apart, and principled, outside a bourgeois ethos hostile to the artist. The success of "Ruth and Irma" has made Bolton reconsider a working relationship with the magazine, but she is not quite ready to capitulate entirely. She begins with the question of whether she belongs in the pages of the *New Yorker*. She now believes that she does, that she is a *New Yorker* writer. Perhaps, Bolton argues, it is hard to recognize her as such because her age and individuality make her appear to be someone who marches off the well-recognized street, the clichéd metaphor that the author still can't quite shake:

> Very likely the stories that you have turned down were turned
> down because they were not as you put it "up your street."—
> I'm not so sure of this. I think, that with a little willingness on
> both our parts to concede that all stories I write are more or
> less up your street (not that all are by any means those that you
> would want to take). But let us say—up your street I'm young
> no longer. I've lived in this disturbed and cock-eyed world
> with a very sensitive response to all that I have seen. Because
> I'm older than most of your writers I have perhaps kept watch
> on more variety of scenes and worlds and general changes
> than most.[22]

Bolton concedes that she was likely too hasty and too free with her words in the first letter, but she insists that White must take responsibility for behavior equally as rigid: "I believe that if you'd not turned them down with such finality that every one of those Economic Royalist stories might with a little change have been very new and perfectly good *New Yorker* material. The observation was correct—the experience was first hand—But you're so *drastic*."[23] Bolton felt put off by acceptances that depended on changes to the manuscript; such demands hindered her inspiration and creativity and led her to magazines who accepted pieces without conditions:

> Well *Harper's Bazaar* had no provisals—They took it as was—
> (And I don't really see a great deal that would have changed).
> The dress-maker story was good—emotionally exceedingly
> well recorded needing I admit certain changes—But if you'd
> said "let's get together" you might very easily have got the
> changes achieved. I was in a vein just then and could have
> turned off in a few months enough stories to make quite a re-
> spectable series. When one is in a vein one is in it—I'm not
> likely to be in that particular vein again—And it's not probable
> that I can get after those people with as much freedom of ex-
> pression and insight into my own methods of attacking them
> as at that particular moment.[24]

Bolton continues with her argument: if White could exercise a little less editorial authority, Bolton could help the magazine by bringing in a fresh perspective, offering a viable alternative to the same tired fiction. Both author and publication could win if the editor would just compromise a little on the editing:

> So let me say this—and without offending you—I feel this that the New Yorker needs me and that I need the New Yorker—
>
> You have really—I believe you'll admit this had a little too much of the brief, topical, conversational stories—all recorded with a view to catching and reflecting the shifting scene as it changes, its slang its drinks its fashions in motor cars and hats etc. etc. But there's not been much below the surface—a kind of slick and brilliant surface account that (may I say it again without offending you) has awfully got my goat. Now I know that I get your goat—(and more than often justifiably in being a bit too pretentious—in striving for those effects that the really first rate writers achieve—and more than often failing abysmally). But I care tremendously for good writing, and for significance. And I think still, that in some of the very stories you have turned down these things exist and could with a willingness on your part to recognize them, and a willingness on my part to be checked here and there in my over elaboration, be turned out as far more interesting and acceptable than a large portion of the stuff that has recently been appearing in your sheets.[25]

Bolton ends with an appeal, an invitation of sorts for a new working relationship: "I somehow feel that between us we've muffed a good partnership—(my fault as much as yours)—I'm so deep, so desperately deep in my new book that we can't—as the phrase goes 'get together' on anything for some time to come—but when I do again begin writing short stories, let us talk the whole damned project over before I turn [away] any work for you."[26]

On August 5, 1947, just a few days before her vacation, White writes Bolton at length, never mentioning specifically the first, less conciliatory letter that suggested that author and magazine go their separate ways. Instead White thanks Bolton for the last letter, assuring her that her suggestions would be interesting to others at the office and that there is nothing in the letter that the editors haven't read before. Indeed, she tells her, reaching for common ground: "What it said about our fiction in some respects echoes the sentiments of the editors.... I am even willing to go along with you in thinking that our very polishing up of the fiction we do use, to be certain that it contains no obscurities or bad grammar, may make for a certain similarity in sound." Even Bolton's appraisal of genre is accurate, White appeases: "Most of us would agree with you that, in general, our reporting is more distinguished than our fiction at the moment, but American factual writing is better than American fiction in all fields at the moment too."[27]

This last comment, however, marks the end of White's concessions. From here on out the letter is a defense of the magazine's editorial practices and its offerings, a defense that does not stem from loyalty but from study. White notes that she has carefully looked not just at her own magazine but at the offerings in other magazines, and thus her analysis has professional distance, if not complete objectivity:

> I must add—not out of loyalty but because I have really studied the fiction published in the *New Yorker* and in the other American magazines. I can't find any other publication that has offered within a three months' period as wide a variation in types of fiction, or in styles of writing, as we have since the first of May, for example, with stories by John Cheever, Kay Boyle, Christine Weston ("Her Bed Is India"), E. B. White, John O'Hara, Niccoli Tucci, Nancy Hale, and Isabel Bolton, all of whom seem to me to have written at the top of their form in that period. We have opened our doors to a piece of Maugham opera bouffe just for variety! And most of these stories went through without more than routine editing, for commas and so on. The foreign writers do have to be turned into English, of course. Thurber and John O'Connor, Irwin Shaw and Wolcott Gibbs, Sylvia Townsend and Joseph Wechsberg are all

regulars, yet no one could say their style or subject matter are at all alike.[28]

To the degree that there is perceptible "standardization," White defends it as "unavoidable, in as much as we have to publish about four times as many short stories as any other publication." Accepting pieces that need editing both builds the pool of available material and speeds the artistic process along, helping writers to get their work into final form sooner. Because of the sheer volume, the necessity of filling columns, not every submission is expected to attain top levels of artistic achievement. "It is foolish of me to try to defend the magazine or to argue for our fiction if it bores you. Lots of it bores me too, but we have to get our 52 issues a year and publish around 250 separate items of fiction in a year—there just are not that many topnotch stories being written."[29]

Fear of being foolish does not stop White from at last addressing the concern expressed in Bolton's first, angry letter—her visceral reaction to the "up our street" cliché—or from underscoring how committed the editors are to the artistic integrity of the fiction they publish:

> The only reason I argue at all is to correct a false impression that I may have given you and to lead up to a point that I do feel necessary to stress. This is that it is terribly important, in the eyes of New Yorker editors, that writers should stay on their own streets. When any writer tries to write something in what he think is New Yorker style, or aims at something that would be "up our street," that's when they are likely to fail for us. It was silly of me to use that "up our street" cliché in writing you—I can't remember to what story I applied it—possibly "The Tindamies" which, if I remember it right, seemed to us rather sentimental, and also unsuccessful in its whimsical touches and its treatment of the racial tolerance theme. But that is not to say that it was not a good idea for you to have written it. If you like it better than anything you've written that's enough; I believe every writer should write to please himself. So please do not be misled by my having used an edi-

tor's cliché probably either as a short cut or in an effort to be polite when I wrote you.[30]

White ends her letter by appealing to their shared values: "I'm just rambling away here because it is interesting to talk with someone who cares about writing." And then, as is common in a White letter, she revisits the topic still one more time, offering one more instance of how the *New Yorker*'s editorial process is misunderstood in the press. Reviews of Christine Weston's short story collection were particularly on the editor's mind. She again returns to the idea that editors are sometimes blamed for authors' sins:

> One thing I've been thinking about recently is the charge many reviewers make that the *New Yorker* imposes slightness on its writers. This was said in reviews of Christine Weston's new volume of short stories about India, "There and Then," a delightful and perceptive little book to my mind. But nearly every one of those stories was slight and when Christine really let go and wrote a full scale story, such as "Her Bed Is India" or "The Devil Has the Moon," there could not have been more rejoicing. We do use the slight, tiny, mood story or reminiscence, in fact we are nearly the only magazine that does open its pages to this sort of thing, but we don't encourage it for heaven's sake.
>
> The moral of all this is please don't try "to meet our editorial standards"—please write as you want, and when you write stories we admire we shall buy them and when you write ones we don't like you can sell them elsewhere.[31]

This marks the end of the showdown; Katharine White gets the last word. Bolton continues to sign first-read agreements with the *New Yorker* for five years, although she publishes only two more stories with them: "The Christmas Tree" in 1948, about the violence inspired by new technologies, and "Under Gemini" in 1949, about twin sisters. After 1950, the archives show only rejections, as Bolton tries unsuccessfully to carve *New Yorker* stories from her longer projects. Sometime late in 1949 or early in

1950, she submits another twin piece, "Earth, Sea and Air," and is encouraged to rework it. White reports the bad news in mid-February of 1950: "I . . . have a great sense of guilt in having involved Miss Miller in this long revise for nothing. Perhaps it should be a lesson to me not to encourage revision of this sort, but I did really think her new idea might work well as she outlined it, and I was very much disappointed to have to agree with the other editors that it did not succeed in the end."[32] A month later, White assures Bolton, who is struggling with depression, poor health (her eyesight continues to worsen), and financial difficulties, that the magazine is always interested in her work:

> *Of course* we would want the chance to read the new version of the start of your novel, and I'm grateful to you for offering us this. So do send in the manuscript right away. The only thing I worry about at all is that if, by bad luck, we did not find the chapter right for short story use in *The New Yorker*, you would consider my having to tell you this another set-back and cause for depression. The point is that it's extremely rare that part of a novel does work out well for a separate story, so it seems to me that you ought *not* to be downcast if we couldn't use it, for it would not mean that the material was not good. You have been one of the few first-rate novelists whose novel chapters *have* made short stories, though, so I am hopeful, and we very, very much want to see your new first three chapters. Do send them right in and we'll read them at once.[33]

That fall, the *New Yorker* rejects "Gabriel's Wings" because, despite the "delightful writing," "the story seems to have no underpinnings" and the characters are too thin and are not rendered "important enough, emotionally." White surmises that this once again stems from the problem of culling a self-contained story from a novel: "I wonder whether this is not because you have here the material for a novel rather than for a short story. I just don't think that in this space we can know enough about Margaret Sylvester to understand her or care enough about her." White notes that she writes so directly because she knows Bolton prefers this.

Despite these failed attempts to produce *New Yorker* stories, White continues to encourage the author to write novels and to find unified stories in them, "for I know that books, not short stories, are what you prefer to write. For purely selfish reasons, though, I hope there will be more stories."[34]

White devotes most of the length of the letter, however, to discussing Bolton's personal dilemmas, offering details (but not a recommendation) for breaking with an agent and recounting specific strategies that James Thurber used to manage blindness and a writing career:

> Any writer who has to learn to write in a different technique because of eye trouble has my deepest sympathy. I have seen Jim Thurber go through it and I hope it will be encouraging to you to know how well he has managed. Of course *he* is practically blind. He does not use the typewriter at all but writes his material in longhand, a few lines to a typewriter page. Then he has this copied and read to him—several times I imagine—for corrections, amplifications, rewriting. With him it has really had to be a transfer from eye to ear and the interesting thing is that under the new system his style has come more complex rather than more simplified, as one might expect. But with you, I'm sure so drastic a change will not be necessary and I think you are wise to learn to type by touch. I do earnestly hope that the new oculist can help you a great deal.[35]

Bolton does at least temporarily discover a strategy: she hires a younger man to help with typing,[36] but the arrangement is short lived. She continues to struggle, particularly with *New Yorker* fiction. "Harold" is rejected in late 1951 ("it does not seem to us to make a story—at least not one for *The New Yorker*"[37]) and in April of 1952, the editors cannot find any stories in her latest book-length work.[38] One month later, Bolton's first-reading agreement with the magazine lapses and is not renewed "since Mrs. White reports that Miss Bolton has decided to discontinue writing short fiction," and fiction editor Gus Lobrano concurs, summarizing that the magazine "bought nothing and rejected two casuals and eleven chapters of a novel submitted under the agreement to date."[39] White continues to correspond with Bolton, clipping a review of her novel in September 1952.[40] Later that same year, White rejects Bolton's "The Companion at Her Side" because it doesn't work "very well as a short story—not at least for *The New Yorker*." White praises one passage but notes that the rest of the manuscript doesn't "seem to us to be as good." Again, she writes, "I'm being thus frank because I think you would prefer it."[41] Almost a year passes before Bolton receives her last rejection for "A Death in Spring," which again the editors cannot see as a *New Yorker* short story, not because it falls out of bounds but because it's too conventional, too familiar, too dated: "we doubt it as a story for us because of the familiarity of some of the material. For instance, you have already done for us, and well, the theme of the intercommunication between twins. Also, as you perhaps know, period stories are not quite so good for us as contemporary ones."[42] White suggests *Harper's Bazaar* or *Atlantic*, magazines not so restricted in terms of subject matter and genre (not limited to the self-contained short story).

Mary Britton Miller's record with the *New Yorker* could be read as an extreme case. The details seem extreme: her age, her health, her financial difficulties, her fighting temperament. Yet the archives show that none of these traits were unusual for editors to encounter as part of their work.[43] Indeed, Miller can be just as easily seen as representative of a large number of writers who alternately balked at the restraints of the *New Yorker* system and benefited from the structure and comfort it provided its writers. Miller is indicative of writers who struggled within the rigorous editorial system. Other writers, however, even those who experienced even greater levels of editorial intervention, identified strongly with the magazine's ethos and submitted to "improvements" on their work. In the section that follows, I again turn to the correspondence between Frances Gray Patton and Katharine White to present a striking example of collaborative authorship.

"Playing It Down": The *New Yorker's* Practice of Speculative Editing

Wolfe had boldly stated that "the chief [*New Yorker*] editor can—and is expected to—rewrite the piece in any way he thinks will improve it. It is not unusual for the writer not to be consulted about it; the editor can change it without him" (274–75). Perhaps responding to this accusation, E. B. White in his *Paris Review* interview conceded that the copyediting was aggressive but maintained that "on the whole, *New Yorker* writers are jealous of their own way of doing things and they are never chivvied against their will into doing it some other way" (Plimpton and Crowther 79). E. B. White's proclamation has the ring of truth; his reputation is as a truth teller. Wolfe is known for his overstatements, but in this case he doesn't go as far off the mark as one might think. In 1933, eight years into the magazine's history, Harold Ross wrote to Katharine White that the only time they encountered difficulties regarding revisions was when they did it wrong. He saw their role as collaborators free to make suggestions. Yet the boundaries of collaboration were hard to draw. *New Yorker* editors did substantially rewrite sections of manuscripts, making significant changes in plot, character, dialog, or setting in order to align individual authorial vision with the *New Yorker's* editorial ethos. Ross later came to regard the magazine as a kind of a writing school. And with some frequency, the editors "chivvied" authors into making extensive changes, though technically, such changes were not made against the author's will: an author could comply with the changes or simply choose to place the story elsewhere.

By 1957, the year she submitted "As Man to Man," Frances Gray Patton was an established writer with some reputation. Although she had written memoir and fiction pieces for the *New Yorker* (and thinly veiled autobiographical fiction), she was widely recognized as the author of *Good Morning, Miss Dove*. Patton was by no means a novice, but she was battling writer's block and thus required some extra editorial care. On June 17, 1957, Katharine White wrote to Diarmuid Russell, Patton's agent, rejecting one story, "A Matter of Semantics," and asking for a delay on a second submission, "As Man to Man," about a father and sixteen-year-old son left home for a summer, in contemporary terms, to bond.[44] White explains the reason for the delay, "we find it a great deal too long and repetitious for its own good." It was also, she notes, "too broad," a judgment that shows up frequently in the archives and generally refers, as we shall see, to a range of literary offenses. However, as White explains to Russell, the story was "based on a nice idea"; it was possibly salvageable, if Patton, whom White judges as "a little out of practice," could agree to some extensive editing:

> I do think that if Fanny is willing to work with us on a revise as she has in the past, it should come out in the end. Therefore I shall get the story copied and write her about it, with a series of notes and suggested cuts. I can't swear it will come out in the end of course, but I hope and believe so. I feel that Fanny is a little out of practice and this may be why we feel this story needs more revision than hers usually do.[45]

Within a week, White sends Patton a long letter, criticizing the story's shortcomings and appealing to the strength of their professional collaboration and personal relationship:

> We do think it needs work, both in its general scheme and in detail. I half have the feeling that you wrote it as a first version and sent it along before you had time to boil it down and polish it.... I'm awfully glad you did send it; it is wonderfully cheering to be working on one of your manuscripts. Now since you and I cannot sit down at a table and talk it over, what I have done is to have the story copied and go over it fast myself, making cuts and changes that I would have suggested to you.[46]

Katharine's letter suggests the extent and nature of the changes,[47] some of which are geared to what Thurber called "playing it down," making the nuances of the manuscript more subtle: "You

will see that occasionally we think you have overstressed your humorous points, once in a while putting the story into a vein of humor so broad that it is not like you." The correspondence between
White and Patton makes it clear that the changes were substantial. Throughout the letter, Katharine reinforces that the choice
is really Patton's, that the decision to accept the editor's changes
rests technically with the author. By having the manuscript cop-
ied, the original will remain intact in case she doesn't approve of
the suggestions: "The changes are of course only tentative ones
and are for you to put into your own words"; "Please do not think
that I believe the version I am sending you now is right; I did it
under pressure—fast and very likely carelessly—sat up most of
last night in order not to delay you longer. The whole thing is
by way of suggestion. I am of course eager to hear your reaction
and I shall be keeping my fingers crossed until I do."[48] Still, the
consequences of Patton's decision are clear. If she cannot accept
these suggested changes, the *New Yorker* will not publish the story:
"Now it is of course quite possible that you may like the story exactly as it stands and may not want to change a word. If so, we'll
understand and I have your original version unsullied, to be returned to Diarmuid. But that, frankly, would be a terrible blow to
me."[49] The move is vintage White: *she* would be the injured party,
or more accurately, the *New Yorker* and its readers would suffer.

Patton does agree to revise the manuscript, but she chooses,
after a phone conversation with White, to make her own revisions, writing the piece over from the beginning to make sure
that the story did not suffer as she cut it. Length as well as coarse
humor form part of the "broadness," so Patton cuts five pages
and then goes over the manuscript again, cutting and rephras-
ing. On July 1, 1957, she sends the manuscript back, indicating to
Katharine White that the chore was pleasurable, in part because
of the editor's encouragement. Patton apparently makes some of
the corrections in ink, some in pencil, originally intending that
those in ink must stand. But in the letter, she reverses her stance,
indicating that all the corrections are debatable.

The rewrite that Patton judged successful was not acceptable to the *New Yorker* editors. Katharine White breaks the news: "I got your revise and two of us read it and it went on to Shawn for his opinion. All three of us were in agreement in thinking it is still far, far too long, and also in places still too broad."[50] Katharine makes clear her own opinion, revealing now the stern editorial demeanor for which she was as well known as for her nurturing. White presents the picture of her own constancy, in the face of an author's instability. She knows the author's strengths and weaknesses. She is capable of extracting her best work from her, as the editor knows best:

> You were so very amiable about trying a revise and about my notes. I must, however, be honest and say that I was myself disappointed in the revision—especially in how little compressing and cutting you had been able to do. It's still an endless long story for its substance and its nature, and it gives an impression of wordiness that is unlike you. . . . I blame myself somewhat for not being firmer on this point in my first letter. But I did emphasize the length ("*ever* so much too long") and said that the last eleven pages needed "drastic cuts" and that the start was too slow and that the center dragged.[51]

Whites scolds Patton, "you rejected some of my suggestions" and notes in passing something else "broad" and troubling in Patton's manuscript—a reference to mental illness. She thanks the author for "removing the idea of insanity" but indicates that there wasn't "enough toning down of the broadness."[52]

This news must have been daunting enough for Patton, but there is still more bad news. The editors raise new concerns and this time insist that they play a stronger authorial role: William Shawn "thought your dialogue was not always convincing and needed a lot tinkering because of your 'extremely feminine idea of how men talk.' But he said he believed that if we had a really free hand in the editing this time, we might be able to make the story one we could buy."[53] In a subsequent letter, White reassures Patton, "I don't know of a woman writer to whom this does not happen occasionally in writing about men."[54] White holds out the option that the author might try another rewrite, but the chances of such a rewrite passing editorial muster are slim: "I think that perhaps this time it would be easier for us to do it than you."[55]

Patton gives her blessing to proceed with the speculative editing. Across several more letters White explains how she and another male editor have worked to make the story less broad: "shorter—more consistent in length with the weight of its matter" and "more masculine."[56] Katharine herself writes "a new final paragraph." Other of Patton's "broad" cultural references are removed: "The Geratol joke has gone, and if you want it back, I'll reinstate it, and if Shawn does not approve, he can say so on the author's proof. The reason for removing it was that the point was made that if there was less joking about alcohol and geriatrics, Alex's real concern about the effects of alcohol at the end might seem more touching."[57] Patton tries one more time to get the Geratol joke accepted but then agrees to its excision. More importantly, she agrees to the toned-down manuscript.

The "As Man to Man" example, and others like it, works as a case study illuminating the rhetorical practice of editing, highlighting the thin line between issues of editing and rewriting, but also between judgments about "craft"—what makes writing better—and gendered, time-bound assumptions like fictional men mustn't sound like women. Examples like this provide evidence of how institutional ethos is negotiated and sustained. This broadening of editorial powers, as I suggested in the opening, was not without its critics, even inside the *New Yorker*'s hallowed hallways. This extensive rewriting obviously required writing skills on the part of the editors. In *Here at The New Yorker*, the gossipy "insider" view of the magazine that deeply wounded Katharine White, Brendan Gill did not discuss the extent to which editors reworked manuscripts, but he did insinuate that Katharine frequently overstepped her bounds, even to the point of actively promoting a policy that all *New Yorker* editors should be writers (116). Thankfully, Gill writes, Ross did not subscribe: "Mrs. White's theory was soon abandoned. It was certainly a poor one and would have been impossible to put into practice; even Ross, as Thurber once noted, never learned how to become a *New Yorker* writer" (117).

Katharine claimed never to have made such a proposal, but even if she had, it's clear that Ross, and later Shawn, would not necessarily have summarily dismissed it. Ross was frequently in the position of having to defend the long arm of *New Yorker* editing, and he did so by emphasizing the positive value of extensive collaboration between writers, artists, and editors. Here, for example, is Ross replying to Gluyas Williams, who, according to White, "express[ed] a determination not to accept ideas from others" (Kunkel, *Letters* 85). This refusal, Ross writes, "distresses and alarms me" (Kunkel, *Letters* 85); indeed, Ross implies, it works against the very spirit that has made the *New Yorker's* literary and artistic excellence: "the one thing that has made *The New Yorker* successful is that it is a collaborative effort, switching ideas back and forth to find the man best adapted to doing them, and I hope to high heaven that you aren't going to be discouraged into not being willing to work collaboratively" (Kunkel, *Letters* 86). James Thurber, E.B. White, Katharine White, and Ross himself were the "idea people":

> I'm employed by *The New Yorker* . . . largely as an idea man.
> That's what I regard myself as, at any rate, and what I think my chief value to the magazine is. That's White's value partially, Mrs. White's and Thurber's. This magazine is run on ideas, God knows, and we naturally hire the people that have them and hire them for that purpose.
>
> My God, a very large percentage of the contents of *The New Yorker*, drawings and text, are based on the ideas originating with the staff and suggested to writers. Now please reconsider your resolution. We don't ever try to cram an idea down an artist's throat. We always send it as a suggestion made on a take it or leave it basis. (Kunkel, *Letters* 85)

Frances Gray Patton was a better sport than Gluyas Williams, or perhaps, she more keenly self-identified as a *New Yorker* writer. She agrees to accept the editorial "suggestions" for "As Man to Man." Indeed, to a great degree, she seems persuaded by the ideal of a transcendent literary standard, one that careful editing nurtured into existence. At one point, she concurs with the editors that the revisions resulted in a better-crafted story, one not marred by feminine influence, one worthy of publication in the *New Yorker*. A real author, she suggests, could see the improvement; only a woman writer would see anything else: "Objections and suggestions so honestly stated couldn't wound any writer who wasn't very 'missish' indeed!"[58] Of course, some of this might have simply been strategic. Had Patton not accepted the changes, the story would not have been printed, a point again made clear by White when she submits the rewritten version: "oh Horror!—if you hate the whole thing, please say so frankly and I shall then sadly return to the original manuscript." In customary form, White ends on a note of encouragement: "I do hope there'll be another story coming in soon and I'm perfectly sure that if there is, there not be more than routine editing on it. It was just bad luck that this story needed more than the usual."[59] It may have been this encouragement coupled with the fact of publication and pay that led to Patton's agreeableness. Elsewhere in the correspondence there are glimmers that suggest Patton wasn't wholly won over by the final manuscript. Tellingly, perhaps, this is the last manuscript Patton submits to the magazine. There are myriad possibilities for this—the film success of *Good Morning, Miss Dove*; the accidental death of her brother-in-law; her increasing involvement in MFA programs; the writer's block brought on by the pressures of all of the above; or Katharine White's retirement. And yet, one wonders. In 1959, Patton offers only this as an explanation to Roger Angell, Katharine's son and successor: "that sort of writing requires a happy climate of a mind and imagination which life doesn't always afford!"[60] Life somehow had grown darker.

Editors with Rules and Unruly Authors:
Katharine White Encounters a "Formidable
Array of Feeling"

By 1947, Katharine White was ready to consider the unthinkable: revising editorial practices. On November 4th, Katharine White composed a long memo to Ross, reporting on the nature and extent of criticism against the magazine: "I am unable to name you a specific review—they have been so numerous in the past year or two that I have never even thought of registering a specific review in my mind." As Katharine dictated the memo, she was on the brink of change, vacillating quickly between defensiveness and inquiry. Some of the complaints came from quarters, the *Saturday Evening Post* for instance, that White felt justified in dismissing: "Of course this sort of thing is said by Maloney in his constant reviews of and references to books by our author. He doesn't count, from our point of view, and is of course unfair, but the very fact that there's a man who is making his living mostly by abusing us is harmful. His stuff is read by those who do not know his psychosis and sounds plausible to outsiders."[61] Maloney's error-ridden reviews seemed easy enough to discount. Unfortunately, however, for the editors, the critiques were not contained to the *Saturday Evening Post*. They were widespread and numerous and showed no sign of slowing. Given the sheer number of critiques, White felt compelled to argue to Ross that criticisms about over-editing may have had merit: "Most of the references may have been unfair but the very fact that they are made at all is bad for us, and where there's so much smoke, there is some fire."[62]

Katharine White realized that reviewers were frequently attacking *New Yorker* editorial policy because a few writers were giving reviewers the evidence to do so. Some contributors resisted the magazine's policies not by refusing to publish with the magazine at all but by reverting to unedited versions when they published collections or novels. Clarence Day was perhaps among the first to do so: "even way back there," when the system was not so rigidly established, Day "thought your queries removed his in-dividuality and he would carefully stet even bad grammar into his book versions if he thought we'd been too pure."[63] Another writer, Christine Weston was "vociferous" about the magazine's editorial practices. She published a series of heavily edited short stories in the *New Yorker* and then made a drama of using her un-edited versions for publication.

Even with this much weight against them, White might not have engaged in such extensive introspection; after all, reviews at some level can simply be dismissed as individual, subjective opin-ions. However, by this point, White was also hearing quite regu-larly and quite heatedly from agents: "Among the agents Russell & Volkening, and Watkins are the most vociferous on our over-editing, and [Diarmuid] Russell harps on it constantly till I dread talking to him. A lot of this is unjust, but some of it is just." More distressingly too, the magazine was hearing from an increas-ing number of contributors; White "naturally [didn't] agree with these reviews," but she did "take more seriously the complaints of the authors themselves." The amateurs, she sniped, should be grateful for the editorial assistance: "A few are very grateful for it, mostly the amateurs like C. O. Skinner." She pointed out that some see the virtue in the fussy editing only when a published piece received high praise, "Isabel Bolton—she complained bit-terly but ate some of her words when her story was a success." Yet, White added, despite this success and her resulting pleasure, Bolton "still feels against our methods," White's pithy paraphrase of the fiery correspondence between them.[64]

White composed a long list of disgruntled authors, "most of them ones I handle," not because she's the most aggressive edi-tor but because they are the ones she knew about. "Here's your list of dissatisfied contributors.... Many of them write so badly that they haven't a leg to stand on but some write well and even the foreigners like to feel their individual style can be kept." John Hersey, White complained, "was the most trying one of all for me in his complaints, because his piece was so badly written." Still, the list included more than just amateurs or those with prose that cries for doctoring: "It's easy as anything to give you these names of the ones who are disgruntled or unhappy but I'll only put down a few I can remember quickly.... I rather think that if we polled our contributors, we'd find more dissatisfied than happy ones on this matter of editing." Katharine's memo ran six pages long, and the list of dissatisfied authors was extensive: Jessamyn West, "kind to [White] but vocal to her agents"; Kay Boyle, and Ross "heard this one direct from her"; Mary McCarthy; A. J. Liebling, and White added clarification with the phrase "you know," that received a handwritten response from Ross, "Yes, I know." White conceded, "Even William Maxwell"—a writer who joined the *New Yorker's* editorial staff—"thinks we over-edit."[65]

Moreover, White herself seemed persuaded that more gifted or established writers may justifiably resent intrusive editorial practices. And pragmatically, she understood what it meant when certain well-received, high-profile authors refused to publish in the *New Yorker*. White was feeling less certain in the late 1940s that *New Yorker* editing had indeed made the pieces stronger, in part because of one influential agent's persuasive arguments based in something that looked like fact:

> Diarmuid Russell has pointed out that our over careful editing prevents our getting stories from writers with great names who don't even think of contributing because they want no queries— people like Hemingway and Faulkner. I daresay he is right on this point. Also he has quoted a book that made a careful study of the solecisms of the great fiction writers, and edited some of these inaccurate passages to make them correct, in order to prove that the slight edited version was less good as literature than the original versions.[66]

It was enough to make her doubt herself and Ross's system. She tried to convey the seriousness of this to Ross: "Eudora Welty—would not allow *any* changes so we've never been able to buy. I have received a vague impression from Bessie Breuer that Carson McCullers, a first rate fiction writer, does not contribute any more because she got discouraged by our methods. (I do not vouch for the fact this is true since it comes second-hand.)" The case was compelling enough that it prompted White to imagine a new editorial policy, one that allowed for a lighter hand in editing: "I am not saying that a single one of these people is right— I only say it builds up to a formidable array of feeling against the detail of our editing and that this makes it so hard to get good fiction that I think we should modify our methods even if some of our stories are less perfectionist." Perhaps, White proposed, there could be a system of editing that distinguished between amateurs and professionals: "We've always been purists and I do not suggest that we give up editing. I only suggest that unless we soon make a considerable revision in our habits in handling the work of professional writers, we won't have any good fiction at all to publish." Of course, she acknowledged, the trick is in distinguishing the real writers from amateurs who assume the same posture: "Margaret Osborn, of course, withdrew a story because of our (my) editing. She is a La Farge, and a crazy woman." Almost immediately, White retrenched, the specter of unedited text apparently rearing as she spoke: "As for the amateurs and beginners, I think we should get carte blanche or nothing and edit them, especially cut them, even more than we now do." White recognized that distinguishing the amateurs would be the problem: "There's a danger here too which is to really be able to spot when a beginner ceases to be a beginner."[67]

For Katharine to suggest a lighter hand in editing demonstrated the mounting pressures she and Ross were experiencing. Ross was a system builder; it was important to him to have an almost militaristic system of checks and rechecks. Facts and the magazine's prized reputation were at stake. Katharine, likewise, was deeply invested in the belief that extensive editing made for high-quality literature. It was a belief she staked her life's work on. Yet, battered by reviews and agents and authors, Katharine White was ready for change: "I feel that too often we have to ask for changes to meet preconceived standards of our own that may be good standards but that, if insisted upon, make our fiction less individual than it would be if edited less and even than if it was far less perfect and precise."[68] Katharine White became persuaded enough that she continued to lobby for some time to change the level of editorial intervention.

Two months after her long memo to Ross, she writes Christine Weston: "I also want to say right off that I am very much in sympathy with the feeling that the New Yorker over-edits. It's one of my strongest feelings right now and it's a battle I'm fighting to try to get less editing."[69] Katharine White lost this battle. She and other New Yorker editors continued to practice on the fault line, reconciling ideals of unspoiled literariness with the magazine's extensive, careful system of editing. They did so by sustaining the old hard line, arguing that the magazine's printed stories, whether by well-known writers or amateurs, represented the result of unprecedentedly high, unflinching literary standards. The editors made no exceptions for named writers, on the grounds that even famous writers now and then produced duds. No writer was above editing. Although it cost the magazine contributors and further fueled criticism in review columns, the New Yorker stayed with its practice of "over-editing," of carving and pruning work so that it would belong "on their street." Of course, to say this is to insinuate that the New Yorker produced substandard literature, a statement that assumes a fairly simplistic premise: real art is produced by individual genius. It must not be tainted by social politics, market pressures, or individual relationships. It can only be harmed by editorial intervention. Add to these the truisms practiced on the manuscripts: art cannot be sentimental, nostalgic, or anything else perceived as "matronly." It must show true grit.[70] Such a conception of art stands vulnerable to the iconoclast's pen: show that it's gendered, show that it's to any degree collaborative, show that suburban or middle-class consumers (women among them) provide for it, and it withers, emasculated. To come to terms with New Yorker art, to appreciate it in any complex way, we must embrace rather than hide the magazine's gendered past.

THREE ∽ MADEMOISELLE, THE NEW YORKER, AND OTHER WOMEN'S MAGAZINES

Several times Truman had tried to get his prose into *The New Yorker*, thinking it the only home for a gifted young writer, and several times he had been politely rebuffed. What he did not know was that he was knocking on the wrong door. The place he was looking for, the place where new writers were not only accepted but welcomed, was not Harold Ross's sometimes stuffy establishment on West Forty-third Street, but a less famous, less likely address altogether: that of the women's fashion magazines, particularly *Harper's Bazaar* and *Mademoiselle*, which for upwards of two decades, from the mid-thirties through the mid-fifties, published the most interesting and original short fiction in the United States.

> Gerald Clarke, *Capote*

The *New Yorker* ethos couldn't handle modernism; its experiments in fictional and poetic techniques were judged "too complex" for the magazine's middlebrow, readership. The so-called little magazines provided the venue for that writing.[1] The *New Yorker* also skirted another major movement in U.S. letters, the Harlem Renaissance. It wasn't that the editors didn't recognize that something was happening uptown from them. They followed several writers only to discover that the literature of the Harlem Renaissance wasn't up the *New Yorker's* street.[2] As biographers and critics of writers such as O'Connor, Faulkner, Welty, and Porter suggest, the *New Yorker* also almost missed the Southern Renaissance. At best one could say that it came late to it. Guy Davenport was rejected on grounds of substance and of modernist style. Michael Kreyling summarizes the obstacles Southern writers faced: the "straitjacket of Southern gothic" was a "descriptive convenience already, in the early 1940s, hardening the arteries of book reviewers" (80). Eudora Welty had a little luck, although much of her work was judged "too complex for *The New Yorker* to handle."[3] In 1938, the magazine could muster little interest in Carson McCullers. They rejected her "Court in the West Eighties," and even after her agent pointed out her Houghton Mifflin fellowship, they didn't see a need to follow her. Still by fall of 1941, McCullers had several stories accepted. By the end of the year, after a rough cycle of editing, McCullers was feeling perhaps a little less inclined to publish there.[4] Ultimately, Southern writers found a more receptive market for their gritty stories in the women's magazines where editors were willing to take risks. Both *Harper's Bazaar* and *Mademoiselle* were actively working to create a network for Southern writers.[5]

Sherrill Tippins's *February House* describes the "atmosphere of 'slick nuttiness'" (23) at *Harper's Bazaar.* Although fiction editor George Davis was eccentric, McCullers found the editing professional: "It was a revelation . . . to observe his sensitivity to the rhythm and structure of prose, his 'unslakable love of words and their correct usage,' and the patience with which he questioned her about a character's motivation or worked with her on a passage or a page over and over until she got it right. This demonstrated respect for the prime importance of literature" (Tippins 23). Davis's temperament precluded a longer tenure at *Harper's Bazaar,* but while he was there he managed to publish material that pushed fictional boundaries while at the same time keeping reader tolerance levels in view. In 1939, after accepting William Saroyan's "Miss Holly," he rejects two other stories by the same author, explaining "I think both stories are awfully good but not for *Harper's Bazaar.* The PRESBYTERIAN CHOIR SINGERS especially would madden many of our readers."[6] Later, Mary Louise

Aswell would capably walk that fine line at *Harper's Bazaar,* like Davis, seeking quality prose and adhering to a system of light editing.[7] During this period, Saroyan had less luck with the *New Yorker.* A dozen or so years later, when Katharine White suggests that Saroyan substantially rewrite a story so that it might possibly fit in the magazine's pages, he explains clearly but gently: "I couldn't possibly rewrite a story. I might sometime write a story *The New Yorker* might like. As you see, however, it is not at all easy for me." Earlier that year, Saroyan corrected a piece in the "Talk of the Town" about one of his dramatic productions, pointing out less gently that they had botched the Armenian: "Your man is a girl, and a damned nice one. Why do you feel it is necessary for your deputies to be boys? It's not *Akh, yavroos,* it's *Ahkh, yarus.* . . . [Your reporter] didn't hear these words. She heard the words she put down. Different meaning, rhythm, value." *Harper's Bazaar, Redbook, Story,* and *Esquire* all provided better venues. Of these, Saroyan felt "cheap," only when he, as he felt, lowered himself to write for *Esquire.*[8]

Mademoiselle too was in the business of publishing quality short fiction and courting up-and-coming and established writers. Sometime in July 1943, Katharine White alerted Ross that *Mademoiselle's* literary acquisitions were translating into higher visibility: "Right now," she writes, "I am interested in trying to analyze the apparent advertising success of 'Mademoiselle' and have suggested to Shuman that he tell our business office that this mag. seems to be cutting us out in some things." Ross was always concerned that the *New Yorker* stay abreast of its competitors: "What I would like to feel is that there is a responsible, close watch of the whole magazine field and that I will be advised if there is anything I ought to know about. It's as simple as that. I don't think I ought to know about every single possible idea or drawing that we may have missed in *Colliers* or the [*Saturday Evening Post*]. I would like to feel, however, that if some phenomenal artist comes along in one of the other magazines I would know it in a reasonable amount of time."[9]

The specific case of *Mademoiselle*, however, did not worry him: "In connection with your analysis of the advertising success of *Mademoiselle*, I would report that it is unquestionably due to a low advertising rate, anyway. The circulation of this magazine shot away up and they offered what agencies consider bargain rates. In that respect it is similar to *The New Yorker* in the early years when were guaranteeing, say, 40,000 and selling 65,000. Advertising rates, as you know, are set automatically for a year ahead, and if your circulation goes up in that year you are giving a big surplus to the advertisers."[10] A year later, Ross seemed a bit more concerned. *Mademoiselle*'s fiction contests were garnering a great deal of attention because their selections were filling the prize-winning story anthologies feeding the growing middle-brow market. Impatient to wade through the increasing number of short stories published, readers wanted not only to know what was best—reviews answered these questions—but to have them readily available in a single issue or volume.

In 1943, Ross specifically asked White to report on the latest, a *Mademoiselle* war story contest. White at this point felt secure that the *New Yorker* still rested at the top of the literary pack. She found the stories uninspiring. Nonetheless, she made a list of seven writers and supplied her notes. One she judged sentimental, another pretentious, and still another sophomoric and unconvincing—contest winners perhaps, but not worthy of reprinting in any prize volume. Two of the writers on her list had contributed to the *New Yorker* (Eleanor Shaler and Ignatius Sacco). These particular stories were not worth publishing. Sacco's "LaGuerra" is barely a story and heavy in Italian dialect; Eleanor Shaler's piece she also judges unworthy. She buried one significant misstep in the middle of the list: the editorial team had rejected Edward Harris Heth's "Of Age." This was particularly egregious because she believed he had the potential to be made into a *New Yorker* writer. She likewise paused at Alison Stuart's "Sunday Liberty" because she worried that this author might have suffered an unwarranted rejection from the *New Yorker*. Another editor, Ik Shuman, remembered that the editors had rejected Stuart's "The Yodeler," one that White thought might have made into the O. Henry Prize stories, the kind of publishing chain of events that would have made the *New Yorker* look bad. She later appended a handwritten note, explaining the good news—the story had not been rejected at the *New Yorker*; they had not been scooped. The tally? Seven writers, two already contributors, three deserving to be wooed by the fiction editors. In June of 1944, White was still tracking stories in *Mademoiselle*, looking for writers the *New Yorker* might persuade to move to their pages.

Part of the culture of literate zeal, editors at women's magazines were serious competitors in the short story marketplace. Why does it seem almost counterintuitive for us in the twenty-first century to take their work seriously? As I suggested in the introduction, the nature of women's magazines has changed significantly post-Kinsey, post–second-wave feminism and its legacy of sexual liberation. By the 1970s, as Jennifer Scanlon documents in her biography of Helen Gurley Brown, literature in women's magazines seemed outdated, old-fashioned: orgasms sold women's magazines, not poetry. The men's magazines— *Esquire* and *Playboy*—came to be seen as the appropriate place to house a modern, unsentimental, bold (read "manly") literature. Yet this wasn't the only obstacle. Academic analysis tended to characterize one dominant theme in a magazine, rather than to look for the tensions among competing discourses. Women's magazines in particular were more likely to be characterized by a single trait (domestic, superficial, sexist, bourgeois). The literature, ads, editorials, features were all read as supporting that single trait. Although the quality of literature in the *New Yorker* was (and is still) debated, finally its reputation survived. It has become coded as cultured. The women's magazines fared differently; they came to be seen as culture's antithesis.

Literate Zeal works alongside other journalistic histories that capture a moment in U.S. cultural history when women's magazines contributed to the making of belles-lettres. There is still deep resistance to accounting for the literary work done by women's magazines. To recognize their contributions, to see these magazines in the same league as the *New Yorker*, undoes a powerful mythology: that the *New Yorker* is an icon of literary sophistication, one that towers above and apart from other boorish, middle-class, large-circulation publications. There are deep assumptions that must be unpinned, or at least investigated, if we are to account for the important work that editors, women in large numbers among them, did to promote belles-lettres in the mid-twentieth century. First is the judgment that women's magazines had no significant content. Second, is the idea that the *New Yorker* is decidedly not a women's magazine. While it is one thing to concede that the *New Yorker* had middlebrow undercurrents, it is quite another to argue its role as a player in the women's marketplace and to see women's magazines as players in the *New Yorker*'s field.

"I Don't Want to Play the Harp"

The *New Yorker* wasn't the only commercial magazine trying to create an ethos—an institutional personality as well as a place—for literature that would impart the idea of literary sophistication and cultivated tastes, that would have the stamp of being the right thing to be reading. *Mademoiselle* magazine published its first issue a decade after the *New Yorker*'s debut, but one can see in compressed form a similar movement from a light and witty magazine to a publication that sponsored serious high letters. *Mademoiselle*'s opening pages, which listed plays and operas and other entertainment, looked quite familiar to *New Yorker* readers in content and typography.[11] The similarities between the *New Yorker* and *Mademoiselle* were striking enough to inspire one job seeker's confusion. On April 22, 1935, a young woman wrote to Harold Ross, inquiring about a job on the "new woman's magazine to do with fashions" that she heard the *New Yorker* was "fostering." Two days later, editor J. O. Whedon responded, "You have been misinformed somehow. The *New Yorker* has no connection with any other magazine and has no intention of starting another. It takes all the time and effort we have to get out this one. There is a new women's magazine out called 'Madamoiselle,' [sic] but we had nothing to do with it."[12] It might amuse twenty-first-century readers to imagine how a young woman could be so confused: *Mademoiselle,* the fashion guide for young women, an offshoot of the *New Yorker*? Whatever could leave such an impression? A look at the first decade of *Mademoiselle* provided me a surprising answer: plenty.

When I first began research on *Mademoiselle,* I expected to see cover stouting fashion, hairstyles, and recipes. That's not what I found, but I also didn't find surprises, at least not in the first few issues, which are filled with fashion sketches sprinkled alongside long columns of true-love romance stories. The dominant impression is not of photography but of columns of text. Its invitation to subscribe invoked a visual image that suggests the persona the magazine was trying to create, drawing, as Condé Nast did some years earlier with *Vogue,* on the image of the magazine as a young woman, a debutante with whom other young women might wish to socialize: "And so *Mademoiselle* has called—she has called once. If you have enjoyed her personality—her bubbly, youthful interest—won't you ask her to call again? She has been formally introduced to you. Now it is in your discretion to make her a member of your circle. She is a newcomer—but is already quite popular" (*Mademoiselle,* February 1935). Such beginnings sync with a commonplace understanding of *Mademoiselle* as typical women's magazine's fare—face creams, fashions, and how to land your man.

Two issues later, the editorial team, led by Desmond Hall, rechristened the magazine, offering its "Platform, or Constitution, or Bill of Rights, or whatever you'd like to call it." The editors begin by irreverently dismissing the kinds of lady's subjects that *Mademoiselle* had no interest in covering: "*Mademoiselle* has no interest in: Prize recipes. Romantic fiction written with a stencil. Articles on how to handle six-year olds, etc. Stuffed shirts. Sublime acceptance of everything the publicity men tell you, and the apparently general assumption that all young women in American actively interested in fashion are either nieces of J. P. Morgan or slaves to patterns" (*Mademoiselle*, May 1935). So what was it that this newly christened magazine was trying to achieve? The editors delineated their platform thusly: their magazine "admits to a strong interest in: A sense of humor. Stories with at least faintly recognizable characters. The value and pleasure that may be obtained from unstuffing shirts. A candid and matter-of-fact approach to the great glamorous legend of Careers for Women. Fashion news that is news and that doesn't make a dress allowance look silly" (*Mademoiselle*, May 1935). Theirs was to be a fashion magazine of a different kind.

Before I begin drawing similarities between the *New Yorker* and *Mademoiselle*, let me begin by elaborating on one important concession. *Mademoiselle* differed from the *New Yorker* in that it restricted its ethos by targeting college-bound or college-educated women, as well as trade school graduates, looking to improve their skills and professional opportunities. *Mademoiselle* readers were women who worked, ideally as what the magazine labeled as "junior executives." In invoking the junior executive, *Mademoiselle* was neither recording a realistic portrait of readers, nor creating a fantasy. The rhetorical work the editors were doing—it is still the rhetorical work editors do—was constitutive: they were naming a niche, a group with significant numbers and buying power, and then inviting readers to identify with it, to grow the market. This same group of women—those leaving colleges or small towns to look for careers in the city—would be exemplified in the popular musical of 1967, *Thoroughly Modern Millie*. Part of the comedy of that production comes from rendering young female desire as either quixotic (innocent young women finding careers in the hard-nosed city) or duplicitous (young women ostensibly in search of careers could only be after that which Marilyn Monroe made famous: diamonds and millionaire husbands). In using the appellation "junior executive," *Mademoiselle* was according seriousness to young female ambition, chronicling myriad success stories to show that careers could be had and that the sophistications of the city were within reach.

Mademoiselle opened its doors to readers unapologetically young. In July 1938, Mrs. M. A. E. of Winston-Salem, North Carolina, complained in a letter reprinted in the "A Penny for Your Thoughts" column: "When I subscribed to *Mademoiselle* about eight months ago, I was not aware of the fact that it was a publication primarily of interest to the very young girl, but rather was under the impression that it was of interest and help to the business woman as well; however, since I have been reading it, I have found out differently. Therefore, since it is in the interest of the 'very young thing' I do not find it particularly helpful." If Mrs. M. A. E. was hoping to persuade the editors to widen the readership, she failed. The "A Penny for Your Thoughts" column ran sporadically, but responses by the editorial team were even more sporadic. In this instance, they were motivated to respond: "*Mademoiselle* is edited 'for the smart young woman' between the ages of seventeen and thirty. We are sorry that Mrs. E. finds us disappointing, but we hope our many other readers under and above this age group will discover much of interest in the issues to come" (*Mademoiselle*, July 1938). This strategy paid. As Katharine White and Harold Ross noticed, *Mademoiselle*'s advertising revenues grew precipitously.

Mademoiselle was less prescriptive on the question of whether its ideal readers were middle-class (white) or upper-class (white) workers.[13] Despite the working focus, the features and ads unabashedly sold expensive leisure products and services, following the formula of giving readers a little more than they wanted, of offering readers an aspirational leisured space. A few readers protested, like I. W. Haverhill of Massachusetts, that only wealthy young women could afford the items advertised. The editors chose not to respond to this letter, or rather they did so by printing two others which praised the magazine's helpful advice on maintaining an attractive appearance while not spending a lot of money. Ads for working women's residential hotels appear with great frequency and range in price: three dollars a night for the Hotel Park Chambers—"the Hotel for Smart Young Women" (Fifty-eighth Street at Sixth Avenue) and twelve dollars per week for the American Woman's Club—"designed by business women *for* business women" (353 West Fifty-seventh Street). Paul Alexander describes the best known of these hotels: "Victorian, stately, ornate, the Barbizon Hotel for Women, where *Mademoiselle* put up its guest editors, stood on the corner of Lexington Avenue and Sixty-third Street, in the middle of Manhattan's Upper East Side. A fixture of the neighborhood since 1927, through the years the hotel had been a favorite of young women attending Seven Sisters schools" (108). There is little in cultural histories about the role these residential hotels played in women's entry into the workforce, but it's clear they were an important element. Young, single women needed places to live once they left small-town homes for the cities. Residential hotels like the Barbizon

> provided a refuge for many of these women, and its owners sought to create an environment that reinforced the values of the families from which the women had come. Codes of Conduct and Dress were enforced, no men were allowed above the lobby floor, and prospective tenants needed three letters of recommendation to be considered. Despite these apparent constraints, the Barbizon later hosted many social, intellectual and athletic activities and ... was also active in promoting women's organizations, providing meeting space to groups such as the National Junior League, the Arts Council of New York, and the Wellesley College Club. (National Register of Historic Places)

Overall, it was the promotion and celebration of careers for women that came to delineate the parameters of *Mademoiselle's* ethos. Women were defined by what they did—and the magazine constantly promoted a range of occupations. The July 1938 career issue, for instance, featured a woman maneuvering pieces across a chess board. Each piece represented some possible career, many traditional, but not all. The inside makes the theme clear: "Dreams of a career, of having the world at your feet, of making millions, of being a 'power'—may be just dreams. But to the girl on this month's cover, the delightful chess 'men' designed in soap sculpture by Lester Gaba represent reality—as she considers the next move to decide her future." Feature upon feature suggested the range of professions for women in a manner impossible to conceive of in a twenty-first-century large-circulation women's magazine. The editors presented statistics that normalized women's work: "11,000,000 women in America—one out of every three women between the ages of 15 and 44—are employed" (*Mademoiselle*, July 1938). There was advice for breaking the "vicious circle of 'no job without experience,'" profiles of three career women (one a secretary, one an interior designer, and one a graduate assistant in mathematics on her way to being "the woman to teach men"). There was a large, detailed pullout chart, offering advice on what to expect in terms of training, duties, aptitude, professional advancement, pay, working conditions, bosses, and compatibility with marriage. The list of fields was jumbled, a very mixed bag: photography, editor, window display, interior decorating, explorer, aviatrix, entertainer, librarian, archeologist, secretary, actress, physical education, medicine, hotel and tea room manager, personal shop proprietor, sculptress, beautician, proofreader, stenographer, publicity, traffic manager, illustrator, copy writer mannequin, social science, home economics, vocational counselor, receptionist, laboratory technician, travel bureau, chemist, teaching, merchandise counselor, physician, textile designer, landscaping, reporter, cosmetics, historical research, journalism, dressmaker, buyer, agent, and labor leader.

Numerous columns were devoted to debunking gendered work stereotypes. A feature in 1952, for example, was entitled "Ladies Allowed!—if not welcomed to the career of chemistry, but the field is rich with opportunities for trained job hunters." The piece opened by correcting a Lawrence H. Summers–like gaff made by Francis P. Garvan, head of the Chemical Foundation, who had declared that women did not work in the field of chemistry. Granted, such articles appear alongside the usual fashion-based articles, brief pieces about wardrobes for work, or the perfectly manicured professional hand. But just as often, such career features are positioned next to another career-oriented article.

One regular feature in the magazine was Helen Josephy's "I Don't Want to Play the Harp," published under this title from April 1935 through April 1937. The captions under the title would alter some, but all played on the differences between a finishing school education and the possibilities in the world of work: "If harp and embroidery needle leave you cold, if you'd rather fly an ocean, split an atom, set a style, here's your department" (April 1935, 30); "If harp and embroidery needle leave you cold, if you'd rather set a style or split an atom, follow this department monthly. The first step is the first job—Here are several practical tips for getting it. Read 'em and Reap!" (June 1935, 32).

After the first few columns, a postscript was added: "Every month in *Mademoiselle*, Helen Josephy tells of opportunities for 'young women with futures.' You can depend on her articles; they are honest, authoritative and complete. You should not miss one of them" (July 1935, 42). By October 1935, the feature began to offer mail-in service as well: "Her wealth of experience makes Helen Josephy the ideal advisor for would-be careerists— and you can avail yourself of her knowledge merely by writing to her in care of *Mademoiselle* . . . and enclosing a stamped, self-addressed envelope. You will receive in return frank, honest, unprejudiced advice" (68). The column of October 1936, "Author! Author," is illustrative of the form and tone of the series in which Josephy argues that attitudes about women working as writers had changed. While once women were advised "to go home and create babies, not literature," the advent of the new century initiated a profound change. Women no longer had to follow the route embarked upon by women like George Sand who "cut her hair, put on some pants and called herself George Sand" to avoid the scandal that might come with any association with a "Bohemian literary life." Female authorship was now so accepted, Josephy proclaims, that "doting mother-in-laws whisper proudly over bridge tables, 'Imagine! Martha has promised to dedicate her first published work to me.'" The "ambitious female fiction writer need no longer sweat it out alone" because there is a whole machinery that supports authorship, from therapists to writing schools to literary agents. "Experts analyze her psyche, help her discover her 'natural' subject matter, teach her technique. Agents take on the dirty work of contacting editors." Even publishers and critics are supportive, enthusiastic to discover and promote a "fresh point of view." New technology expanded rather than threatened the literary marketplace: "typewriters across the continent clatter," producing "novels, short stories in the 'slicks,' movies, plays." Josephy delineated the broad range of genres women might productively engage: "The young woman seeking a more ordinary work environment can compose series for magazines and newspapers, radio continuities, one-act religious plays, skits for women's clubs and even filling in balloons for comic strips." Aspiring women writers needn't believe that genius is required. The "Harp Department is essentially pragmatic and vocationally minded," and, moreover, the "legend that literary genius, in a trance-like seizure, can turn out a perfect story or a full-blown novel without previous apprenticeship, has been blown to bits" (October 1936). In all her columns, Josephy argued for women's presence in the field, discussed the practical and economic issues associated with the profession, and profiled a number of diverse practitioners.

While always aware of "vocationally minded" writing, *Mademoiselle* also extended its interest to writing of high literary quality—and then claimed always to have had that mission. Here, for example, is fiction and poetry editor Ellen A. Stoianoff in a foreword to *Mademoiselle Prize Stories: Twenty-Five Years 1951–1975*, published in 1976: "From its inception in 1935, *Mademoiselle* has tried to publish fiction of high literary quality.... A number of major American writers, including Truman Capote, Flannery O'Connor, Sylvia Plath, Joyce Carol Oates and Doris Betts, were virtually unknown at the time they made their literary debuts in *Mademoiselle*" (vii–viii).

Given this focus on careerism, it was not entirely surprising that the editors chose to sponsor contests that encouraged or showcased women's work. While its first College Board contest encouraged fashion design, it wasn't long before *Mademoiselle* incorporated beat reports from campus journalists and implemented its high-profile guest editorship program. Fiction contests furthered the work of earlier columns that promoted writing and editing as careers for women. While earlier feminist criticism focused on sexism in the magazine's fiction (examples surely are there, as well as in the other magazines included in the smart genre),[14] I have focused on the competing messages that normalized careers for women. In *Mademoiselle*, the fashioning of the career woman was not merely part of the magazine; it was its most salient feature.

Marrying Smart Culture at *Mademoiselle*

The platform made clear that the editors of *Mademoiselle* wished their magazine to be seen as an example of the "smart" magazine genre, that they wished to (and would) compete with publications like the *New Yorker* or the *Smart Set*. If the *New Yorker* saw itself as a kind of Baedeker for smart young men (think Eustace Tilley), *Mademoiselle* modeled itself similarly, targeting college and career women, instructing them on locating the perfect college, finding a suitable career, landing the best job, selecting the most appropriate clothing and makeup, traveling to the most desired destinations. As part of this mission, it also supplied tips about opera, theater, and, importantly here, provided reading material. While such reading material would always include romance, it was by no means restricted to the genre. Early on, *Mademoiselle* readers enjoyed a campy "smart" element, including for instance an art sketch entitled "A Page of Leerers."

Marriage was frequently made the material of smart humor, as in the irreverent "imaginary marriage" columns that played with the idea of strange matches. One column imagines the coupling of Greta Garbo with Mahatma Gandhi. Another column in the series fantasizes about the marriage of Gertrude Stein to boxer Max Baer. Yet another recommends the union of socialite Elsa Maxwell and Leon Trotsky.

The presence of such columns points to levity, a certain spirit of play possible at a new magazine, play that frequently invoked the juxtaposing of gay or bisexual culture side-by-side with heteronormitivity. Truman Capote's biographer Gerald Clarke makes a convincing case that women's magazines offered such a plastic work environment because of the support of chief editors and publishers who weren't overly invested in micromanaging the literary enterprise.

> Though the business offices of [*Harper's Bazaar* and *Mademoiselle*] grumbled about the highbrow and often startling stories [George Davis] chose, such as a Ray Bradbury fantasy about a vampires' Thanksgiving, his top editors, two extremely formidable women, Carmel Snow at *Harper's Bazaar* and Betsy Talbot Blackwell at *Mademoiselle*, were resolute in their support.... Davis had far more freedom working for the fashion glossies than he would have had at *The New Yorker*, *The Atlantic*, or any other magazine whose primary concern was words. He was allowed to publish pieces by Virginia Woolf, the Sitwells, and Collette, to commission Christopher Isherwood and W. H. Auden to report on their trip to China at war, and to devote much of two issues to Carson McCullers' stark and, at that time, shocking novella *Reflections in a Golden Eye*. (81–82)

Clarke speculates that this freedom stemmed from the low regard the editors had for literature: "The publishers, who looked upon fiction and poetry as nothing more than padding for the pictures and ads ... shrugged their shoulders and gave in [to Davis], assuming, perhaps correctly, that their readers were wise enough to avoid large and offensive blocks of type" (82). This explanation, however, doesn't hold particularly well. It would have been far easier for *Harper's Bazaar* and *Mademoiselle* to follow *Vogue*'s lead, publishing nonfiction only, particularly nonfiction with a leisure theme.

It seems more likely that Snow and Blackwell committed to literature because it was part of an expanded mission—and because it sold magazines. In her memoir, Carmel Snow comments: "I think I determined from the moment I read the first installment [of *Gentlemen Prefer Blondes*] that if I were ever the editor of a magazine I would publish fiction, which *Vogue* refused to publish. Though our business as a fashion magazine was to show fashion, our business as journalists, it seemed to me, was to make an exciting book" (50). Snow was an astute business woman. In 1925, when she was still working at *Vogue* magazine, *Harper's Bazaar* published in serial form Anita Loos's *Gentlemen Prefer Blondes*; its presence in the magazine tripled the newsstand sales (Rowlands 90). It was a lesson Snow remembered.

Women's magazines had a largely female audience (good for fiction), and they offered (relatively) more accommodating working conditions for gay men. In providing work for talented gay editors, women's magazines benefited from an extensive network of talented artists and intellectuals.[15] Truman Capote's experience provides perhaps the most striking example of differences between the working environment at the *New Yorker* and *Mademoiselle*. Biographer Gerald Clarke clearly takes delight in envisioning Harold Ross's reaction to the distinctively self-fashioned Capote: "If his appearance did not shock, his childlike voice did—it was so high, went one unfriendly joke, that only a dog could hear it.... 'For God's sake! What's that?' Ross himself demanded when he peered out of his office and saw him drifting down the hall" (71). Clarke's suggestion that the *New Yorker*'s work environment was more restrictive is corroborated by other accounts. For example, here is Brendan Gill on the subject:

> If challenged, [Ross] would have argued that he would never risk hiring a homosexual, on any of a dozen preposterous grounds; the fact was that he hired them often and willingly and took ruthless advantage of their subservience to him.... For the purposes of the magazine, Ross needed a certain kind of homosexual, whom he thought of as the only kind. To pre-

serve the skimpy fiction that he was not surrounded by his sup-
posed natural enemies, he ignored everything about them except their work. . . .They worked hard and for comparatively low
wages, in part because they could afford to, having no wives
and children to support; moreover, they were able to keep longer and more irregular hours than men whose wives expected
them to be home for dinner at a certain time each day and perhaps also to come home early on occasion to entertain the little
ones at birthday parties. In a word, they were bachelors, and as
such, a resource readily manipulable by Ross. As for [this] nest-
building faculty . . . it was indispensable in the early days of the
magazine. (29–30)[16]

Whatever the source of the irreverent humor at *Mademoiselle,*
the smart attitude pervaded the magazine. *Mademoiselle* rarely lost
sight of a readership of women who were new to the city but ready
to join their young male colleagues "about town." Consider, for
example, the long, semihumorous piece entitled "Lady Barfly,"
which offers advice on the right way to drink in a bar.

For all their attempts to be self-consciously "smart," the editors and writers for *Mademoiselle* were quite serious about careers
and obstacles that stood in the way of women's careerism. The big-
gest of those obstacles was marriage especially the new rhetoric
of "marriage as a career." The May 1938 issue carried an article by
Gretta Palmer, "Marriage Is a Career," which lamented the ways in
which marriage had changed. "The New Domesticity" was much
more scientific, "a grim and humorless demonstration of how the
Bedeaux system can be applied to the home of today." Gone were
the days "when a girl got married for fun," "to enjoy life with the
man of her choice." This generation of women "do an amount of
work that would appal a navy and President Roosevelt rolled into
one" (Palmer 43). Palmer lamented that even women's colleges
have buckled to the powerful ideal of marriage as a career:

Vassar, founded to give women an identical education with
men, succumbed during the depression years and now provides its clamoring students with courses in budgeting and

interior decoration and baby culture. Stephens College has scrapped the whole old-fashioned curriculum in favor of intensive training the womanly arts. The Brides' School in New York City was founded to cater to debutantes who demanded instruction in how to make strawberry mousse and hospital beds. Even the pigtailed students of the Pulton preparatory school borrow babies by day, to practice on them during their hours at school. (43)

To make matters worse, the editors continue in the next month's issue, young women in colleges are buying into the new domesticity: "from a questionnaire sent out to college students, *Mademoiselle* learns that 83 per cent of the college women questioned look forward to matrimony." Only "10 per cent contemplate careers after graduation, and finally, that remaining 7 per cent consider marriage and a career feasible." The authors present *Mademoiselle* as one of the lone standouts and invites like-minded women, that elite 17 percent, into this ethos. They produce a manifesto of sorts on the potentially most powerful obstacle to careers for women:

> We cannot reconcile with reality the findings of our Marriage-Career questionnaire. We believe that marriage and a career are compatible: more, we believe that every woman, married or single, should be educated for a career when and if necessity or inclination warrants it.... To the hundreds whom we see (and the thousands whom we can't)—and to the young women who already have jobs but wish for better ones, to girls in school, to young married women who want or need to augment the family budget—to all of these, her readers, *Mademoiselle* dedicates this Career Issue. (*Mademoiselle*, July 1938)

This particular issue invites readers to abscond from the 83 percent and join the enlightened 17 percent who understand that true careers are found *outside* the home. The career focus would continue through the 1950s.

Marriage occasionally found a happier reception in *Mademoiselle*'s pages, but only if coupled with a career. Consider, for ex-

ample, the rough treatment of women (both those without outside careers and those who choose not to marry) in Dorothy Dayton's "Marriage or Career?" (July 1935):

> A large part of my career has been given to interviewing
> women on how to have careers. Everything they've said
> has been a lot of hooey. Married women who've never really
> wanted a career at all use marriage as an excuse for never
> having done anything else. Single women, who still feel
> apologetic for not having got their man, use careers as an
> excuse for their spinsterhood.
>
> In the meantime, the thousands of married women
> peacefully pursuing their careers seem to be the only ones
> who have graduated from the cro-magnon stage of the
> woman question. With the little man at home to spur them
> on, they make real progress. (18)

Such columns were certainly not accepting of other patterns of
community and other sexualities: "If you're careering, but hus-
bandless, you're always looking for a husband. It may be subcon-
scious and you may not admit it, but it's true—unless, of course,
there's something radically wrong with you" (Dayton 19). The
stance was clear: educated progressive women aspired to work
outside the home and ideally to enter working partnerships
with their spouses, a value made clear by profiles of couples who
worked together (for examples, two artists or two schoolteach-
ers). Working women (single or married), or the aspiration to
become a young, cultured woman about town, a career woman,
represented the class marked to enter *Mademoiselle*'s pages.

Who's Afraid of Tom Wolfe?—Or, the Early *New Yorker* as Woman's Magazine

Tom Wolfe's "Tiny Mummies," published in 1961, harpooned
the *New Yorker*'s style, rehashing the debate over whether the *New
Yorker* edited literature into or out of existence. Yet this was only
one weapon deployed by Wolfe in his satiric attack. Wolfe had
yet another barb in reserve, which he let fly just in case: if the

magazine had any living presence at all, he taunted, any gasp of life, it assumed the lowest form, that is, the shape of bourgeois women's trade fare, filled with "the wettest bathful of bourgeois sentimentality in the world," (280) with the kind of "stories the other women's magazines used to run thirty years ago" (281). Wolfe used the specter of women's magazines, and dated women's magazines at that, to dramatize the *New Yorker*'s fall from its new literary pinnacle. Wolfe didn't need to tease out the argument; he simply needed to make the connection. *New Yorker* readers could choose their poison, a magazine fussy, pretentious, literate, and dead, or one alive, but, well, old and matronly. Wolfe might be taken as an outlier, if he were the first to stake the line. As Trysh Travis's research documents, he was not. He had simply relighted and ignited a touchy subject. In March 1965, *Newsweek* had judged the magazine "prissy"; three years earlier, Seymour Krim of the *Village Voice* had been less genteel, referring to the editors as "punctuation castratos," an image that pales next to another he posits, the image of a magazine that, in publishing James Baldwin, was "spread[ing] its legs and offer[ing] its body," searching for a "force that could buoy it up and inseminate its jellied blood with meaning." Compared to the *Village Voice*, Wolfe suddenly seem dull, as does James Thurber, who in 1958 complained about the *New Yorker*'s "matronly girth" (16).[17] The narrative that haunted Shawn's *New Yorker* had been established: the rough-hewn, manly Ross had run a quality magazine; after his death, the effeminized Shawn had, starting in 1961, delivered it over to women.[18]

Wolfe evoked this guilt by association with women's magazines thirty or more years after women began entering the editing profession in record numbers and six years before the launch of *Ms.* as an insert in *New York Magazine*. Wolfe located and exploited a weakness in the logic. In order to achieve literary heights, the *New Yorker* had to mark its difference, not so much from other class publications but from gendered and mass and "slick" publications of its time. In other words, in order to achieve literariness, the *New Yorker* had to claim to grow beyond the pale of the industry it was a part of. It had to make transcendent claims about editorial independence, factual accuracy, and aesthetic, written judgments, all of which criteria would have staked its difference from other class publications. In retrospect, the logic seems natural, unassailable, rather than an example of nostalgic reconstruction: Of course, the *New Yorker* is different from women's magazines, in every dimension, in the kind of people who produced it, in its editorial staff, in its readership, in its advertising staff who never stepped on the editorial floor. Yet the details tell a different, more nuanced story. Wolfe was correct enough to be persuasive. The *New Yorker* was publishing pieces by women that appealed to women. Wolfe erred, however, in his belief that this represented a historical change for the magazine. The *New Yorker* from the beginning was one of several class publications to emerge at the time, and like these other publications it depended on traditional women's material to broker literacy for an aspirational upper-middle class.[19] It marketed itself to women's desires. In this, it was very much like other magazines that published literature. As Ruth Adams Knight wrote in *Lady Editor*, the distinction between fiction magazines and women's magazines "may be a distinction without a difference.... All-fiction periodicals are also in a strict sense, women's magazines. Research has proved that it is feminine interests that moves them from newsstands, even though there may be large number of men among the ultimate consumers" (102). Later in the century, charged with increasing the circulation of the *New Yorker*, Tina Brown may have understood the magazine's past, its history, its reputation, better than her critics knew. Her cover for the special women's issue of 2004 featured Eustace Tilley as a woman, the idea for which was perhaps suggested by an earlier photo of Janet Flanner in the well-recognized pose. In 2004, the gesture failed. What Brown failed to perceive was the degree to which the *New Yorker*'s reputation, its romanticized history, had replaced the original article. Yet a look at the original confirms that the New Yorker's success depended not on the values of the transcendent literacy that increasingly defined it—so tenacious is this ethos now that the New Yorker markets its own literate image on calendars, mugs, and the like—but on the talents and on the leisurely, gendered desires of both the men and women who produced, contributed to, and read it.

Lingerie, Lipstick, & Letters

One might argue that the content of the New Yorker—its features, its "art," as well as its advertisements—differed in significant ways from publications such as Mademoiselle or Harper's Bazaar, publications presumably slavish to visual representation of commodities marketed toward women. Yet such a claim is overstated. In scholarship on women's magazines, it is standard fare to read critiques of the beauty industry. One might expect the advertising in the New Yorker to be significantly different, but it isn't. The New Yorker, pre– and post–World War II, is filled with advertisements for women's clothing and beauty products, and they are not so unlike those in women's magazines. In New Yorker ads in 1937, women scientifically measure their legs to verify the effectiveness of hosiery. They look for nail polish that somehow reflects intellect. (Stupid women presumably wear garish shades, a derogation usually linked with class or race; here all are conflated: smart, rich, white women wear subtle shades.) Neither underwear (or at least support garments), nor deodorant were considered beneath the New Yorker readers. The New Yorker balanced such ads—as did Vogue and Harper's Bazaar—with ads for sleek cars and exotic travel destinations.

The relationship between the business and the editorial sides of the New Yorker has long been one of the magazine's transcendent tropes. Beginning with Dale Kramer's book and continuing with Kunkel's revised history, the magazine's historians have followed Ross's lead and insisted on a narrative of editorial purity. Advertising had to happen to keep the magazine afloat, but it would not, as Ross would not allow it to, infect the magazine's content.[20] The *New Yorker*, though it had to rely on advertisements, could thus rise above crass commercialism. Fair enough. Yet in 1927, just roughly two years after the *New Yorker* debuted, it established a column on fashion (granted without the commercial art photographs that *Vogue* made famous) written by Lois Long, who previously had been writing nightclub reviews under the penname "Lipstick." Long was an English major from Vassar who began her career as a copywriter for *Vogue*, later replaced Dorothy Parker as drama critic for *Vanity Fair*, and then moved on to the *New Yorker*, a fledgling publication. Brendan Gill argues that her writerly intentions distinguished her from other writers: "L. L.'s attitude was a novelty; most writing about fashion then, like most writing about fashion now, amounted to scarcely more than the sedulous puffing of certain favored shops and designers. L. L. cared not a straw for anyone but her readers. Her intention was to instruct and entertain them by the extraordinary device of taking clothes seriously and writing about them honestly" (206). Others, including Katharine White, argued that Long's brilliant style, her distinctive voice, set her apart from others who wrote on women's fashions. White wrote to Long's daughter: "You can be very proud of both your parents. I heartily agree with Shawn that Lois was an innovator—the first fashion writer to be a true critic of fashion and to write about fashion as an art that should not be degraded by bad style. I have missed her outspoken views and emphatic, clear writing since she had to retire because of poor eyesight."[21] There's no doubt that Long had a wonderful, biting sense of humor. Consider, for example, this bit from her review of New York fashions on May 29, 1937: "Take a sum like $7.95 in your little hot hand and Altman can make a best-dressed woman out of you. They go to town there about old-fashioned, printed longcloth in tiny Oriental patterns. In black, dark green, blue, or red, with tiny Taj Mahals over it, longcloth fashions a simple dress with a white braid belt and white star buttons. A white linen bolero goes on top, and you could lunch at the Ritz in it with equanimity. (Or maybe you'd rather lunch with Eunice.)" (Long 46). Clever enough, but much of her writing follows in the vein and vocabulary of fashion reviews: "Then there are what they call 'garden coats,' with long, circular skirts, slim waistlines, and short sleeves—wonderful to slip into after that cooling shower, or lounge in, or even wear for very informal dining" (Long 46). Whether or not Long really stood out is debatable. It's clear she was certainly one of the most carefully edited, as edited versions of her columns in the *New Yorker* archives show.

Why would the *New Yorker* include such a feature? What do historians who wish to apotheosize the magazine do with such stuff? In *The Smart Magazines*, George Douglas ventures that when Harold Ross gave Long the column, "which at one time he vowed not to have," he was undoubtedly "responding to some unspoken demands of local advertisers" (153). This seems a possibility, or perhaps he was simply acting on the reception of the earlier article that had first moved the magazine from a failing startup to a young magazine on solid footing, an article penned by a debutante, offering a glimpse into the world of debutantes. Regardless, Ross involved himself with the details of Long's work, in part because he involved himself in every facet of the magazine, in part because the advertising department pressured him to, and in part because Long's somewhat erratic working habits compelled him to:

> Miss Long: November 28, 1927
>
> Will you please talk to me about Russek's? Mrs. Angell says it is not a very high class store—or was not the last time she visited it two or three years ago. Spaulding tells me that they have made great efforts to bring it up the last two or three years and he rates it as superior to Macy's from our standpoint. He says that they have very good imported merchandise.
>
> Am I asking too much when I suggest that you tell the girl at the operating desk when you are coming back? I looked for you all over the place—to find that you had gone out—Ross. (Kunkel, *Letters* 33)

To Lois, whom I never see: April 21, 1934
    I have been asked by the management with tears in its eyes to plead with you to get your copy in on time as it is costing worry, money, energy and all those things. For CHRIST'S SAKE WON'T YOU PLEASE DO SO? It is true, Lois dear, that these big books now are a lot of work to get out and do mean that some of the pages have to go through and get OK'ed and printed ahead of the rest. 5PM Tuesday must be the deadline on Avenue copy beginning this week (I should have written you this three or four days ago but I guess you have been advised of this) and please, please, please observe it. Don't throw us down, little girl.
    Ross[22]

Long remained employed at the *New Yorker* for several reasons. She was in the beginning writing several columns for the fledgling magazine, covering nightclubs, restaurants, theater, and fashions. She was a savvy fashion reporter with an eye for the new. In one letter, Ross congratulates her for scooping the *Garment News*.

Most importantly, as the letters to the editor attest, "Lipstick" had a following almost as strong as the Constant Reader (Dorothy Parker). Lois Long received large quantities of mail each month. Most of the letters were invitations to fashion shows or to try new products, but some readers wrote in seeking her advice. The mail grew so voluminous that early on Ross hired a secretary committed to this department. Long's fashion column brought recognition and subscriber loyalty.

Long's column brought in advertising revenues and readers, just as similar ones did for publications like *Vogue*. "As a boy," Ross writes to one acquaintance, "I never dreamed I would have to deal with any publication running critical pieces about women's underwear. Here I am, though. My viewpoint on these departments is that they are necessary evils" (Kunkel, *Letters* 48). Long understood this necessity and used it to argue for higher pay in a memo to Ross:

I consider that each department is worth more than fifty dollars.... Particularly the Fashion Stuff. Discarding the fact that the business department, who pays salaries, has profited more from that department than from any other, the Avenue stuff requires more time, more experience, and more accuracy than Tables. I consider it worth seventy-five alone, on the present rate of salary....

With love and without mercenary motives, Long[23]

Because fashion was a money maker for the magazine, it came under the close scrutiny of the advertising department. In 1931, Ross sent a series of queries to Long, passing along "requests"—demands actually—to visit certain stores or attend openings. Indeed, whenever a business pulled its advertising, Long could expect a query, along the lines of this: "The following is an extract from a memo received from the business office. What about this for God's sake?" Occasionally, Ross would meet a businessman socially and hear that advertising had been pulled. "What about it?" he would ask. Long mostly ignored such requests, leading Ross to send a message like the following: "I would like to have answers to my memos of April 4th, 9th, and 10th."[24] To this, Long responded in characteristic, facetious style, citing the idealistic division between dirty business and lofty editorial goals:

Ross: Here are your memorandums. Damn it, the business department has had its fun—now can we please have some peace and quiet for six months? Twice a year, regular, you let them get you down. If it weren't for me and my fierce integrity and Duty To My Readers, I honestly think you might give in sometime. Shoulder to shoulder, dear.

Love Long[25]

Long survived these incidents and continued to profit from the *New Yorker's* steady inclusion of fashion and increasing commitment to it. By 1943, almost twenty years after its inception, it is clear from Long's correspondence that the *New Yorker* was competing with *Vogue* and *Harper's Bazaar* for the college fashions market.[26]

By the time of Harold Ross's death from lung cancer in December 1951, Long was something of a celebrity because of her high-profile career (she had augmented her magazine work with weekly radio shows about shopping) and equally high-profile marriage to and divorce from *New Yorker* cartoonist and artist Peter Arno. When her daughter wed in Long's home in late March 1951, the *New York Times* headline read: "Patricia Arno Wed at Mother's House: Daughter of Style Editor and Cartoonist Is Married Here to Roy B. Moriarty Jr." Long was writing for the *New Yorker* at the time of Tom Wolfe's lampoon—she did not retire until 1970—but she was certainly no newcomer. She was a distinctly feminine feature that had been with the magazine almost since its inception.

As Mary Corey demonstrates, the *New Yorker* was—and the same might be said of most all other publications in the pre– and post–World War II period—"far more a feminist endeavor than it was venue for feminist discourse" (156). Her close analysis of the postwar *New Yorker* reveals a magazine that "portrayed women variously, now as gold-digging party girls, now as middle-aged children or parasitic housewives, but also as independent career women who infused their enterprises with a special brand of feminine instinct" (Corey 152). Such ambivalence was represented initially by the composition of its editorial staff. Harold Ross was a man's man who represented the tradition of the tramp reporter and the GI newsman. He was married to Jane Grant,[27] a Lucy Stoner who helped dream the magazine into existence and who worked as a reporter to support the Ross-Grant household during the magazine's early fiscally rough years. Although Ross and Grant divorced before World War II, their collaboration continued in fits and starts, perhaps reaching its peak when Grant proposed the "Pony" edition of the *New Yorker* designed for troops overseas (see Yagoda 181–82). Katharine White's long tenure on the magazine likewise translated into a strong, female editorial influence. Katharine was no Lucy Stoner, but she did exercise and exhibit feminist sensibilities. The *New*

Yorker thus depended on the talents of women and represented women variously. In doing so, it was no more or less sexist than other publications of the period. It was certainly not unique. Progressive women editors there and elsewhere knew the industry's limitations. For example, the first editor of *Vogue*, Josephine Redding, encountered "moments when, tried beyond endurance and flying in the face of the advertisers, she would spill her outraged common sense into the editorial pages of the magazine" (Chase and Chase 36). Edna Woolman Chase, a successor to Redding and longtime editor of *Vogue*, felt the "almost medieval coercion" behind Consuelo Vanderbilt's "spectacular marriage," "the super-de-luxe, unparalleled jumbo spectacle of its time," an event promoted and used to hawk products from pills to home furnishings (Chase and Chase 39).

The *New Yorker* achieved broad circulation, its widest to that date, in the postwar period, when the magazine "had more women readers than men and was thought by some to have actually become a women's magazine" (Corey 151). This is certainly the feeling Wolfe locates and intensifies. At the very time that the *New Yorker* was working its way into American literary history, at the same time that it was developing a well-deserved reputation for literary excellence, at the same time that it was experiencing what might be called its apotheosis into haute literacy, it *was and had always been*, to a significant degree, a woman's magazine, a cousin to *Mademoiselle* and *Harper's Bazaar*, not old and matronly like a Helen Hokinson sketch, but in *Vogue*, if you will. It is only when critics buy into Wolfe's modernist value system, one that clearly defines literature as a category that excludes female experience and sentiment,[28] that the very label "women's magazine" becomes the ultimate slight.

CONCLUSION ∽ LADY EDITORS, KATHARINE WHITE, AND THE EMBODIMENT OF STYLE

"To My wife Katharine, who combines in her person all the elements of style, from the Co-Authors"

> Inscription on Katharine S. White's personal first edition of Strunk and White's *Elements of Style*

Editing the Fashioned Self

Female rhetors have long been aware of the importance of dress, costume, to their rhetorical ethos and thus their rhetorical effectiveness. In *Appropriate[ing] Dress*, Carol Mattingly chronicles how "visual presentation" of women's bodies is integrally tied to their effectiveness as speakers—and even as writers—in the nineteenth-century public press. Both location (a proper sphere) and dress (a modest, feminine style) were standard criteria brought to bear on female rhetors' performance. Female rhetors, in response to these criteria, used their own carefully designed costumes or fashions "to negotiate [these] expectations restricting them to limited locations and excluding them from public rhetoric in order to challenge and reconstruct the power hierarchy" (Mattingly xiii).[1] In other words, women dressed the part— either the part they desired or the one they deemed necessary for rhetorical effectiveness—or they dressed against a part they rejected, and in doing so they composed new public identities as they entered new public arenas.

It would seem that editors, who practice behind the scenes, out of the limelight, would not have to worry about fashioning ethos through costume or dress. Instead ethos would seem to be more about setting "the agenda, standards, and tone for a publication," as Kunkel says:

> In the narrowest sense, editors lay twitchy hands on someone else's work, fixing it, patching it, polishing it, and generally trying to keep it upright. In the broadest sense, however, they set the agenda, standards, and tone for a publication. They hire and fire; they pick stories, and the writers to go with them. They must have enough ego to confidently steer talented people, but the will to subordinate it. They must assuage prima donnas, compel laggards, and sober up drunks. Equal parts shaman and showman, they must have an unwavering vision for their publication, convey it to a staff, and sell it to the great yawning public. (*Genius* 241).

Ideally, the rhetorical work done by editors would consist of fashioning the prose and reputation (not the bodies) of others. Brendan Gill presents the standard vision: "For a time, I served as an editor as well as a writer, but the experiment proved uncongenial to my vanity.... To be an editor is to be an invisible, unheralded Pygmalion; it is not in my style to fashion Galateas who are assumed to have fashioned themselves" (161). Editors are people "who are content to perform feats of editorial sleight-of-hand behind the scenes and who, should it occur to a writer to thank them, would pretend that their ingenious 'save's' were but the usual tidying up of grammatical loose ends" (B. Gill 161). Certainly for many women editors, this vision was appealing. In theory, it allowed them to escape the sexist gaze. They could simply work.

Yet as the Pygmalion and Galatea reference suggests, such work is rarely gender neutral, the workplace likely never so. Women editors experienced sexism on the job, even from those they admired and worked with most closely, even from those who generally respected their talents. Edna Woolman Chase, for example, describes her relationship with Condé Nast: "Through the years we came to a working agreement. If he sometimes urged me to engage ladies for the editorial staff because they played good bridge, or dressed well, or danced with grace, I would abide by his wishes and put up with them for varying lengths of time, even though I found them something less than world beaters as editors." He, in turn, would defer to her if she felt he had taken a "scunner" against a candidate (Chase and Chase 72–73). The bigger problem was that "lady editors" never escaped the determination of the first term in the phrase. Neither writers, agents, readers, nor the public were content to allow these editors to go out unaccompanied by that adjective "lady," and with that adjective travelled an image. Successful editors were publicly invoked and, body and persona, brought into the marketplace. They had to be dressed—fashionably. So women editors learned. While men were expected to provide vision and a kind of rough business sense, women were to provide style—both through their classed or practical schooling *and* through their physical presence.

Given these expectations, the best women editors could do was to try to control their image, authoring themselves a persona and fashioning themselves. But even this strategy had limits: they could choose black sequins, on one of those famed hats let's say, but they were not always "read" in the ways they had hoped. Fashion, as Joanne Entwistle summarizes, has a "complex relationship to identity: on the one hand the clothes we choose to wear can be expressive of identity, telling [or *suggesting to*] others something about our gender, class, status and so on; on the other, our clothes cannot always be 'read,' since they do not straightforwardly 'speak' and can therefore be open to misinterpretation" (*Fashioned Body* 112). Sometimes, in the case of lady editors, their individual representations were simply ignored, replaced by a sexualized and trivialized type. Consider, for example, Theodore Roethke's "Reply to a Lady Editor," presumably written in response to a *Harper's Bazaar* editor who had the audacity to ask him for the poem "I Knew a Woman," a poem whose sexual suggestiveness he thought the editor must have missed (Roethke was operating under the misconception that *Harper's Bazaar* wouldn't possibly publish such a poem, if they understood it). The opening lines of the poem set the condescending tone, emphasizing "verse" as something merely consumed, not understood, by women and suggest that this poet will not be dished up as women's piece goods: "Sweet Alice S. Morris, I *am* pleased, of course, / You take the *Times Supplement*, and read its verse" (Roethke 133). The poetic reply explains reminds "Sweet Alice S. Morris" of her "true nature": ladies in this world are designed to simply lean back, no need to engage in poetic enterprises, since any attempts are bound to result in mere women's fare. Women can only trivialize poetry. They are the stuff of poetry, not the authors, not even true consumers.

Lady editors could not have helped but know they were being read, figured, and ridiculed. If they seemed obsessed with fashioning themselves, it is perhaps not so much because of the women's fashion business where they found employment, but rather because, like their 1980s counterparts (or today's MLA black-clad job applicants with edgy earrings), they realized the necessity of "power dressing" for work.[2] Not surprisingly, in memoirs and biographies of women editors the themes of fashioning and dressing are prominent. In the foreword to her memoir, *Always in Vogue*, published in 1954, Edna Woolman Chase recounts how she finally succumbed to pressures to complete a memoir that would offer the highlights of her long career. Coauthored with her daughter, Ilka Chase, Edna's memoir offers the story of a life interwoven with the history of the magazine that came wholly to define her. It is a story of transformation from a state of unsophisticated unawareness to a fully developed sophisticated, artistic consciousness such as that mirrored in the pages of *Vogue*. *Vogue* was first edited by Josephine Redding, who named the magazine. Other than an ability to aptly name a thing, Redding, as Chase quips, seemed to have few other qualifications: "Her other qualifications for the editor of a fashion

magazine were less evident. In a day when the chic feminine figure was corseted until breathing was a matter of hearsay rather
than experience, Mrs. Redding's square little body was cozily un-
confined, supported on common-sense shoes and topped, summer and winter, day and night, by a broad-brimmed hat. Under
no circumstance was the hat ever removed" (36).

Chase continues with a favorite anecdote about paying a sick
visit to Redding. The punch line? Even "propped against her pil-
lows, clad in her nightgown," her hat remained in its place. Redding's person—the odd assortment of "'evening dress' paired with
her flat-crowned broad-brimmed creations" reflected the office
which housed the magazine—"informal and non-professional"—
as well as the magazine itself, the nonchalance in its makeup, the
disarray of its page designs: "we once illustrated a love story of a
girl on an army post with drawings of plump, belligerent trout on
hooks. The idea that an illustration might plausibly implement the
text had yet to gain footing" (33). *Vogue* had one feature to boast
of, its typography, a credit not to Redding, whose eclectic person
would never have attended to such detail, but to founder Arthur
Baldwin Turnure, for whom typography was a passion (Chase and
Chase 30).

This story about Redding and her awful hats offers Chase
the opportunity to relate a good anecdote, a chance she rarely
misses, yet it does more: it establishes the integral connection
between an editor's body and her body of work. So crucial is
this trope to this memoir and, I will argue, to magazine histories generally that Chase notes in her foreword that to her "great
regret," she and Ilka were "unable to obtain a likeness of Mrs.
Redding, the magazine's doughty first editor" (11). *Vogue*'s history, it seems, is not complete without some representation of
the body that presided over the magazine's early years. Chase's
own story is structured by this trope: to understand her transformation from a Quaker childhood to a long career as editor of
a fashion magazine, one had to witness her remarkable transformation, her growth into sophisticated consciousness. As Chase

states: "It was a curious alliance, for *Vogue*, from its first issue, had been published by and for sophisticates and I might have been cast as the typical 'little girl from the country' arrived in the big city to make good" (25). To make matters worse, Chase, while "not an unattractive young woman," would never be "as fashionable as the drawings in *Vogue* ... the chic, the prevailing, the only permissible bust measurement, the perfect thirty-six, I did not possess. No matter how many ruffles I pinned to my corset cover I still retained a childlike, desperately unchic flatness" (32). She was thankfully, she jokes, not "stout," presumably an insurmountable career obstacle: "Once *Vogue* showed two or three dresses for stout women, but we were so shaken by the experience we haven't repeated it in fifty-seven years.... We acknowledge that a lady may grow mature, but she never grows fat" (Chase and Chase 33–34). Still, her presentation of a flawed body, combined with rural dress, proves an obstacle: before Chase can describe to her readers the work she did, the magazine she built, she must offer an explanation for how she evolved into a city-chic woman of a certain class, how she went from being "a kind of little widget, young, eager, and ignorant" (42) in 1895, the year she joined *Vogue*'s staff, to become a lady editor. The answer she offers is not genius, not even temperament, but rather instinct, energy, and perhaps oddly enough, religious simplicity and integrity:

> I had a great deal in my childhood—but certainly the world of fashion was alien to our ways; yet instinctively I must have been clothes-conscious. I can remember ... visiting my Great-aunt Abigail and Great-uncle Gilbert Swain.... It was very quiet—Quakers do not speak at service until the spirit moves—and I was very bored. I looked around the room and decided how I would rearrange the furniture if it were mine. I looked at my aunt and uncle sitting in their sober Quaker clothes and thought that that was a fashion I didn't care for at all, and I began considering how I would re-dress them. (Chase and Chase 26)

This instinct, however, is one that is tamed by the memoirist. Her youthful impulse to redress her kin doesn't stand up to mature reflection. The fashion world has schooled her to appreciate plainness: "As I think back upon their appearance, Aunt Abigail in her soft, puce-colored silk, with the snowy kerchief of fine muslin drawn in neat folds over her bosom, and Uncle Gilbert in his high stock, they seem, to my now sophisticated eyes, to have possessed a true elegance that no amount of ornamentation can achieve." Youth can be misdirected, as she was: "in those days I was much more impressed by the fashionable, bustled silhouette of my young mother when she came from New York to visit us, and by small cousins from Philadelphia in their embroidered white frocks and heavy silk sashes tied on their little behinds" (Chase and Chase 26–27). It is her years of experience that developed her eye for tasteful, sophisticated fashion and that gives her the authority to instruct others. That the editor of *Vogue* would operate under such strictures seems commonsensical. The place of body image in fashion magazines has been widely critiqued. What's been less explored is the role of such body politics in a magazine like the *New Yorker*. Again, I turn to Katharine White.

Figuring (Out) Katharine White

In biographical accounts of Katharine White, several people recall a woman who spoke incessantly about her various illnesses, a portrait furthered by Brendan Gill, first in a preface to an interview with E. B. White in the *Paris Review*, later repeated in his book, *Here at The New Yorker*. It was nothing that the Whites' own children wouldn't say. Katharine's daughter, Nancy Stableford, attributed her mother's obsession with illness to her stepfather's influence: "When Andy came into her life, he was already a pretty good hypochondriac, and she quickly caught it" (qtd. in L. Davis 194). Roger Angell too discussed the Whites' obsession with illness with his mother's biographer, Linda Davis, describing how his mother and stepfather "had created an exclusive world of two inhabitants who spoke their own special language—the language of illness. It was a world that left other people on the outside" (qtd. in L. Davis 195). As late as 2005, Angell in a tribute to his stepfather, titled "Andy," memorializes the Whites' "joint hypochondria," characterized by its "energy" and its exclusions:

> The narcissism and intimacy of their exchanged symptoms could be infuriating, since it excluded everyone else, but it was so dopey that you laughed and forgave them. When you turned up at their house after an absence, they'd ask you about your kids and your job and your recent doings, and almost in the same breath bring up a lingering migraine or this morning's fresh back spasm. Someone in the family—someone who'd been reading astronomy lately and remembered the "red shift" phenomenon as a measure of radiation and distance—named this the "White shift," and it stuck.

The problem with the analysis, as beautiful a testimony to intimacy as it is, is that Katharine's talk about illness didn't just bind her to her husband: it bound her to others like Jean Stafford and Nadine Gordimer, who commiserated with her. White's editing style was woman centered; it stressed rather than elided personal relationships.[3] In print, she invoked whatever traditional female role—mother, friend, teacher, muse, disciplinarian—might encourage writers to work and submit their work. Katharine could be steely in person. She communicated in print with more ease, divulged and deployed more of herself.

I won't attempt to argue that the Whites didn't dwell on illnesses; they certainly did, particularly as they aged. I'm more interested in the rhetorical effect her frequent articulations about illness had—and why it seems so inappropriate, particularly for Katharine White, to articulate them. Not surprisingly, Katharine White didn't consider herself a hypochondriac, as her response to Brendan Gill indicates:

> You don't say that O'Hara was one of the greatest hypochondriacs of all time.... I will refrain from any details about An-

dy's and my health since your note in The Paris Review seems
to imply that we talk of nothing else. I would only like to register that no doctor I have ever had would say that I have ever
had an imaginary ill. Poor Andy is saddled with a decrepit wife
who had now become terribly expensive because of nursing
care but whose mind hasn't entirely given up. I myself don't
consider Andy a hypochondriac and think he is a neurotic and
is onto himself about his fears. Curiously enough most of his
fears have turned out to be true.[4]

Rather she was something else, something more simple: an old
woman, growing older, and in a "decrepit" rather than graceful
fashion: "One is continually struck by her graphic and frequently
ugly description of herself in old age" (L. Davis 213). With hon-
esty and striking directness, Katharine, who began and ended
her career as a writer, revealed an unglamorous side of the cocktail generation, an aging perspective.[5] Like others during this
time she drank. She smoked. She likely didn't exercise enough.
She loved her work perhaps a little too much and frequently took
it home with her.

White's health problems began to multiply in her fifties.
She ran a fever for most of the summer of 1945, "each week the
doctor kept saying that next week he would have [her] infection
stopped. This went on almost all summer." In spring of 1947, she
registered problems with sciatica, a problem she attributed to
sleeping on a bad bed during her stay in Florida. That September, she experienced changes in her spine, a problem that goes
untreated until almost nine months later when she undergoes a
spinal fusion surgery. Two months after the spinal fusion, she
began working from home. This was a pattern that recurred.
Just about every two years she experienced another health issue,
some mild, some not. In 1950, she had influenza; in 1952, the
year William Shawn assumed the editorship—White was almost
sixty—she contracted infectious hepatitis. The winter of 1954
was troubling not so much because of a single illness but from a
confluence of caretaking, personal, and work-related stress. It's

the one time Katharine was reported as "nervously ill," or on the verge of a nervous breakdown. She was sixty-two years old: she herself had mumps and the flu; her husband had shingles, a broken nose, and "other troubles"; her ninety-two-year-old aunt required Katharine's care, as did her sister, who was experiencing financial setbacks (L. Davis 167). During all of this White continued working as an editor for the *New Yorker*.

E. B. White's biographer Scott Elledge pinpoints 1957 as the year that Katharine deteriorates into invalidism. Katharine White officially retired in June 1961, at the age of sixty-eight, reducing her role to that of consultant. That summer, she suffered from a gangrenous appendix, removed just before it perforated. According to her biographer, it was then that her health suddenly declined: "Though she had suffered serious illnesses ... before retiring, it was only after Katharine left *The New Yorker* that her health collapsed. Almost overnight she was transformed from a vigorous sixty-eight-year-old into an old woman" (L. Davis 192). For Roger Angell, his mother's decline was likely a psychosomatic response to retirement. The problem with this explanation, however, is that it ignores a quite real blocked carotid artery, which she had been noticing the effects of for some time before it was diagnosed. Katharine White's biographer wonders why the angiogram wasn't performed earlier: "Considering the wealth of information that can be got from an angiogram ... it is curious that Katharine White's doctors had not earlier thought to give her one. At the age of sixty-eight, at a time when she had made a critical transition in her life, she had been subjected to eight months of uncertainty, fear, and immobilizing symptoms. And then, having prepared herself for a brain tumor, she was informed that she had something altogether different" (L. Davis 192). All of this must have seemed like a warm up to the plague that hit in 1963, a skin disease, made worse by prednisone treatment. White spent a great deal of 1964 in the hospital with lesions covering her skin. At one point, she shed her entire skin, "like a snake" in her husband's words. This illness was apparently the result of the experimental use of Butazolidin, as she notes, the medicine that disqualified the Kentucky Derby winner and the only medication that offered her relief from bone spurs. The prednisone used to treat the skin condition caused more complications: "her skin swelled, most of her molars fell out," as did some of her hair (L. Davis 213). In the hospital, the sheets were raised so they didn't contact her body; she had to "stand naked before twelve dermatologists who were being lectured to by her doctor." She couldn't bathe herself; her husband did it for her (L. Davis 213–14).

In a letter to William Maxwell after Katharine's death, E. B. White composes perhaps the most poignant vignette of his wife's late years. Overwhelmed in the days after her death, E. B. White writes the piece as a therapeutic exercise. "The mail is torrential and I don't know what to do about it. So I thought I would just sit down and write one person a long letter. It isn't going to work, but I had to get something off my chest."[6] Not surprisingly, the letter is really an essay, one shaped by the image of his wife's infirmities and her energy. The piece builds on the details of Katharine's day-to-day activities, painting a picture of a woman still working, despite physical obstacles. The image is familiar to anyone who has nursed an aging relative (granted, the Whites had the benefit of a household cook). As is often the case with home care, the day is punctuated by nurses, medicines, and the daily routine of getting bathed and dressed:

> K's day started at six, when she was awakened by the night nurse, given a pill, and escorted to the bathroom. At seven the night nurse departed, and I arrived at seven-thirty with the breakfast tray and the *Bangor Daily News*, a salt-free, sugar-free beginning to the day....
>
> At quarter to nine, the cook went up to the bedroom for a lengthy conference, planning the meals for the next 24 hour period. At nine, the day nurse arrived, and Katharine was bathed and anointed with the cortisone ointment that controlled her subcorneal pustular dermatosis.[7]

In light of all these significant, incontrovertible illnesses—in White's words, "no doctor I have ever had would say that I have ever had an imaginary ill" (qtd. in L. Davis 190)—it seems odd that White's biographer reached so far for a way to explain her subject's hypochondria. The only plausible explanation seems to be the penchant in the 1970s and 1980s for psychological biographies and for armchair psychology generally. Linda Davis looks to Hypochondria: Toward a Better Understanding to illuminate Katharine White's psychology: "Hypochondriacs are widely regarded as people who suffer from imaginary illnesses. But as long ago as 1928, a British psychiatrist, R. D. Gillespie, proposed that the preoccupation was not only with imagined ills but with actual 'physical or mental disorder[s]' as well. What distinguishes the hypochondriac from anyone who is normally anxious about his health is that he is ... 'preoccupied excessively; he is not merely interested in his condition, but interested with conviction, which makes him immune to all influences that are contrary to it.'" In this sweeping definition, one can be "both physically sick and hypochondriacal" (L. Davis 193).

Roger Angell is careful to assign the trait to husband and wife. White's biographer is not quite so generous. She takes Katharine White to task for suggesting, in a private letter, that Andy might lean toward hypochondria. Davis writes: "It is surprising to find Katharine White—generally the most protective of wives—talking this way. For, although she is compassionate toward her husband, defending Andy in her latter remark, she is also uncharacteristically selfish—in effect, sacrificing her husband's image and protecting her own" (190). Somehow, Katharine has crossed a line in suggesting that E. B. White, the brilliant writer, might have "a bad head," he might be neurotic, although clearly she wasn't the only one to notice. Unwifely, selfish, iconoclastic—she's taken down Mr. White, the writer, the voice, the conscience of the New Yorker. Even a biography that celebrates Katharine's life and is generally sympathetic toward her cannot quite excuse this, although clearly her husband did. The

general tenor of all these commentaries is that there is something annoying, disturbing, or simply foolish about discussing
illnesses, about referring so concretely to the aging and ailing
body. Katharine's aging and ailing body was particularly trouble-
some. Although E. B. White had been troubled by memory issues
for some years, his Alzheimer's disease had a sudden onset and
fairly fast resolution. He had chronic allergies and was inclined
toward depression, but it was easy somehow to imagine him as a
trim and spry outdoorsman, a kindly farmer: "His youth, and his
'Andy'-ness" seemed "intrinsic and inexpungeable" (B. Gill 294).
Katharine's professional image was more difficult to maintain.

Those who are quick to apply the label of "hypochondria" to
Katharine White seem to disregard the crucial exception—the
idea of immunity from contrary influences, the inability to see
anything but illness. This doesn't seem to be the case. Katharine
never stopped seeing work. The surprise for me is not so much
that White spoke about her illnesses—an impossible subject to
ignore if one is confined to bed or unable to wear clothing—
but that she worked through them. Overall, the image that E. B.
White paints in the letter to Bill Maxwell is not one of an invalid
but of a woman who controlled her surroundings. "At about half
past ten, she came down the front stairs on her canes, switched
to her walker at the bottom, and went clumping into the living-
room to take charge. At noon, she arranged flowers for all the
rooms in the house. They were miracles of quick, rough construction. She never babied flowers."[8] Katharine's work is not restricted to the domestic; it was simply tucked in behind her real
work, corresponding with contributors and with "anyone connected with her darling magazine." The house and its furnishings are revised to allow her to work despite restricted mobility:

> During the last years of her life, Katharine conducted her af-
> fairs seated on the north end of the livingroom sofa, next to a
> dropleaf table that supported a lamp, cigarettes, stamps, book
> matches, pens and pencils, Guaranty Trust deposit slips, and
> a wild assortment of scatterings. She had no desk in front of

her. Everything that arrived in the mail, along with the *Times*, she pushed to her left, so that it landed on the sofa, on top of everything else that had accumulated there. When she lit a cigarette, she reached to her right for the book matches, then discarded the book on the sofa to her left. She never used the same book of matches twice—always reached to her right for a fresh book. The ashes from the cigarette dropped to her blouse.

After a while, a small round table was set in front of her, because it had a place for her to put her feet up, and the doctor wanted her to keep her feet elevated. The table then received the morning mail, which was often quite heavy, since she never ceased corresponding with her college classmates, her writers, her relatives, and her strays—people who had wandered into her life and found it a pleasant place to hole up in . . . The things on the sofa grew higher and higher, the stuff on the little round table slid off onto the floor. Katharine sat quietly in the middle of the mess, dictating letters in a steady firm voice, never missing a "comma" and "new paragraph."

The pile grew and grew. It did not seem to bother her in the least, except she could never find anything that she wanted because she simply placed one thing on top of another. I stood this as long as I could, then one day went out to my bench and built her a long coffee table out of pine and painted it the same color as the wall. She seemed mildly pleased with this development and began placing things on the coffee table, which stretched almost the full length of the sofa. Inside of a week, she had it groaning under the weight of seed catalogues, back issues of the *New Yorker*, carbons of letters to Senator Muskie, duplicates of orders to Hammacher Schlemmer, fly swatters, lengthy correspondence with department stores taking them to task for abandoning cotton and wool and substituting polyester, old copies of the Horn Book, a wooden glove box full of I do not know what, newspaper clippings of editorials that she planned to take issue with, unanswered letters from grandchildren, and on and on.[9]

It's clear both from this description and from the archives left that despite illnesses, White continued a voluminous correspondence with contributors turned friends. Linda Davis's biography is based on Katharine White's private letters housed in the Bryn Mawr Library, letters written when she was older and ill. The letters in the *New Yorker* archives are written by a younger woman, and while illness certainly is mentioned from time to time—the letters frequently merge personal and professional concerns—it is not an overwhelmingly obvious theme. Indeed, routine vacations intrude with more frequency.

Katharine White's editorial persona and image changed radically over the forty-eight years she worked for the *New Yorker*. She started work at the magazine when she was just shy of thirty-three, the wife of a lawyer and mother of two children. E. B. White, who over the years composed several verbal portraits of Katharine, characterized the young "Mrs. Angell" in his *Paris Review* interview many years later:

> Ross, though something of a genius, had serious gaps. In Katharine, he found someone who filled them in. No two people were ever more different than Mr. Ross and Mrs. Angell; what he lacked, she had; what she lacked, he had.... She was a product of Miss Winsor's and Bryn Mawr. Ross was a high school dropout. She had a natural refinement of manner and speech; Ross mumbled and bellowed and swore.... She enjoyed contact with people; Ross, with certain exceptions, despised it—especially during hours. She was patient and quiet; he was impatient and noisy. (Plimpton and Crowther 83)

Early references to Katharine all stress her refinement, her women's school education, her sereneness. The "sharp-tongued, witty" Dorothy Parker was an obvious foil. As Katharine later explained, "At that period it would have been automatic, when she first began contributing, that I edit her manuscripts but Ross explained to me that she was so malicious he wouldn't want me to be hurt by her mean talk. 'She'd murder you,' he said." Katharine suspects as well that Ross believed she "wouldn't be successful" because she wasn't Parker's "kind of person." Indeed, Katharine acknowledges, it would have been easy (and likely) for Parker to ridicule her "as a Bostonian and an austere and unwitty woman"; "I was the kind of person who would have been fair game to her." Katharine writes to set the record straight. If Parker made sport of her, Katharine didn't know it: "we met at parties and outside the office she never said a mean or malicious word to me. She was invariably kind and friendly and appeared to like me. In fact, at such occasions we had several long and interesting conversations."[10]

Mrs. Angell is fairly short-lived in *New Yorker* history—just a four-year tenure. In 1929, at the age of thirty-seven, Katharine divorced Ernest Angell and married the younger E. B. White. This combined with the publication in the same year of E. B. White and James Thurber's *Is Sex Necessary*, a send-up of sex guides, sexualized Katharine's image, something Brendan Gill simultaneously invokes and dispels in *Here at* The New Yorker: "Katharine White is a woman so good-looking that nobody has taken it amiss when her husband has described her in print as beautiful, but her beauty has a touch of blue-eyed augustness in it, and her manner is formal" (294). He delights in telling a story about a Thurber prank. According to Gill, Thurber pretended to be a reporter trying to arrange a picture of the Whites. When E. B. White agreed to the photo, the "reporter" recommended a pose: "Why, I think a shot of Mrs. White leap-frogging naked over you." White was outraged, or so Thurber confessed: "The Whites were not amused" (qtd. in B. Gill 283). But Gill clearly is, and whether the story is real or apocryphal seems beside the point. What's clear is that the Whites were for a short time a scandal, an awkwardness underscored each time the new Mrs. White, with no explanation, signed her name to a memo. The Whites were not without a sense a humor; humor formed a significant part of their joint work. And they were not beyond seeing themselves as objects of humor.

E. B. White, however, was a romantic; his representation of

his wife frequently invoked this sensibility. Interestingly, E. B. White builds his romance by highlighting his wife's career, her work, thus evincing that gendered habit of mind that for a time at least yoked the ideal woman with the career woman. His poem, "Lady Before Breakfast," uses classic devices (e.g., Serena, the sonnet form) to paint the new woman who uses the tools of literacy to exercise agency over her own life and the lives of others:

> On the white page of this unwritten day
> Serena, waking, sees the imperfect script:
> The misspelled word of circumstance, the play
> Of error, and places where the pen slipped.
> And having thus turned loose her fears to follow
> The hapless scrawl of the long day along,
> Lets fall an early tear on the warm pillow,
> Weeping that no song is the perfect song.
>
> By eight o'clock she has rewritten noon
> For faults in style, in taste, in fact, in spelling;
> Suspicious of the sleazy phrase so soon,
> She's edited the tale before its telling.
> Luckily Life's her darling: she'll forgive it.
> See how she throws the covers off and starts to live it!
>   (White 70)

Katharine recognized the mock heroic devices, but she read the poem in the light it was intended: "It is a judgement about me—it's me as I was when I was vigorous, and I like it" (qtd. in L. Davis 251). Later, writing to James Tanis at Bryn Mawr Library, E. B. White would focus on Katharine's voice and her disciplined approach to work: "Thank you for your warm letter of 30 July and please forgive me for being so late in replying. I am not steady, like Katharine, when it comes to letter-writing—she always managed it so well and so calmly. Somewhere in my attic I have a cassette that contains a brief recording of her voice made while she was dictating a letter—I must look it up, it is so comical, with it meticulous attention to punctuation marks and paragraphing and its immaculate delivery."[11] In his *Paris Review* interview, White characterized his wife's work as a forty-plus year love affair: "During the day, I saw her in operation at the office. At the end of the day, I watched her bring the whole mess home with her in a cheap and bulging portfolio. The light burned late, our bed was lumpy with page proofs, and our home was alive with laughter and the pervasive spirit of her dedication and her industry. In forty-two years, this dedication has not cooled. It is strong today, although she is out of the running, from age and ill health" (Plimpton and Crowther 83–84). Roger Angell inherits some of these same images. The notable "White shift" occurred later in the Whites' lives, but Angell in "Andy" writes nostalgically:

> A moment's effort can bring back for me the way things were at home in the better days, a couple of decades back—say on a late morning just after the mail has arrived. Their studies face each other across the narrow front hall, with the doors open. My mother, in soft tweeds and a pale sweater, sits at her cherrywood desk, one leg tucked under her, with a lighted Benson & Hedges in one hand and a brown soft pencil in the other as she works her way down a page of Caslon-type galleys, with her tortoiseshell glasses down her nose. Her desk is littered with papers and ashes and eraser rubbings.

Such are the family reminiscences. Others remember a formidable Mrs. White. Over time, Katharine grew more confident, both through the exercise of her work and the authority derived from her marriage to an author whose reputation grew over time. The Whites became stable personages, rather than the scandalous icon of a young writer hooking up with a divorced lady editor. By the late 1940s, it was common for Katharine to put into a letter something like "Andy thought so too," either to intensify praise for a piece or underscore a weak point. She used his name almost as an exclamation point. In her blurb on Dorothy Parker, White suggests some of the cover provided by her famous husband. If Parker was kind to Katharine, it was in part because of her association with Andy: "[Parker] admired E. B. W.'s writing," the suggestion being that Parker extended the admiration to his wife.

Katharine's tone in letters and memos was direct and confident. She was not afraid of a fight. Some contributors and coworkers were put off by the style or took offense, as the case of Isabel Bolton exemplified. Others, like Frank Sullivan, discerned abruptness but not ill will:

> Some place in a long and rambling letter I mailed you yesterday I said you once "snarled" at me, in returning a piece I sent you about all those NY skyscrapers. That has been on my mind all day, that's the kind of thing I worry about, and I have to add this postscript to tell you that of course that "snarled" was a jocosity.... I'm sure you already know that but I couldn't rest easy until I told you. You never snarled at me in your life, or mine. I doubt if you ever snarled at anybody. I do not see you at all as a snarler. Now that's off my mind.[12]

Those who came to know White through Davis's biography and White's own letters—as I have—might find this picture almost incomprehensible. As Davis aptly summarizes: "Curiously, Katharine White's letters give no indication of her formidableness: one who knew her only through her letters would find there a freer and more openly affectionate person than the woman others knew in life. In her letters, which gave her distance from people while simultaneously providing her with an intimate and tangible means of communication, she was able to put her arm around you, a gesture she found difficult in the flesh" (144). For all the emphasis on Katharine White's hypochondria, Davis is actually more persuasive when she demonstrates the degree to which the editor's letters, a particular mix of personal and professional, invite her writers to trust her with their own health and family preoccupations. As many nineteenth-century women did, Katharine White knew the powers of invalidism; she had breathed that culture. Davis understands part of the power of invalidism: "a part of her thrived on being ill, and on getting attention. Illness had a place in her life. She made room for it, accommodated, if not invited, it" (197). Katharine's references to illness (and family troubles, big and small) are numerous but still private; they create intimacy, no less genuine or powerful than an embrace. She likely would have been appalled had someone asked her to wear a pink ribbon or walk in white sneakers down a public street, side by side with others in a t-shirt advertising a cause. It's difficult to imagine her standing wearing a red dress, holding a Campbell's soup can, doing a benefit promotion for women and heart disease. Those who come to know Katharine White through memoirs, such as Gill's, might lean toward the former portrait and see her as she feared Dorothy Parker might, namely as an austere, unwitty Bostonian. Katharine White was a strong personality who intimidated (or infuriated) some, but the woman one finds in the archives is largely a warm correspondent.

Later in her life, Katharine thought about how she would like her work to be remembered and figured. She would likely have been pleased with E. B. White's posthumous description of her surrounded by books and papers and other implements of her work: "There were days when I could hardly see Katharine for the bulge."[13] She herself preferred images that excluded the body, even a body comically represented. The suggestion of the work being done would have been enough. In July 21, 1975, she writes to Bryn Mawr Library, rejecting an image by Steinberg even though she admired his work: "I had told you about a drawing of his which I loved but which I thought would be unfair to Bryn Mawr to use—the one of the Amazonian woman hurling a javelin wrong end to. Bryn Mawr women don't hurl javelins or anything else wrong end to, or so I assume; and all of them don't look like hideous Amazons, although I can think of a few who might qualify for that description." Katharine was certainly aware that she was a type, a Bryn Mawr woman, and she was proud of this association. Yet, for her own work, she imagines a different representation, one that focuses not on the person, the editor, but on the work itself: "It's difficult to know what the symbol for editing is. All I can think of is a typewriter with endless batches of type floating off in some wild direction, the way that Steinberg pictures sometimes do; or a picture with a New York skyline background, seen through a window and a shelf full of reference books, including Webster's Unabridged. That would be characteristic of my former office."[14] This is not the image that Steinberg creates, although he does make one perhaps that would have been even more to her liking. It features simply a hand, at first glance a man's hand perhaps, and a pencil.

Katharine White lived long enough to witness the backlash against women's literary aspirations, to feel the effects of "the rhetoric of hats" used against midcentury lady editors. Like other women who took with literate zeal to their work, Katharine White preferred the ideal of a transcendent literacy, one that could move beyond the weight of gender, age, and sexuality. The bulge of a manuscript suited her. She clothed herself in letters.

In "Nostalgia: A Stitch in Time," a retrospective piece for the December 2002 edition of *Vogue* magazine, Margaret Atwood makes a connection between fashion design and writing, between abstract creativity and the substance of work. "If you think," the comparison between fashion and writing is "far-fetched"—and here she seems to be talking to the intellectual media, or maybe even her academic critics, who she fears would certainly pooh-pooh such a connection—"consider: Both involve pattern, structure, and design, and so many of the metaphors used about writing derive from sewing. *Textile* and *text.* *Spinning a tale. Tissue of lies. Fabrication*" (Atwood 80). From her lion's perch atop the contemporary literary scene, Margaret Atwood seems to thumb her nose at the literary world, claiming a connection between fashion and women's worlds spinning deeper even than history: "The chief resemblance is a very simple one. Out of a hint, an idea, a longing—a bodiless concept, an airy nothing—you make a thing you want, the way you want it to be. And if what you want is black trilobites all over your skirt, so be it" (80). Both fashion and fiction make substantial (instantiate?) ideas, desires; they allow for individual expression. Style rests at the heart of both enterprises. Neither, however, can control how style is read. For all her careful crafting of letters and her devotion to work, Katharine White and other women editors were unable to fix the focus on the work itself. Behind those typewriters sat bodies. The times demanded that they have just the right elements of style. Those stylistic expectations both constrained women's imaginative work and opened possibilities for it. Scholars wishing to write a history of women's repression will find ample evidence in twentieth-century magazines. They will also find evidence to the contrary, particularly if they look at the scene of production, where ideas were fashioned.

AFTERWORD ᘒ KATHARINE WHITE'S BEQUEST, OR RUMINATIONS ON AN ARCHIVE

"I consider . . . the *New Yorker*'s record . . . something to boast of."
Katharine White to James Tanis, April 20, 1971

Sometime around 1968, Katharine White, then seventy-five years old and suffering from a variety of illnesses, including the skin "deficiency disease" that had caused her to lose her "entire skin," turned her still considerable vigor to two projects. The first of these was her gardening essays, which she was struggling to collect into a book. In a letter to Jean Stafford in 1968, White explained that the writing for her "mythical garden book" had been "stymied." Although health would seem the obvious obstacle, there was another. Katharine was attempting "to try to elevate" her work out of the category of garden literature and into the genre her husband perfected, the occasional essay. The task was challenging her: "It will never get done. But I still struggle. The new chapters are harder—not garden stuff and all, but portraits of familiar gardeners and family gardens."[1]

Her second project was seemingly easier, organizing her *New Yorker*-connected books and personal correspondence with contributors. Her goal was to present the collection as a gift to her alma mater, Bryn Mawr College. Some of White's inspiration for the project was practical. The Whites, not surprisingly, amassed more material than they could house. Katharine described the situation in dramatic terms: "I am sending them now instead of after my death, chiefly for safe-keeping against fire. Our house is a fire-trap."[2] Katharine had begun revising her will and was trying to determine what to do with all her books, many of which were first editions, given to her in thanks and tribute to her work on manuscripts. In reviewing the collection, she considers only briefly their value in explicating herself as a subject to be written about: "I am vaguely thinking of asking Bryn Mawr whether they would like a total collection (Andy's and mine) of 1920 to 1950 short stories, novels, humor, fact books, verse and poetry, and picture Albums as a bequest in my will, which I'm rewriting at this moment. The books are dimly a record of my career as an editor, but I can't imagine the children or any college would want or have room for it."[3] What she could imagine—and believe in—was the value of books as central to literate culture and values. Since living in Maine, the Whites had given many of their "extra copies" to the public library, "which of course never has enough money to spend on books." The donations opened space on the book shelves and provided a needed tax break, but the gifts also contributed to a shared sense of purpose. They took pride in the library's holdings and in their contributions to literacy education, particularly in times of encroaching visual media. The town, Katharine White wrote, "has one of the highest per capita records for circulation in the state of Maine. Because we have kept the books up-to-date and good, and because the town is isolated from most pleasures—no movie house, no amusement halls of any sort—the people in town, young and old, have turned to reading. However, as more TV sets come into the village, the rate is beginning to slip a little."[4]

The Whites' long-term donor relationship with the public library underscores the fact that Katharine saw her *New Yorker*-related books as something more than tributes or dim records of her editorial career. These books were items that could contribute to the common good. These particular books, however, were different: they were first editions, and thus had monetary value:

"The books themselves with their inscriptions and first editions are the best part of my gift to Bryn Mawr."[5] They were also valuable as artifacts of an emerging American literature. In the years until her death in 1977, Katharine would become more and more convinced that the *New Yorker* had a significant role to play in American literary history, and she took, as she described it, a vicarious pride in the *New Yorker* and the work it produced and the new literary tradition it was forging. As early as 1957, when offering a signed copy of the *Subtreasury of American Humor*, an anthology she coedited with her husband, Katharine reflected on the absence of American literature in her college education: "It is odd that in thinking back to my days as an English major I cannot remember ever having been assigned a book of American literature, let alone American humor, as either required or recommended reading."[6] In 1959, Katharine had given the library a copy of the humor anthology, writing that it might provide possibilities for future generations of Bryn Mawr students: "I hope that a few students may even want to sample some of the great American humorists from early days down on."[7] Seventeen years later, as she worked on assembling the collections, she took the opportunity to lecture the Bryn Mawr librarian James Tanis on the importance of American literature, and fiction generally, in the English curriculum: "From 1911 to 1914 there were no English courses that covered any literature later than Miss Donnelly's course on the Romantic Poets, and there was no course offered on American literature given at the college when I was there. The more I think of it, the more scandalous it seems to me. There was no course offered on the novel, English or otherwise, either."[8]

Safeguarding a Tradition

There was little doubt in Katharine's mind that the *New Yorker* had historical value, yet she worried about its place in a tradition focused on British literature. She worried particularly because in her long life she had witnessed changes in literary tastes: early *New Yorker* writing was no longer in favor. It would take scholars to rescue the early humorists from the dustbin, and scholars needed material from which to work. The *New Yorker* records required preservation in a library so that literature not appreciated in its time might be later discovered by scholars.

Katharine had been privy to early efforts to preserve the editorial correspondence. She explains to Tanis that "Harold Ross was determined that the letters from contributors and editors should be deposited in an orderly way, after they had been held a certain number of years for legal purposes, in some big library well able to take care of them. He appointed a member of the staff to look into this and four libraries were suggested with a strong recommendation, as Ross was working on in the last year of his life and it was very dear to his heart but did not live to see it accomplished."[9] By the early 1970s, the *New Yorker* history was rapidly disappearing, disintegrating in basements and other neglected spaces. Her letters thus articulated both personal urgency and a sense of duty, an extension of the editorial work that energized her and other lady editors of her generation. Her letters repeatedly make the case the magazine's history was in peril, that "*New Yorker* files ... were disintegrating in the furnace room,"[10] "getting very brittle from the heat—or so Bill Maxwell and Ebba Johnson tell me."[11] Katharine White expected that William Shawn would follow through with Ross's initial efforts, but Shawn was slow to place the magazine's professional correspondence in any of the archives that Ross had identified; Shawn's lack of action on the matter became more and more disturbing to her: "Oddly enough William Shawn, who is much more of a scholar than Harold Ross ever was, has not seemed to feel this urgency about finding a good place for deposit. Unlike Ross, he tends to want nothing to be known about *New Yorker* procedure.... I don't understand this."[12]

White was clear about what she could offer to Bryn Mawr—only her personal correspondence and her personal copies of books. She reiterates to Brendan Gill the same message she had already conveyed to Tanis: "I am not allowed, of course, to send my *New Yorker* editorial letters, which are more interesting, as they belong to *The New Yorker* and will eventually end up in some library once Shawn can decide to which library to send the New Yorker files."[13] There was, however, only a slight distinction: when Katharine sent letters from the *New Yorker* office—or from Maine when she was working from afar—she included personal details. Her letters in retirement are filled with work-related details; she was still reading and commenting on manuscripts. Katharine was aware that only part of the *New Yorker*'s history was safeguarded with the archiving of her papers. Authors maintained "original manuscripts" that were "returned to them automatically after a certain number of years."[14] Still, original manuscripts aside, the collection was large and valuable: "What remains that is important is the editorial correspondence, including Ross's, which has been locked and sealed since his death." As the current editor, Shawn was the only one with the authority to determine where (or if) the records would be archived. She doubted that Bryn Mawr could be a consideration, although she offered to pass along the college's interest in housing the collection, "I will, when I feel I can bother Bill Shawn, mention that Bryn Mawr would like to have the *New Yorker* files but I myself would not think it a suitable place until you can afford to add to the staff an experienced manuscript cataloguer."[15] It was a good call: the finding guide for the *New Yorker* collection housed in the New York Public Library is 800 pages long.

The Whites had always been collectors, or perhaps just pack-rats. Katharine understood part of her project as simply collecting and depositing: "I have news for you and Mrs. Gibbs, which may or may not be welcome, since it means still more work. I am almost ready to send on a new batch of letters, smaller but to me even more important than the last one, because at last we have turned up in the attic a big missing link with many Ross memos and letters when he was writing me fairly often after we first moved to Maine."[16] As she began the difficult but pleasant task of going through her papers and books, she had some difficulty seeing that her job was simply boxing the material; she found it difficult to leave the organizing to Bryn Mawr. Katharine had played a key role in collecting her husband's works for Cornell University Library. E. B. White's allergies were stirred by the attic dust (the attic, at times in the correspondence, seems almost a scene from a horror movie). He also felt the task of collecting was interfering with his writing. Katharine stepped in to take charge. In 1964, George H. Healey, the curator of Cornell University Library, wrote to instruct the Whites to box everything, explaining to E. B. White that Cornell would welcome truly any of their papers. He urged the Whites not to throw anything away, no matter how insignificant they considered it. At the time they received this memo, it was difficult for either to believe that the ordinary details of their private or professional lives could be of literary value. On August 17, 1964, Katharine asked Healey for clarification:

> Because Andy saved *everything* from the 1920s on, most of the letters are of the kind any American husband or father or journalist might receive. Does Cornell really want a letter from a Boston hotel telling him that he left a shirt behind when he checked out? Or a letter from a man who accepted his offer to buy a boat? Or the dossier of the architect who supervised winterizing our old house? Or the family letters showing the financial straits or the contents or the sorrows of his brothers and sisters?[17]

The question, for Katharine, is rhetorical; certainly, Cornell would, as her husband said, grow to feel as if it has had "enough of him and his small affairs." Both Whites were surprised by Cornell's answer: Yes, send *everything*. Katharine learned a valuable lesson, one she would repeat: "I'd like to point out that some of the personal letters from the staff—my secretaries and others—would tell a scholar or researcher or writer working on a biography of, say, Harold Ross or Thurber, or a history of *The New Yorker* [a lot]. . . . [They] might well learn more from letters to me from people on the staff with totally unknown names than from letters of well-known writers."[18]

Saving everything, however, raised different concerns, privacy among them. Katharine reassured contributors and friends who authored letters that the letters would be used only after the parties had died. Ironically, it was Brendan Gill she assured in 1972, just before the publication of his tell-all book that would so devastate her:

> Lest you fear that there are personal letters from you in this growing file in the Bryn Mawr Library that houses the rare book room, I don't think I ever received any letters from you after the time I began to collect them.
>
> As for the letters, such as this letter of yours with the wonderful O'Hara obituary, which I shall send to Bryn Mawr, I can assure you that no facts from the letters can be used without permission and of course nothing can be quoted without your permission. The terms of the gift are very explicit and if anything happens to Maxwell so that he can't give these permissions (if Andy and I can't) the permission will be given by somebody Maxwell delegates to.[19]

Finally, Katharine was not content to simply box; she became something of an amateur archivist. She was constitutionally unable to leave the work of organizing to others, and she found it impossible to resist the opportunity to build and shape American literary history. She set about annotating a book list for her collection, adding brief notes on a few of the authors with whom she worked. When she was unable to remember details, she probed for them, as she does in her letter to Brendan Gill in 1972:

> I wasn't on to how important these personal letters were until just a few years ago. I have no note on you in my book list and I'd like to add, for your future biographer, the details for your first story accepted. I think I edited it and sent you the check. Wasn't it a piece about seeing Sinclair Lewis in a Hartford theatre? Was it a movie house or a theatre? I do remember writing you that we would buy it if we could make certain changes, which I must have outlined. Or did I send the manuscript back edited as we'd like to see it? I do remember an excited phone

call from you in the middle of the night saying O.K. At least it *seemed* the middle of the night for Andy and I were in bed and asleep and we didn't go to bed early in those days. I also would want to put down the many, many jobs you did for the magazine after you joined the staff. Talk rewrite, Talk original stories, Cinema critic, Theatre critic, book reviews etc. There must have been many others I don't know about. Also of course your contributions of short stories and much else. Like Andy and Gibbs you did just about everything. Did you edit any departments regularly? Probably. And what year did you join the staff?[20]

Bryn Mawr was accepting of the gift and the arrangement, thanking Katharine for whatever efforts she made. She, in turn, felt her work was valued, although she had some reservations about the quality of what she was producing, particularly given her age, particularly since she was working without the benefit of a *New Yorker* fact checker. In a letter to James Tanis, she writes:

Thank you for your kind and gracious letter, which made me almost believe that all these notes on *New Yorker* people that I labor over may some day be worthwhile to someone. It's a labor of love and in the long run I fear it will be only marginally helpful to scholars. Some of the letters themselves, and later the books, will be more so. If Mrs. Gibbs finds inconsistencies in my remarks, tell her to please remember that I am now eighty and that all my facts will have to be rechecked by whoever uses my notes or the letter file and booklist—if anyone ever does. However, I guess my *impressions* are as valid as ever.[21]

For almost a decade before her death in 1977, Katharine labored at this project. Her work was punctuated by illness. April 1970 was a month particularly marked by interruptions. On April 1, E. B. White apprised Bryn Mawr that Katharine had been hospitalized with congestive heart failure. It's clear that he had taken a good look over some of the material, perhaps in anticipation of taking over the project. Looking over the large volume of personal correspondence that Katharine had been amassing at their Maine farm, he found more than merely a "dim" record of her career: "I've been leafing through the letter this morning and have been impressed by what an interesting and informative correspondence she has conducted over the years, thanks to her close relationship with writers at work and at play. I think any Library would be glad to have them—I could hardly tear myself away from some of these."[22] Two days later, Katharine was back at work on the Bryn Mawr bequest:

> I want to enlarge upon Andy's letter of April 1st, and explain why I am foisting on Mr. Tanis at this most inconvenient of moments a box of personal letters from *New Yorker* writers and staff members. They are annotated but not arranged and sorted as Andy said, and can't be by me before they are mailed. They will arrive all higgledy piggledy.... I also send this box off now because at the same time I am collecting ancestral papers promised to Yale and Bowdoin and I feared that if I should die, these letters might get mixed up with the ones for Bryn Mawr or Cornell.[23]

Another few weeks passed, and Katharine was back in the hospital. E. B. White again explained the delay, relating Katharine's determination to finish the project:

> Katharine asked me to drop you a line, to let you know that she is back in the hospital, and that there will be another delay in assembling the letters and papers for Bryn Mawr. She is quite ill, and at the moment quite incapable of going through her papers. But I hope to have her back home in a few days, when she will resume the work involved in preparing the gift. It is much on her mind and she is determined to see it through. Should she be unable to tend to the matter herself, I shall take it over from her. But at present she wants to do it without any help from me.[24]

By the first of May, Katharine was corresponding with Bryn Mawr again, worrying about the coherence of her notes: "Please remember that during the entire year I have been drugged with pain-killers and cortisone and tranquillizers likely to make one write foolishly and illegibly."[25] In summer of 1972 and again in May of 1975, Katharine reported on her progress; through age and infirmity, Katharine continued her work to safeguard a literary tradition:

> I have been sick and so has my husband. He was in the hospital briefly. This is why the box of letters I'm sending today has been very much held up.... I had hoped to go over everything in the box but I'm sending them along without waiting to re-read my own comments to see whether my own remarks are silly or inadequate or inaccurate, but I just have not got the strength or time to go over this now.... I simply have to get this box out of the house in order to make room on my desk for E. B. White cartons of letters, as my present task is to go through these cartons of E. B. W. letters and papers that are headed for Cornell, in order to extract temporarily any letters *from* him for possible use by the editor of his projected book of letters.[26]

> Between us, my husband & I have had a sick winter and I have been very scattered and vague about my work but I am much better now and hope to buckle down and get a lot more work done, both for Bryn Mawr Library and for myself. We have also added quite a few books to the *New Yorker*-connected book list and this I will send when I have it up-to-date.[27]

Setting the Record Straight

Katharine experienced a different kind of setback with the publication of Brendan Gill's *Here at* The New Yorker: "The Brendan Gill book, which you may have read, has had a devastating effect on me, and on many others, and I feel that I am one of the ones most injured."[28] Gill's book certainly didn't mark the first time that Katharine felt attacked. Two years earlier, she had written to have some correspondence removed from her collection:

Thank you very much for your careful answers to my many small queries.... I think I would just destroy my memo and any notes from him [Eric Day], unless you really want to keep them. They have no real bearing on The New Yorker—only on me as a despised "career woman." I have no objection to your keeping them if you want to but to me they seem related to KSW only, and not therefore connected with The New Yorker except that my career was there. I don't really know why I sent them on in the first place.[29]

There's a light check in the margin, suggesting that Mrs. Gibbs—hired to do the collection—removed them.

It's clear that Gill's book provoked a much more embattled response, perhaps in part because Katharine and he were still corresponding, apparently friends. Just a year or so earlier, he had praised Katharine's work at the magazine, and she had written to thank him for his kind words: "I didn't half thank you for calling me 'the literary conscience' of the early New Yorker. It touched me and helped boost my spirits in some low weeks. It was Ross who called Andy 'the conscience of the magazine' and that term I guess was true. All I deserved was A for effort. I guessed wrong in many a case on literary merit, I feel sure.... Thank you, too, for your kind references to me which I can only pray that I deserve. One never knows."[30] In this case, Katharine certainly didn't know about the negative portrait Gill was composing. She didn't see it coming. Her first impulse was to sue for libel, but she was advised against it because his publisher had doubtlessly made him couch his claims. Gill's wasn't the first memoir to be published, and thus Katharine had already been working to correct what she saw as the falsehoods printed along the way. Katharine was not particularly in favor of memoirs that offered peeps into the magazine's operations—she preferred to open archives to scholars—but she warmed to Ford's The Time of Laughter. Ford didn't take the Whites by surprise. The acknowledgements indicated that both read the book in manuscript and offered "corrections and valuable suggestions" (Ford 221). In one case, even when he didn't make a change that E. B. White suggested, Ford footnoted the objection (227). Katharine White also judged Ford's intentions. While Brendan Gill's book came across to her as a memoir in the name-dropping, exposé tradition, Ford's was a sentimental tribute to a Golden Age of American humor in the 1920s. Ford took up operations at the *New Yorker* only insofar as they played a role in literary and dramatic history. Perhaps most endearingly, Ford treats the Whites as an influential *team*, giving credit to both husband and wife, without taking credit away from Ross, whom Katharine felt increasingly called upon to defend: "More than anyone else save Ross himself, Katharine S. and E. B. White were responsible for *The New Yorker*'s enormous impact on American letters. Their unerring taste guided it through the formative years, and White's poetry-in-prose became the hallmark of the magazine" (Ford 124). Katharine White saw more problems in James Thurber's *My Years with Ross*, which she characterized as:

> notably inaccurate, both on Ross himself and on facts and figures about the magazine. Going over these cartons of his, I found many letters from Thurber to us both. I'll try to get copies of these for you later. They are important for biographers of Thurber because some of them, written when he was writing "The Years With Ross," show with what animus he approached the writing of that lively but sorry book, which has been taken as gospel truth by most of its readers. It is easy to see that half the time Jim Thurber really hated his subject and tried to cut him down to a minor and ignorant and stingy figure in American letters, which he was not.[31]

It pained Katharine to read reviews of these works and stand by silently as they sold copies. In the case of Thurber's book, she was grateful to the critic Rebecca West, one of the few who said that Thurber's depiction of Ross did not match her knowledge of him.

Gill's book was of another order and reinforced for Katharine the necessity of her bequest. It's impossible to overestimate the degree to which the book drove her. After her death, E. B. White wrote to Bill Maxwell, hoping to protect Katharine post-

humously from the damage inflicted on her psyche and reputation: "I have in my attic a fat folder of notes Katharine made,
in her last year, of the Brendan Gill book."[32] Gill wounded her
deeply by repeating (or perhaps even inventing) a rumor that "it
was Katharine White who was prepared to lead a palace revolution" (192) to oust Ross. This was, she wrote Tanis, "Totally untrue. I was almost fanatically devoted to Ross & three times over
I persuaded Fleishmann not to oust him by saying that if he left,
I would leave with him & so would most of the others."[33] Katharine White was especially sensitive to any criticism that she dis-
sented from Ross's vision for and decisions about the magazine.

There is much in Gill's book to disturb the Whites: Gill rendered E. B. White ("Andy") quaint and foolish; he continually
painted Katharine as powerful and power hungry: "At the time
she resigned her full-time position, she was in charge of fiction
on the magazine, but her influence extended far beyond that department; she had helped to invent the magazine as a whole, she
and White were owners of a good deal of its stock, and she took
care to make her weight felt at every turn" (B. Gill 291). While Gill
acknowledged the Whites' working partnership—"Katharine
and Andy White worked so closely over the years as to become,
in most people's minds, one person" (290)—he insinuated that
there were rifts in the marriage: "Mrs. White believed herself to
be giving up the best job held by any woman in America when
she followed her husband to Maine, and no doubt she was right"
(119). From Katharine's letters, it was clear that she was happier
in New York City than in the country, but she was wholly committed to what E. B. White needed in order to write and had suc-
cessfully made arrangements to continue her work from afar.
Even if she did feel some resentment about the move, she wasn't
the kind of person to air such a sentiment. To have Gill articulate her disappointments, and publish them, was galling. While
Gill's book was a tribute to Shawn and a celebration of the New
Yorker, he selected details that he must have known would strike
a nerve or two because they undermined the New Yorker ethos. For

example, the magazine prided itself on fact checking, a journalistic principle very dear to Harold Ross. Gill implies that the fiction editors didn't know what they were doing, particularly when
they accepted his Catholic stories, that they never checked his
facts: "It became evident that the editors of The New Yorker knew
little about Catholics and especially about Catholics in religious
orders. . . . I could cheat with impunity and I did" (93–94). At every turn, there was something that galled her, motivating her to
write to correct the record:

> I am outraged by his report on Ross and Gibbs—the matter of
> Gibbs's wife's suicide was not at all as Gill wrote it—and I am
> outraged by the triviality of his report on Lobrano, who was
> for years a tower of strength as an editor and not at all the silly
> man Gill described. . . . I have tried to annotate the book but
> I have to do it over and try to make it less passionate. Eventu-
> ally these notes will come with the book to Bryn Mawr. . . . The
> best thing in it is Shawn's short summary of Ross, which he
> wrote not having read the manuscript. Nobody read it until it
> was in proof and had gone to press, so the magazine could not
> insist on Gill's correcting statements that were false.[34]

White wasn't alone in her strong reaction to Gill's book: "For
a while I was very much depressed after the book appeared, but
I have lots of letters of indignation from contributors and staff
(some of which will eventually end up at Bryn Mawr) which
cheered me a little. Gill has injured so many people by what he
said of them, and has ignored so many who count in New Yorker
history that the book does not give a realistic picture of the magazine. Shawn has called the book 'a disaster.'"[35] She took comfort in the belief that others on the staff reacted negatively: "The
comments on the book by his colleagues, particularly the younger
ones, have been by no means entirely favorable. They tend to
think that Mr. Gill, by all but ignoring the considerable changes
in the tone and content in the magazine in the last 15 or 20 years,
has given continued currency to a stereotype of snobbery, artifi-
ciality, cliquishness and metropolitan provincialism that is long

outdated" (Buckley 25). Still, the book did well. Gill was witty and engaging. The New York Times reviewer Christopher Lehmann-Haupt conceded that the book was "extremely bitchy" and even a little "depressing"—"scarcely a paragraph of 'Here At The New Yorker' goes by from which someone doesn't emerge with teeth-marks or tiny daggers in his or her flesh"—but he confessed that the book kept him in a "continual state of mirth" (25). Gill's book seemed particularly damaging given the uncertain climate during which it emerged. The New Yorker was facing a budget crisis; adver-tising revenues had declined to "an alarming figure." The mag-azine needed supporters, not detractors. On every public occa-sion, the press repeatedly questioned New Yorker executives about the effect of Gill's book: "Finally, Milton Greenstein, a vice presi-dent on the editorial side said, 'Let me put an end to the Gill book once and for all. The book is full of inaccuracies and if you're go-ing to take Gill's impressions of The New Yorker and ask the board to answer for it, you're out of line" (Dougherty 52).[36] To all this criticism, Gill pled genre: "Of course it doesn't pretend to be a history.... It's a memoir and intensely personal" (qtd. in Buckley 25). Unfortunately for Katharine White, Gill's book enjoyed great popularity (it was reprinted in 1997), a popularity born of the con-troversy it stirred, both within the very private confines of the New Yorker hallways and in the very public corridors of the press.

E. B. White reports being unnerved by Katharine's intense response; he felt she had lost her composure. He was able to re-turn her to her senses, as he saw it, but when she died, she left him with a problem, what to do with Katharine's fat file on Gill's book: "When she finally rounded up all her vast material for the Library, she deliberately withheld the Gill book, along with her notes, and left instructions saying that she didn't want Bryn Mawr to have the material until, or unless, she could put it in a different form. Then she died, and now it's up to me to decide what to do with it. I will, if I live, which is getting harder by the minute."[37] In the wake of the Gill book and Katharine's death, E. B. White had changed his thinking about what he was willing to archive. He advised Maxwell: "If you are sending KSW letters to Bryn Mawr, I think it's best to exercise a certain degree of editorial control over them. I know that libraries want *everything* and they feel it is shocking for anybody to destroy anything. I'm on the other side of the fence. I burn my own stuff without a second thought and sometimes with a wild sense of elation. The particular letter of K's that you mention does not need to wind up in Bryn Mawr—I leave that to your judgment."[38]

Literate Zeal is a history made possible by Katharine White's dedication to publish American literature and to save the personal and professional letters that built such a rich belletristic history. In addition to White's archive at Bryn Mawr, I visited the *New Yorker* collection at the New York Public Library, which houses her official editorial work. It has been more difficult to locate archival materials for *Mademoiselle* or *Harper's Bazaar* or *Vogue*. For the large-circulation class publications I've focused on in *Literate Zeal*, the difference in what has been preserved is profound. For women's magazines, in terms of an archive that goes beyond the preservation of issues, there is almost nothing to speak of, none of it cataloged.[39] The contribution by women's magazines to U.S. literature was short lived, in part because it was so dependent on the personalities of individual editors rather than on a declared editorial mission. The women's magazines made dramatic transformations when the editorship changed. *Harper's Bazaar*'s participation in the high letters market ended with Carmel Snow's tenure. In 1958, Snow had agreed to publish *Breakfast at Tiffany's* in *Harper's Bazaar*, but by the time the work was ready to come into print, she "had been booted out by the Hearst Corporation, and her niece, Nancy White, had taken her place" (Clarke 308). *Harper's Bazaar* was worried about the darkness of the novel and specifically about its treatment of female sexuality. Capote made changes, but not enough to settle the nerves of the new editorial team. *Breakfast at Tiffany's* was not published in *Harper's Bazaar*: "Without much ado, *Harper's Bazaar* had ended its long and distinguished history of printing high quality fiction. Although he subsequently sold his story to *Esquire*, Truman never forgave the new, Snow-less *Bazaar*. 'I'm not angry, I'm outraged—that's an entirely different thing,' he told a reporter. 'Publish with *them* again? Why, I wouldn't spit on their street'" (Clarke 308). Through the 1940s and 1950s, however, *Mademoiselle* and *Harper's Bazaar* provided a place for U.S. writers to place their work, even work judged outside the mainstream. Both publications were catering to the range of middle-class women readers that would, during and after the World War II, swell the *New Yorker* subscriber lists and fuel the fiction and poetry market. While George Davis has received some attention for the work he did with *Harper's Bazaar* and *Mademoiselle*,[40] the work done by other editors has gone largely undocumented. Rumor has it that a cache of Leo Lerman's correspondence has survived, held in trust by someone who works at Condé Nast. The stories of editors such as Mary Louise Atwell or Cyrilly Abels or Rita Smith will need to be pieced together from archives of individual authors such as Janet Flanner (the Harry Ransom Center, University of Texas) or William Saroyan (Stanford) or Emily Hahn (Indiana). While some work has been done by scholars and literary journalists—Alexandra Subramanian's excellent dissertation on the editorial relationship between Cyrilly Abels and Katharine Anne Porter comes to mind[41]—there is ample opportunity for researchers interested in recovering and synthesizing this history. For now, most of this story remains hidden in scattered archives, and thus unwritten. In light of this sad archival state, Katharine White's work on her bequest seems all the more laudable. The Whites scurried in their later years to leave a rich legacy, one seemingly complete. It is not. From the correspondence, we can learn the nature of editorial work, but we can't see exactly what changes might have been suggested in face-to-face meetings or in phone conversations. Only lightly edited proofs survive, those that had already been through a rigorous editorial process, and only for some manuscripts.

There is one artifact in particular I hoped would materialize from the Whites' attic, that cassette that records Katharine's voice, dictating a letter "with its meticulous attention to punctuation marks and paragraphing and its immaculate delivery." It didn't turn up. I have had to imagine her voice from her letters. No archive is a perfect whole, but the legacy Katharine White labored to leave is substantial. It gives us a glimpse not just into her work but into the work of a generation of women who took to the project of literacy and letters with zeal.

NOTES

Preface: Haute Literacy

1. If William Shawn, the editor of the *New Yorker* for over thirty-five years, were the bragging type—he was instead famously modest—he might have boasted that by 1970, he "had already had 50 books dedicated to him" (Stingone v). See also this short selection of titles: Kunkel, *Genius in Disguise*; Kramer; Thurber; Mehta; and Berg.

2. Bok's memoir is treated at length in chapter one. For more on Bok, see Steinberg; and Krabbendam. For more on *Ladies' Home Journal*, see Damon-Moore; and Scanlon.

3. The story of Harold Ross and the *New Yorker*, as Trysh Travis explains, "satisfies at many levels: it is rich in vivid and funny details, it neatly encapsulates cultural change, and the irony at its heart (how could a man who has to ask, 'Is Moby Dick the whale or the man?' be the editor of the *New Yorker*?) is unresolvable without recourse to the tantalizing mysteries of 'genius'" (258). For Jane Grant's role in the founding of the magazine, see Henry, "Gambling on a Magazine and a Marriage." See also William Shipman's introduction to an exhibit of Jane Grant's papers at the University of Oregon Libaries.

4. So successful was Blackwell in this mission that she was eventually honored as a director of the Columbia University School of General Studies. Unlike some other editors of the period, Blackwell did not write a memoir and has not been the subject of a biography. She was, however, profiled in Rayner's *Wise Women* (38–47) (Francine du Plessix Gray wrote the foreword) and appears in glimpses in editorials. Blackwell's father was a writer and her mother a "fashion stylist" at Lord & Taylor. Blackwell's son became an executive at *Newsweek* (Sanders and Hersam Acorn Newspapers).

5. "Smart" used in this sense evolved from its eighteenth-century roots as "one who affects smartness in dress, manners, or talk" (OED). For more on "smart magazines," see Douglas.

6. Sponsors "lend their resources or credibility to the sponsored but also stand to gain benefits from their success, whether by direct re-

payment or, indirectly, by credit of association." Brandt chose the term "sponsors" because of "all the commercial references that appeared in these twentieth-century accounts—the magazines, peddled encyclopedias, essay contests, radio and television programs, toys, fans clubs, writing tools, and so on, from which so much experience with literacy was derived" (*Literacy in American Lives* 19–20). Brandt studies the effect of these sponsors on the sponsored, while I am trying to get behind the scenes of sponsorship.

7. These magazines formed a belletristic "extracurriculum" that was both liberating and restrictive. I borrow the term "extracurriculum" from Anne Ruggles Gere's *Intimate Practices* (and she in turn borrowed it from Frederick Rudolph) to highlight the "literary clubs" and other activities that supported collegiate life or learning generally. See also Gere, "Kitchen Tables and Rented Rooms"; and Hobbs.

8. For an analysis of how illiteracy gets sponsored, see Mortensen.

9. In *Literacy in American Lives*, Brandt refers to how literacy can be viewed as a "raw material." As she argues, it makes sense that literacy came to be something highly desirable in the mid-twentieth-century: "Turbulent economic and technological changes force changes in the nature of work, rearrangements in systems of communication and social relations, and fluctuation in the value of human skills. With the unique kinds of economic and technological changes of the twentieth century, those fluctuations came especially to affect the value of literacy.... Rapid-process production, technological innovation, modern weaponry, corporate consolidation, the growth of consumerism, the rise in knowledge industries, and the spread of computer technology all made controlling and communicating words and other symbols vital to the production of profit" (187–88).

10. This value they shared with belletristic critics in the academy who viewed literature in the manner of Matthew Arnold and John Ruskin "as a moral and spiritual force and a repository of 'general ideas' which could be applied directly to the conduct of life and improvement of national culture" (Graff and Warner 6).

11. This view still has currency and market capability, as illustrated by work like Azar Nafisi's *Reading Lolita in Tehran*.

12. Katharine employed several signatures over her long career, including Katharine Sergeant, Katharine S. Angell, K. S. Angell, Katharine S. White, K. S. White, and, on strategic occasions, Mrs. E. B. White. Not as much has been written about Katharine White as has been about her better-known colleagues—her husband E. B. White or Harold Ross and William Shawn. This is not to say that Katharine White has been ignored or even that she remains obscure: she appears, of course, in the academic histories of the *New Yorker* or in memoirs by writers. She has also been the subject of two book-length works: a dissertation by Ner-

ney, published just five years after her death, and Davis's "solid, respectful, affectionate biography." Davis in particular did yeoman's work, interviewing many who knew White, including her children, and corresponding with E. B. White. White's correspondence with Davis is part of the voluminous record of K. S. White's "personal" papers at Bryn Mawr, although the line separating Katharine's professional editorial life and personal life was almost nonexistent. This was a woman who lived, breathed, and loved the *New Yorker*, a prioritizing that didn't go unnoticed by her children or her husband.

13. See, for example, Rowley's argument concerning the editing of Richard Wright: "The surviving drafts of Wright's works in the Beinecke Library at Yale, as well as his unpublished manuscripts and correspondence, reveal the almost impossible context in which he was writing. The conflicting forces were such that the Richard Wright we know is a censored, mediated, packaged Richard Wright. Like a ball of wool, there is a complex tangle of threads wound around Wright's work and its reception. It is not easy to disentangle" (625). Rowley focuses on *Native Son* and *Black Boy*, both of which owe early success to Book-of-the-Month Club. As she documents, the selection of *Native Son* came with strings: "selection was contingent on Wright making some changes—mostly in the form of excisions" (627). In 1991, fifty-one years after initial publication as a Book-of-the-Month Club selection, the unrevised galley version was published for the first time. Specifically, Rowley underscores the editing suggested by the fiction writer Dorothy Canfield Fisher: "Canfield Fisher, more than any other of the Book-of-the-Month Club judges, took it upon herself to 'improve' *Native Son* and *Black Boy*. What this meant, essentially, was to make them into narratives that were less shocking to white readers" (628–29). See also Arnold Rampersad's comments on the unabridged Library of America edition.

14. See, for example, Meyerowitz.

15. I borrow the term "gendered imagination" from Kessler-Harris's *In Pursuit of Equity*, which provides a framework for analyzing "habits of mind"—ideas about normative experience (jobs, education, lifestyle, wages)—that were uncontested to the point that they seemed natural to both men and women. At any given time, there is more than one "gendered imagination" at work; these imaginative constructs often conflict, indeed define themselves out of difference and conflict (for example, "not a housewife" or "not a feminist") and lead to new terms and definitions ("stay-at-home mother," "woman who works at home," or "career woman").

16. "Class publications" is not a critical term but a twentieth-century trade term whose history I take up in chapter one.

17. This elision prompts us to ask, as the feminist rhetorician Nan Johnson does, why the contributions of women in any era are "missing

from the map of the history of rhetoric in the first place" (10) and "what cultural interests contributed to the blotting of women's words from the record" (13)? Cultural memory has played tricks on us, granting to only one or two publications the literary laurel, the prominent place on the bookshelf that is literary history. *Literate Zeal* proposes an alternate way of composing this history.

Introduction: Literacy, Gender, and the Rhetorical Work of Editing

1. Brownmiller's memoir is largely about the various factions within the Women's Liberation Movement. This demonstration was planned by the group Media Women and carried out with cooperation from other groups (Brownmiller, *In Our Time* 81–94).

2. Published by E. P. Dutton, *Lady Editor* is really three short books by three different writers: Marjorie Shuler wrote part I, "Journalism"; Ruth Adams Knight wrote part II, "Magazines," the section of the book on which I'll focus; and Muriel Fuller wrote part III, "Book Publishing."

3. Rereading *The Feminist Mystique*, I find that Friedan did on occasion creep beyond textual analysis, including quotations from interviews with women editors, those she calls "old timers," to document the shift from an emphasis on the "New Woman" to an emphasis on the infantilized housewife. Still, her main evidence comes from combing through the editorial contents of women's magazines, as seen in her listing of a typical issue (July 1960) of *McCall's* magazine (Friedan 34–35).

4. Or so the Goulds claim: their memoir *American Story* serves as the source for Bashford and Strange's and Zuckerman's histories. This is just one of many examples that demonstrates how letters and memoirs (even those whose validity is questioned in reviews) become naturalized into our histories.

5. One might reasonably question whether women who taught in the early twentieth century *were* able to effect rhetorical agency and advance progressive agenda in the classroom.

6. Jacqueline Jones Royster describes this as the process of "triangulat[ing] analyses, analyses of *ethos* formation, of the context for rhetorical action, and of the rhetorical event itself" (47).

7. It wasn't simply college graduates entering the field, working women could and did embark on editing and publishing careers through two other common venues—retail and secretarial experience.

8. As Deborah Brandt observes, in general literacy levels in the early twentieth century surpassed what was necessary for work. The surplus thus existed not only in terms of number, but also in terms of "potential": "first as consumers and then as producers, American literates became fuel for the information economy" (Brandt, *Literacy* 188–89).

9. See Alpern.

10. See also Adams, *Progressive Politics and the Training of America's Persuaders.*

11. Peter Mortensen and I look at school-based arguments against marriage in chapter six, "Independent Studies," in *Imagining Rhetoric* (145–88). Almira Hart Lincoln Phelps, for instance, recognized that for some women marriage was a duty they were called to fulfill. She advised her students, however, to avoid it if at all morally possible.

12. The *Ladies' Home Journal* Sit-In Steering Committee drafted a delightful set of potential articles, "the kind of material that the *Ladies' Home Journal* never printed. . . . 'How to get a divorce,' 'How to have an orgasm,' 'How to get an abortion' . . . 'What to tell your draft-age son' and 'How detergents harm our rivers and streams.'" They also printed a list of demands, speaking for fairness in representation in pay and against ads and features that glorified youth, romance, marriage, and celebrity (Brownmiller, *In Our time* 84–87).

13. It is unquestionably a sexist term whether used by Bok or Brownmiller; Knight did not use it in a pejorative way.

14. For more on the feministic ideas, see Mastrangelo.

15. Jane Grant, for instance, was a self-proclaimed Lucy Stoner who wrote, "Confession of a Feminist." See Merrick.

16. In addition to these high-profile women, there were many other women working in lower-tier editing positions. Occasionally, we see glimpses of these women. Here, for instance, is Edna Woolman Chase naming the subjects in a photograph taken at *Vogue's* offices and printed in Edna Woolman and Ilka Chase's *Always in Vogue*:

> Marie [Lyons] was one of our first college graduates and because of this background was engaged to head our copy room as a sort of vice president in charge of semicolons. We had been moseying along using merely the arithmetic of the punctuation world, commas, dashes, and periods, but someone must have decided it was time to graduate. Marie was assertive about her ability in semicolons and got the job.
>
> Equipped with a good mind, a generous appreciation of her own talents, and a not too sensitive regard for the feelings of her fellow workers, she did not warm the atmosphere around her, but was able and influential in bringing onto the staff some of our best people: Ruth de Rochement, Claudia Cranston, Marjorie Hillis, and for a brief, stormy, but exhilarating period Dorothy Rothschild, who, as Dorothy Parker, was to develop in to the *enfant terrible* of American letters.
>
> Seated at the next desk . . . is Marie's contemporary in the copy room, Grace Hegger. Marie was clean-cut, blue-eyed, blond, bursting with energy and not easy to get along with. Grace, on the other

hand, was what we used to call la-di-da, full of airs and graces and affectations, with large green eyes and hair that was a curly nimbus of gold and copper lights.

When she married her first husband, however, she buckled down and turned out several books. As the husband was Sinclair Lewis it was perhaps natural. In a copy of *Main Street* that he gave to the Heyworth Campbells, Lewis wrote, "With merry Christmas greetings and with salaams to all of *Vogue*, from which I stole one of the best wives I've ever had." . . .

The third young woman in the photograph, Martha Moller, felt about the magazine as I did and stayed with us until she died, in the early summer of 1952.

No one has ever taken her place. She became my secretary soon after she joined us and remained with me for almost seventeen years. Finally, feeling it was unfair not to, I saw her established in a more executive position in the organization. (80–81)

17. While *Mademoiselle* believed in "careers for women," Blackwell, in the fortieth-anniversary issue made clear that she and others on her staff were not feminists "crusading for women's right to work," nor were they "battle-axes encouraging competition with our men (the tough-as-tacks career girl is a fast fading memory)," she claims "and good riddance." Instead, she considered herself and other staffers "realists suggesting how to use your talents and training to meet higher living costs, serve the best interest of your family and community, round out your way of life." Her staff, according to a *New York Times* article in 1971, tended toward liberalism and thus tended to disagree with their editor (Rayner 44).

18. Not everyone has such lofty remembrances. Janet Burroway, a 1955 alumna, conjures a "Betsy Talbot Blackwell, who sailed between the mirrors of the editorial room waving her cigarette holder, adjuring us to 'Believe in Pink'" (3).

19. At some point, this mood would change, as Friedan suggests with this undated interview: "Behind her cluttered desk, a *Mademoiselle* editor said uneasily, 'The girls we bring in now as college guest editors seem almost to pity us. Because we are career women, I suppose. At a luncheon session with the last bunch, we asked them to go round the table, telling us their own career plans. Not one in twenty raised her hand. When I remember how I worked to learn this job and loved it—were we all crazy then?'" (56).

20. Blackwell credited a "team" with the magazine's success, including editors who would have had more formal training in letters. See Rayner 45.

21. For more on Hale, see Okker. See also Harris and Garvey.

22. See especially Adler: "As I write this, *The New Yorker* is dead. It

still comes out every week, or almost every week.... The magazine was already, at least arguably, declining under Mr. Shawn" (11). Shawn's tenure ran from 1951–1987.

23. It works to an extent: feminist media critics have revised theories of the way that these magazines worked in women's lives. Eva Moskowitz, for example, argues that women's magazines did not lull women into a state of contentment but instead provided a space to "document women's discontent" (67).

24. Of course, Katharine White originally set out to be a writer (see L. Davis 53) and even at this point *was* occasionally writing, a fact that she needed to justify as part of her work on the magazine: "If I do try to write in my extra time during the coming year, it should be an attempt to carry out some projects I have in mind for *The New Yorker* which Mr. Shawn has o.k.'d." White also recommends to Fisher some "people who are [writers]. Why not a piece by Marianne Moore, who is Bryn Mawr's most distinguished writer among the alumnae? As an undergraduate editor of *The Lantern* I was able to wheedle a contribution out of her, so surely you ought to be able to now, for the Bulletin. She writes more than she did then, and she writes wonderful prose. Another idea I had would be a piece from one of the Lucy Martin Donnelly Fellows—Elizabeth Bowen comes to mind." This letter is actually dated 1958, though it is clear from the context that the letter was written on February 10, 1959, Katharine Sergeant White Papers, Special Collections Department, Bryn Mawr College Library, box 30, folder 2. "'Ideally,' she would say years later, 'all editors should also be writers'" (L. Davis 73).

25. Scribner articulates three different metaphorical frames for literacy. In addition to the "state of grace" metaphor, she explicates "literacy as adaptation" and "literacy as power." To these three metaphors, Connie Kendall adds a fourth, equally as powerful and equally as relevant to this rhetorical history, "literacy as pleasure." Paper delivered at the 2008 Rhetoric Society of America Conference, Seattle, Washington.

26. As Scribner notes, the "metaphor of literacy-as-grace ... has boundary problems.... To what extent are beliefs about the value of literateness shared across social classes and ethnic and religious groups?" (14). The editors I study here look to literacy as a way of transcending cultural difference.

27. It's a trope that continues in literature about the period. Consider this passage for example, from Gore Vidal's essay on Dawn Powell: "It was Dawn Powell's fate to be a dinosaur shortly after the comet, or whatever it was, struck our culture, killing off the literary culture—a process still at work but no less inexorable—and re-placing it with the Audiovisual, as they say at Film School. The Hemingway, Faulkner, Fitzgerald, Dreiser, and Powell American generation was the last to be central to the culture of that part of the world where Gutenberg reined" (24).

28. For a discussion of the role that reading and writing play in family lives see Deborah Brandt's "Remembering Writing, Remembering Reading." Brandt discusses the pleasurable role that reading plays in sustaining family intimacy. Based on the wide interviewing Brandt does of subjects, she also reminds critics to "consider how parental literacy, at least at times, can be a sign or source of trouble for children" ("Remembering" 460).

29. "Literacy narratives are those stories … that foreground issues of language acquisition.… They include texts that both challenge and affirm culturally scripted ideas about literacy" (Eldred and Mortensen, "Reading" 513). Early twentieth-century texts respond to and transform nineteenth-century debates about schools and other institutions that foster literacy, about socialization and propriety, about employment and class mobility. This definition has been enriched by work by Morris Young and Sarah Robbins. Robbins is interested in nineteenth-century "benevolent literacy narratives" and "domestic literacy narratives and the ways such subtypes interact in a "network" with sentimental discourse. This "network" still figures prominently in twentieth-century women's magazines. Young teases out the connection between literacy narratives and citizenship, arguing for "the major revisions that must take place within American culture to account for the literacy and rhetorical practices of people of color" (7). Part of that revision must also include accounting for the ways in which literacy has come to be defined as a white middle-class practice, value, and prerogative.

30. For more on creative writing in colleges and universities, see Adams, *Group*; Meyers; and McDonald.

31. In addition to Rubin's *The Making of Middlebrow Culture*, which provides a contextual history and critical appreciation of the various commercial projects (e.g., digests, book reviews) designed to entice middle-class men and women to read literature and partake of other commodities of high culture, see Radway. Both works ask us to revisit the critical axioms that such efforts were merely the watering down or debasing of literature and culture.

32. New York Public Library, Manuscripts and Archives Division, *New Yorker* Records (1924–1984), box 438, gen. corr., folder P-Pez, May 21, 1946.

33. Ibid., September 6, 1946

34. Ibid., November 7, 1946.

35. Ibid.

36. Ibid., November 9, 1946.

37. New York Public Library, Manuscripts and Archives Division, *New Yorker* Records (1924–1984), box 481, Frances Gray Patton folder, March 7, 1949.

38. Ibid., November 10, 1951.

39. Ibid., July 9, 1954.

40. Letter from K. S. White to Frances Patton Gray, New York Public Library, Manuscripts and Archives Division, *New Yorker* Records (1924–1984), box 730, January 24, 1950.

41. I am persuaded on this issue by Suzanne Clark's argument in *Sentimental Modernism*. For a connection between sentimental rhetoric and the *New Yorker*, see my "Modern Fidelity" in S. Clark 49–68.

Chapter One. Between the Sheets: Editing and the Making of a *New Yorker* Ethos

1. See I. B., "The Genius for Banality."

2. "The 'selling' of the modern college and university system began not only in high school and other 'official' venues that prepared students for advanced study, but also in popular venues, among them mass-circulation magazines.... Such magazines provided the possibility of a literary experience for readers that powerfully shaped knowledge of and preparation for higher education, even as reading itself was constructed as a popular, informative, and pleasurable activity" (Reynolds 163, 165).

3. Postmodern rhetoricians were directed to this formulation of ethos in part by revisiting and reappraising the much-maligned Sophists. For example, the feminist rhetoricans Susan C. Jarratt and Nedra Reynolds draw on sophistic rhetoric to construct a theory that stresses character formation: "Rather than focusing on the split between a genuine, fully formed character and its representation, sophistic rhetoric explains the process of character formation through learning to speak to the interests of the community" (44). Jarratt and Reynolds look primarily to the practice of "selecting 'illustrious' and 'edifying' examples" (45). Their analysis suggests that sophistic rhetoric would demand that critics would practice—and presumably investigate in other's practice—"a constant awareness that one always speaks from a particular place in a social structure—an awareness common to rhetoric and to postmodern feminists" (Jarratt and Reynolds 47). This and other work recovers a definition of ethos that "predates its more familiar and related translations as 'moral character' and 'ethics'" (Hyde xiii).

4. The striking exceptions to this broad generalization are studies that recover the editorial contributions of underrepresented groups. Without this sympathetic identification, however, the stress falls on the manipulative nature of editorial work, particularly any kind of editing that involves mass circulation. At the Rhetoric Society of America Conference in 1998, Sally Gill, once a copywriter for a San Francisco advertising agency, argued that critics had melodramatically vilified the rhetorical work of commercial writers. She uses as an example ad writers, whom rhetorical critics painted in overly broad strokes as "manipula-

tors skilled in the practice of brainwashing": "It sounds terribly sinister. As far as I could tell, however, none of the writers and art directors with whom I worked approached their work the aim of wearing down resistance and hypnotizing people. . . . We worked with the assumption that people are skeptical about advertising, bored by most of it (with good reason)" (S. Gill 200). Gill is not suggesting that critics study commercial writing outside the context of consumer culture—an impossibility—but rather that rhetoricians augment such analysis by studying the insider view, "the perspective of the ethos" (201) that is collectively forged between agencies and audience.

5. In 1951 and 1954 respectively, Dale Kramer published *Ross and The New Yorker*, and Edna Woolman Chase published *Always in Vogue* (her daughter, Ilka, was her coauthor). A cluster of titles followed in the 1960s—Corey Ford's *The Time of Laughter* (1967); Jane Grant's *Ross, The New Yorker, and Me* (1968); and Bruce and Beatrice Blackmar Gould's *American Story* (1968). In 1975, Brendan Gill's *Here at The New Yorker*, coupled with Kramer's and Ford's earlier works, sparked a veritable *New Yorker* memoir industry.

6. The source is so widely known that almost every review of the book or film notes the connection to *Vogue* under the editorial hand of Anna Wintour.

7. Some give Bok credit for discussing venereal disease, however cryptically. In January 1909, Bok printed an article about Helen Keller "giving medical statistics of the results of syphilis and gonorrhea, but not mentioning either disease by name" (n. p.). For a reprinting of the article see "Ladies and Syphilis," *Time*, July 19, 1937.

8. For more on the awards, see the Columbia Law School's website, http://library.law.columbia.edu/ttp/TTP_Bok.htm. The award is referred to as the American Peace Prize, the Bok Peace Prize, and the Bok Peace Award, and it is awarded to "the American individual or organization presenting the best practicable plan by which the United States may cooperate with other nations for the achievement and preservation of world peace."

9. R. D. Townsend, in his review of *The Americanization of Edward Bok* in the *Outlook*, highlights Bok's critique of immigrant experience: "looking back, he sees that he had to practice thrift in a land of waste, that there was too much emphasis on quantity rather than quality, that lack of thoroughness was the 'curse of America,' that the public schools failed to provide rightly for the education of a child of foreign birth, that there was not respect enough for law and order, that America did not teach its young voters rightly as to the significance of the franchise" (514). Such criticism from Bok is buried in a single chapter (there are thirty-nine in the book) entitled "Where America Fell Short with Me." As the reviewer (only the initials I. B. are provided) for *Nation* noted in

what is essentially a positive review, Bok never "heard of the world of ideas.... His criticism of the America in which he lived and which he seems to have understood so well, is always merely trivial" (I. B., "The Genius for Banality" 784).

10. In the 1948 edition by Millicent Fenwick, the usage section (chapter 18) becomes a glossary of sorts, akin to the structure of *Fowler's*. "Usage" becomes part of the subtitle proper.

11. Less frequently, the word "special" was used to describe the category of work that fit in the *New Yorker*. "Mr. Ross feels that the short stories we use have to be quite special in type—*New Yorker*-ish—if that word means anything to you" (New York Public Library, Manuscripts and Archives Division, *New Yorker* Records [1924–1984], box 135, William Rose Benet folder, April 1928).

12. New York Public Library, Manuscripts and Archives Division, *New Yorker* Records (1924–1984), box 3, William Rose Benet folder, circa 1930. Benet's response, written on *Saturday Review of Literature* stationary, defends the poem: "You're cuckoo! That's the best poem I've written in six months and I knew more about poetry before I was born than you or anyone else will know when you die. But I wouldn't have sent it in at all save that Mrs. White kept pestering me for stuff. Whaddya let one letter about poor Holden's amusing piece give you the willies for?"

13. New York Public Library, Manuscripts and Archives Division, *New Yorker* Records (1924–1984), box 135, gen. corr., folder B-Baz, 1928.

14. Ibid.

15. Ibid.

16. New York Public Library, Manuscripts and Archives Division, *New Yorker* Records (1924–1984), box 195, Louise Bogan folder, June 1, 1934.

17. Ibid., November 16, 1934.

18. Ibid.

19. New York Public Library, Manuscripts and Archives Division, *New Yorker* Records (1924–1984), box 246, Louise Bogan folder, 1936.

20. Ibid.

21. Ibid.

22. "Whatever It Is" and "Four Quarters" appear in *A Poet's Prose*, edited by Mary Kinzie (Athens: Swallow Press, 2005), 55–58, 376. Ibid., April 13, 1936.

23. As Douglas notes: "The appeal to an elite was always something of a mannerism or affectation; [smart magazines] were and needed to be 'commercial'" (11).

24. Katharine White writes to Patton: "I attach a few notes to explain changes or to ask for them in light of Mr. Ross' reading of the piece. He is our editor-in-chief and the notes marked 'R' are his. It may be that you don't want to place Stonesboro in any given state because I imagine that it is a made up name, but possibly it would be a little better

to place the locale." When Patton changes the locale to Virginia, White writes back to let her know that that the change is unacceptable, that there are really only two options (New York Public Library, Manuscripts and Archives Division, *New Yorker* Records [1924–1984], box 438, gen. corr., folder P-Pez, 1946). See Kunkel's *Genius in Disguise* for examples of how Ross fact checked drawings and jokes.

25. New York Public Library, Manuscripts and Archives Division, *New Yorker* Records (1924–1984), box 246, Louise Bogan folder, 1936.

26. As Yagoda notes and as Katharine White frequently argues, very early in its history, the *New Yorker* was publishing fiction that seriously treated "dark" themes.

27. In her correspondence with V. S. Pritchett, White "noted the scarcity of humorous pieces" and having seen his comic tale "The Saint" in a British publication invited him to send "some equally amusing stories" to the *New Yorker* (Bloom 212).

28. Katharine White to Corey Ford, September 23, 1967, Katharine Sergeant White Papers, Special Collections Department, Bryn Mawr College Library, box 4, folder 9. White's son and editorial successor Roger Angell also stressed balance between humor and realism and emphasized the presence of humor as an indication of the magazine's currency: "'Since last August, we've seen more humor coming in than in 20 years,' said Roger Angell, the author and fiction editor. 'We've already bought enough to last us until May. It all started the day Nixon left office. I think people suddenly started to cheer up'" (Buckley 25).

29. New York Public Library, Manuscripts and Archives Division, *New Yorker* Records (1924–1984), box 388, gen. corr., folder Br-Briz, June 21, 1943.

30. See also Yagoda: "if the *New Yorker* has had a golden age, it was the decade preceding Pearl Harbor—a time in its history when it was poised gracefully between the formless and sometimes brittle levity that came before and the unquestionably meritorious, occasionally splendid, but frequently solemn, ponderous, self-important, or dull magazine that stretched from the Second World War on up to the 1980s" (56).

31. The idea of metropolitan provincialism in the *New Yorker* comes from Fillmore Hyde. He wrote about it for *Time* magazine (April 26, 1937). Allegedly, Ross saw it and hired him.

32. New York Public Library, Manuscripts and Archives Division, *New Yorker* Records (1924–1984), box 222, Louise Bogan folder, October 23, 1935.

33. Ibid., October 28, 1935.

34. New York Public Library, Manuscripts and Archives Division, *New Yorker* Records (1924–1984), box 964, Katharine S. White Notes on Writing, 1938–1941.

35. Katharine White to Corey Ford, September 23, 1967, Katharine

Sergeant White Papers, Special Collections Department, Bryn Mawr College Library, box 4, folder 9.

36. According to Katharine, she was advised not to take the job: "Before applying at The New Yorker, I asked the advice of Henry Seidel Canby, then editor of the Saturday Review of Literature. He said that The New Yorker was nothing and that I would make a great mistake to join it because he thought it would never amount to anything. I listened to him and then went back and immediately applied for the job" (qtd. in Davis, Onward and Upward 55).

37. It likely would have irked Katharine to no end to find two errors in the first line of her obituary: first, the misspelling of her name, and second a typo, "rceative" for "creative."

38. Katharine White to Corey Ford, September 23, 1967, Katharine Sergeant White Papers, Special Collections Department, Bryn Mawr College Library, box 4, folder 9.

39. University of Illinois Library, Maxwell Collection, box 013-009a, June 7, 1979.

40. Katharine's first anthology project was a coedited volume on humor, not a New Yorker sponsored project, although many of the writers were contributors. Subsequently Katharine worked on, and sometimes initiated, a series of anthologies, including The New Yorker Book of Verse (1935), Short Stories from The New Yorker (1940), and The New Yorker Book of War Pieces (1947). Such anthologies were part and parcel of middlebrow publishing culture and competed with other "what to read" projects—Reader's Digest, Book-of-the-Month Club, Best Short Stories, and so on.

41. New York Public Library, Manuscripts and Archives Division, New Yorker Records (1924–1984), box 38, Editorial: Katharine S. White, 1941–1945.

42. Ibid.

43. Ibid.

44. New York Public Library, Manuscripts and Archives Division, New Yorker Records (1924–1984), box 512, Frances Gray Patton folder, January 5, 1952.

45. Ibid.

46. Ibid., January 10, 1952.

47. Ibid.

48. Ibid.

49. Ibid.

50. Ibid.

Chapter Two. "The Precision of Knives," or More Than Just Commas

1. Yagoda adds one missing from Grant's list, Vanity Fair, "left out, perhaps, because it was just too obvious to mention" (36).

2. New York Public Library, Manuscripts and Archives Division, New Yorker Records (1924–1984), box 38, Editorial: Katharine S. White, 1946–

1947, November 4, 1947. At *Good Housekeeping*, *McCall's*, and *Cosmopolitan*, Herbert R. Mayes was editing: "If a story contained incorrect references or dates or was minus diacritical marks, we held it our obligation, for the author's sake and our readers', to make obvious corrections. Editorial excellence has been called the art of noninterference, but if we thought a story unreasonably long and the need to make cuts vital, we made those cuts, usually with the permission of the author" (155–56).

3. By the 1950s, publishing in the *New Yorker* meant something to young writers; it was, as Langdon Hammer explains, a concrete *image* of authorial worth (78).

4. New York Public Library, Manuscripts and Archives Division, *New Yorker* Records (1924–1984), box 415, Applicants A–Z, July 23, 1945. For tributes to Gould, see Scott; Klinkenborg; Wade; and M. Clark.

5. On May 16, 1945, Katharine White writes to recommend to another publication Jean Batchelor, a *New Yorker* writer who is "anxious to get into editing and needs a job at once." White explains that the *New Yorker* "is not taking on women now in an editorial capacity because, as you can realize, we are having to hold any openings for the men we must take back when they return from war" (New York Public Library, Manuscripts and Archives Division, *New Yorker* Records [1924–1984], box 415, Jean Batchelor, 1945). In a letter to a young woman who applies for an editorial position, one staff member writes back, "The *New Yorker* is a highly specialized activity and hardly a place to start or learn magazine work. It is a performance with some other publication that attracts our attention.... About forty members of our staff went into uniform, and they are beginning to return and they, of course, have priority to fill staff vacancies. Such vacancies could not be filled by a beginner. We are sorry to have to write you such a blunt letter, but we feel it would be unfair to you if we didn't state the situation clearly" (New York Public Library, Manuscripts and Archives Division, *New Yorker* Records [1924–1984], box 415, Applicants A–Z, September 10, 1945). And again, another letter on August 21, 1945, was sent to a man serving abroad: "Trouble is, we've got to think first about the ex-members of our staff who have been in uniform and are expected to arrive back soon. Some of them have already arrived. Others are in hospitals and anxious to get back to us. We have about forty such men all together" (New York Public Library, Manuscripts and Archives Division, *New Yorker* Records [1924–1984], box 415, Applicants A–Z, 1945).

6. Many applicants to the *New Yorker* affected the tone of smartness, usually unevenly or overdone. Compare the "smart" tone of Gould's letter to these two (unsuccessful) candidates. The two reproduced here, from the New York Public Library, Manuscripts and Archives Division, *New Yorker* Records (1924–1984), box 415, Applicants A–Z, 1945, are by young women, but young men's applications exhibited the same literary offenses and shared the same fate:

Dear Sir:

Please give me a job. Audacious as my writing you may see, I do so because I do not believe in starting at the bottom. I want to work at the kind of job I really want while I am still young enough to cherish some illusions and wear a size eleven. For over ten months I have been Getting Experience on the local paper. This has meant wearing my feet and fingers to the bone.

I write obituaries until my face turns a saffron hue. I count undertakers among my friends. When I write of servicemen, they are the casualties. This is no life for a growing girl.

Honestly, I do not write badly.

My education was curtailed when I left the University of Michigan my Junior year; I will not graduate next June. My learning consists of a fund of useless information. I was a liberal arts major. However, I did work on the staff of the university magazine, patterned, I believe, after the New Yorker.

Isn't there some sort of position which I might occupy? I guarantee that I shall learn quickly and easily. If, after a probationary period of your own naming, I do not qualify, I shall return sadder, yet wider, to Springfield.

Dear Sir:

I am that dream girl sent straight from heaven to be your human factor and to bring order out of the confusion that has been steadily mounting since 1925. [She footnotes this: "Funny Coincidence Department—1925 is the year of my birth."]

Why get an efficiency expert when I can compose the five digits that make up 6,000 with more finesse. Hell, I can type too.

I have written and chased for The News one day a week for nearly a year but if you hold that against me you can jolly well get someone else to write your 6,000's,

THE HUMAN FACTOR [her name is at the top]

P.S. I am also durable and lasting (except on Friday nights).

7. Wolfe has since reprinted the piece in his national bestseller *Hooking Up*, and this is what the in-text citations refer to.

8. In contrast, William Styron took the opportunity to defend Wolfe: "I was quite amused to read in *Newsweek* that William Shawn feels that Tom Wolfe's brilliant study of himself and *The New Yorker* 'puts the *Herald Tribune* right down in the gutter …' I have become fairly resilient over the years in regard to criticism, but since the only real whiff of the gutter was in a review of one of my books in the pages of *The New Yorker*, I found Shawn's cry of Foul woefully lacking in pathos" (qtd. in Wolfe 289). Styron concludes his letter by citing scripture.

9. To put it mildly, the *New Yorker* felt the sting. Renata Adler de-

scribes it as one of the "seven crises" (84) to hit the magazine: "Many members of The New Yorker staff, Mr. Shawn in particular, acted, for the first time in my experience, but certainly not the last, so foolishly as virtually to foreclose any outcome but the one they were trying to ward off.... The story, of Wolfe's piece and The New Yorker's reaction to it, was taken up by other publications. Mr Wolfe appeared on a lot of talk shows" (85–86). Clippings of the various news stories are preserved in a thick file in the New Yorker archives at the New York Public Library.

10. By most accounts, the debate over "originality" begins in part with the publication in 1759 of Edward Young's Conjectures on Original Composition. Although Young's Conjectures is often cited as one of the earliest works equating literariness with originality, the argument is not quite so absolute. Young still advises "imitation" of older works as a model, "for nothing Original can rise, nothing immortal can ripen, in any other sun" (251), but challenges writers not to become copies of the ancients but instead to compose their own original morality, which he judged a key trait of literariness. In the nineteenth and twentieth centuries, the equating of art with originality becomes naturalized, buttressed by tightening definitions of plagiarism and more stringent copyright laws. Eldred and Mortensen's chapter 3 presents a summary of this history. In the field of writing studies, LeFevre argues an alternative.

11. In 1943, Miller published In the Days of Thy Youth to little notice. Twins were a recurrent theme in Miller's work, attributable to the fact that she herself had lost a twin sister: "for years after that, Mary Miller recalled years later, her life was 'blotted out—everything became dim, unreal, artificial.'" This tragedy, however, was one of several early in Miller's life. Miller, her twin sister, older sister, and two brothers were orphaned when Miller was just four years old. She is reared first by her grandmother, then by an aunt, and finally by a governess ("Mary Britton Miller Dies at 91; Wrote Novels as 'Isabel Bolton,'" New York Times, April 4, 1975).

12. Her second novel, The Christmas Tree (1949) was written in a similar style. The Time magazine reviewer made much of the shift in style: "Author Bolton has much to say. She says it in a style which Mary Britton Miller should have tried sooner," a veiled reference to the author's age ("Mother Danforth's Story" 106).

13. Anita Brookner, however, finds the appraisals of Isabel Bolton by Wilson and Trilling (and presumably Grumbach) "overheated": "Her writing strikes one as exactly halfway between professional and amateur, and, given the period in which these novels are set, roughly those meager years following the war, they seem escapist, moneyed, almost frivolous." Two years earlier, in a review of Bolton's New York Mosaic, Lisa Michaels had come to just the opposite opinion: "She describes things

as 'gay' or 'splendid.' But she is by no means frivolous. She possesses a ferocious judgment."

14. New York Public Library, Manuscripts and Archives Division, *New Yorker* Records (1924–1984), box 444, Isabel Bolton (Mary Britton Miller) folder, May 16, 1947.

15. Ibid.

16. New York Public Library, Manuscripts and Archives Division, *New Yorker* Records (1924–1984), box 444, Isabel Bolton (Mary Britton Miller) folder, 1947.

17. Ibid.	25. Ibid.
18. Ibid.	26. Ibid.
19. Ibid.	27. Ibid., August 5, 1947.
20. Ibid.	28. Ibid.
21. Ibid., July 31, 1947.	29. Ibid.
22. Ibid.	30. Ibid.
23. Ibid.	31. Ibid.
24. Ibid.	32. Ibid., February 1951.

33. New York Public Library, Manuscripts and Archives Division, *New Yorker* Records (1924–1984), box 503, Isabel Bolton (Mary Britton Miller) folder, March 30, 1951.

34. Ibid., September 19, 1951.

35. Ibid.

36. Ibid., November 9, 1951.

37. Ibid., November, 15 1951.

38. New York Public Library, Manuscripts and Archives Division, *New Yorker* Records (1924–1984), box 710, Isabel Bolton (Mary Britton Miller) folder, April 21, 1952.

39. New York Public Library, Manuscripts and Archives Division, *New Yorker* Records (1924–1984), box 1291, Legal folder, May 12, 1952.

40. New York Public Library, Manuscripts and Archives Division, *New Yorker* Records (1924–1984), box 710, Isabel Bolton (Mary Britton Miller) folder, September 1, 1952.

41. Ibid., December 15, 1952.

42. New York Public Library, Manuscripts and Archives Division, *New Yorker* Records (1924–1984), box 718, Isabel Bolton (Mary Britton Miller) folder, November 9, 1953.

43. There's a study on physical disability and writing ability waiting in these archives. In addition to Bolton and Thurber, Ved Mehta provides precise accounts of how he, as a blind person, wrote and edited his manuscripts. The *Oberlin Alumni Magazine* reports on how Eleanor Gould managed her sudden deafness and on her relationship with Mehta: "She has worked on all twenty of the books by the blind Indian writer Ved Mehta, even though since she became deaf he and she have been able to communicate only through a third person" (M. Clark).

44. Mr. Page's wife is behind this enforced bonding: "Mr. Page suppressed an oath.... at last, he glimpsed the core of his wife's strategy. Her summer plans had been laid, with feminine cunning, toward only one end—to leave him alone with Alex" (Patton, "As Man to Man" 30).

45. New York Public Library, Manuscripts and Archives Division, *New Yorker* Records (1924–1984), box 755, Frances Gray Patton folder, June 17, 1957.

46. Ibid., June 24, 1957.

47. This correspondence shows both the promise and limitations of the *New Yorker* archive, with its amazing 800-page long finding guide. Most of the speculative changes were made on the manuscript itself, which is not part of the archive, although a lightly copyedited final version survives.

48. New York Public Library, Manuscripts and Archives Division, *New Yorker* Records (1924–1984), box 755, Frances Gray Patton folder, June 24, 1957. Herbert Mayes was less conflicted on the point of editorial changes as merely suggestions: "Not often, but sometimes," he corrected, changes are made "without permission, because editors and readers have rights too" (155–56).

49. New York Public Library, Manuscripts and Archives Division, *New Yorker* Records (1924–1984), box 755, Frances Gray Patton folder, June 24, 1957.

50. Ibid., July 11, 1957.

51. Ibid.

52. Ibid.

53. Ibid.

54. Ibid., September 9, 1957. In the next chapter, I will focus on why representations of gender have become such a concern for the editors, but here, I want to focus on the nature of the substantive revisions.

55. Ibid., July 11, 1957.

56. Katharine White to Frances Gray Patton, August 30, 1957, Katharine Sergeant White Papers, Special Collections Department, Bryn Mawr College Library, box 9, folder 12.

57. New York Public Library, Manuscripts and Archives Division, *New Yorker* Records (1924–1984), box 755, Frances Gray Patton folder, September 9, 1957

58. Ibid., July 13, 1957.

59. Ibid., September 9, 1957.

60. New York Public Library, Manuscripts and Archives Division, *New Yorker* Records (1924–1984), box 771, Frances Gray Patton folder, June 30, 1959.

61. New York Public Library, Manuscripts and Archives Division, *New Yorker* Records (1924–1984), box 38, Editorial: Katharine S. White, 1946–1947, November 4, 1947. See also a memo to White from Ross on

September 12, 1947: "Mr. Lobrano tells me that O'Hara is planning to write a letter to the *Saturday Evening Post* about the Maloney piece having what seems to be a good idea for an approach. Mr. Lobrano also says that you detected thirty errors in the Maloney piece and said you could find more. I suggest you send in a list of the errors if you want, and we will give them to O'Hara" (New York Public Library, Manuscripts and Archives Division, *New Yorker* Records [1924–1984], box 38, Editorial: Katharine S. White, 1946–1947).

62. New York Public Library, Manuscripts and Archives Division, *New Yorker* Records (1924–1984), box 38, Editorial: Katharine S. White, 1946–1947, November 4, 1947. More examples from the November 4th memo: "Diana Trilling seems to me to have talked about our over-editing in a review a year or two ago. One review of Weidman's short story book this fall said we had had a bad influence on his style and subject matter (unjust remark of course)."

63. Ibid.   66. Ibid.

64. Ibid.   67. Ibid.

65. Ibid.   68. Ibid.

69. New York Public Library, Manuscripts and Archives Division, *New Yorker* Records (1924–1984), box 470, Christine Weston folder, January 9, 1948.

70. For a nuanced and sustained critique, see S. Clark.

Chapter Three. *Mademoiselle*, the *New Yorker*, and Other Women's Magazines

1. Women were also influential editors of little magazines. See Marek.

2. For example, in 1938, William Maxwell sent word that the editors were rejecting Langston Hughes's poem "Madrid—1937" on the grounds that its tone was much too solemn for the *New Yorker*. A memo to Hughes's agent, Max Lieber, on December 8, 1938 reiterates that the problem rests not just in Hughes's tone but also in his choice of subject matter. Hughes would fit, it seems, if he were to submit a particular type of story with a particular tone and topic. Maxwell suggested to Lieber that Hughes should try something a bit more light-hearted, perhaps something that would capture the perceptions of white people as seen through the eyes of black people, which Maxwell knew that Hughes was very capable of producing with great effect (New York Public Library, Manuscripts and Archives Division, *New Yorker* Records [1924–1984], box 479, Max Lieber folder, December 8, 1938). Hughes's literary career did not contract in this way, but instead it unfolded into a wide range of artistic expression.

3. New York Public Library, Manuscripts and Archives Division, *New*

Yorker Records (1924–1984), box 439, Russell and Volkening folder, December 30, 1946. See also Kreyling.

4. Gus Lobrano tries to reassure her, writing the whole problem off as a bit of sloppy handwriting: "I should have written before this to reassure you about those notations on the proof which you misinterpreted.... That word which appeared here and there in the margins wasn't 'bad.' It was 'had.' So you see we weren't being tersely and nastily critical, but rather were merely suggesting that in several instances the pluperfect tense might be better than the simple past tense. I hope this clear things, including our character, up" (New York Public Library, Manuscripts and Archives Division, New Yorker Records [1924–1984], box 360, Maxim Lieber, December 29, 1941).

5. In addition to Gerald Clarke's biography of Capote and Michael Kreyling's work on Welty, see Subramanian; Tippins; and Rowland. Vogue published nonfiction by McCullers in 1940 and 1941, all on war themes.

6. Stanford University Libraries, Department of Special Collections, William Saroyan Papers, Mo870, box 43, folder 6, letter from George Davis to William Saroyan, April 5, 1939.

7. Aswell accepts one of Saroyan's better stories, "Knife-Like, Flower-Like, Like Nothing at All in the World," with just this revision: "May I cut a little from the first page? All the readers found the opening confusing, and we find that a few judicious cuts plus a substitution here and there of 'Pete' for 'him,' clears it up completely" (Stanford University Libraries, Department of Special Collections, William Saroyan Papers, Mo870, box 43, folder 6, letter from Mary Louise Aswell to William Saroyan, May 28, 1942). By all accounts, Aswell was an accomplished editor; there is, however, no archive of her work that I am aware of. That story can only be found in collections of authors with whom she worked. In the Saroyan archive, I could find only this letter. For more on archival limitations, see the "Afterword" to this book.

8. For Saroyan's correspondence related to the New Yorker, see Stanford University Libraries, Department of Special Collections, William Saroyan Papers, Mo870, box 75, New Yorker folders. Saroyan's troubles with Esquire are documented in the correspondence with Harold Matson who served for a time as his literary agent (Stanford University Libraries, Department of Special Collections, William Saroyan Papers, Mo870, box 117, Ann Watkins folder). His frank assessment of that magazine is outlined in a letter to Whit Burnett of Story magazine: "My brother brought home a copy of the February Esquire last night, and I have been looking at it. I do not believe it is possible to escape this fact: the magazine is absolutely puerile, rankly fake. I know it will be a success, and I am sending stories to the editor, but the magazine smells: all that rotten wealth implied, and the emphasis on well-pressed pants, etc. I would like to be able to write a good story for a good magazine for a hundred

dollars; but when that is out of the question, I will try to write down to a certain level sensibility, merely in the hope of getting the cash … and if I don't get the cash, then for a week, a month, sometimes for a year, sometimes two years, I go around kicking myself where I ought to be kicked. But I am trying. I want the cash. I wrote a story this morning for *Esquire*, for the slick paper, and the proximity of insipid wash drawings of female bare rumps, etc. (The male magazine. That's a pretty nice gag.) Writing the story, I felt lousy, absolutely like a whore" (Stanford University Libraries, Department of Special Collections, William Saroyan Papers, Mo870, box 109).

9. New York Public Library, Manuscripts and Archives Division, *New Yorker* Records (1924–1984), box 38, Editorial: Katharine S. White, 1941–1945, circa July 6, 1943.

10. Ibid.

11. The archives show that the *New Yorker* had for some years been trying to get a patent or copyright on various print features of the magazine. *Vogue* similarly was creating tables of content that reflected the kind of witty quirkiness that became signature *New Yorker*, perhaps because, as Penelope Rowlands points out, people responsible for makeup and design moved back and forth between publications with some frequency (115).

12. New York Public Library, Manuscripts and Archives Division, *New Yorker* Records (1924–1984), box 220, Applications A–G folder, April 24, 1935.

13. Women of color are featured only in profiles about embassy work or work with the United Nations, both of which were heavily promoted by the publication.

14. See McCracken; and Corey.

15. See Chauncey's explication of changing definitions of homosexuality (13). Although Chauncey focuses on working-class gay subcultures, he speaks generally about an urban migration: "Some men were even able to use their gay contacts to find jobs, particularly in those occupations in which many gay men worked or that tolerated a relative degree of openness on the part of their gay workers" (275).

16. Gill is not the most reliable narrator—the inaccuracies in *Here at The New Yorker* were much noted in reviews—and so it's difficult to subscribe too much to his judgments, particularly when he assumes, in one particularly outrageous instance, that men who are "quiet and orderly nest-builders … took pleasure in being roared at and bullied and pushed to their limits" (30). Gill is critical of Ross's stance toward gay men—"He was a throwback and not always an appealing one" (29)—but Gill admits that discussing the subject makes him "feel a bit edgy" (30). He does, however, recognize (at least superficially) the way in which gay men contributed to the *New Yorker*'s editorial staff and informed

the magazine's aesthetics. Eustace Tilly, the aesthete on the *New Yorker* masthead, was clearly modeled after men-about-town. The comings and goings of men-about-town were often reported, particularly by Wolcott Gibbs, so much so that *Mirror* columnist Walter Winchell "suggested that the column should be called not 'This New York' but 'Jerome Never Looked Lovelier'" (B. Gill 121–22).

17. For more on images of womanly and manly journalism as applied to the *New Yorker*, see Travis, who notes a change in journalism toward agonism and a corresponding lack of change in the *New Yorker* stance: "To mainstream critics, *The New Yorker*'s inability adequately to address the contemporary scene reflected a stylistic timidity coded as feminine" (258). Oddly enough, it was the manly Ross who was much less willing to take on the political issues of the day.

18. Not everyone, of course, told this story. Brendan Gill's *Here at The New Yorker*, often maligned for its "bitchy" tone and inaccuracies, made Shawn the hero, albeit a hero who doesn't know when to quit. At least one reviewer found this an attractive narrative: "I like Shawn as a hero. He changed The New Yorker from a humor magazine into a magazine with humor, from a smarty-pants parish tipsheet that dreamed its way through the Thirties as though there was no Depression and no Fascism, into a journal that altered our experience instead of just posturing in front of it. . . . Wolfe's articles on *The New Yorker* in 1965 were hyperthyroid twaddle . . . a sniper attack by squirt gun" (Leonard BR1). Malcolm Cowley's assessment of the old *New Yorker* is that it was "nostalgia mixed with condescension."

19. "Among the organizing principles of this community were intellectual acumen and good taste," which translated into, as Trysh Travis describes, a community of editors, writers, and readers, united by "a sense of emotional connectedness, of mutual respect and trust, and love" (253). Travis addresses this dynamic: "given what we know about the nature of for-profit twentieth-century magazines and their relationships with their anxious middle-class readers, can we ever see [readers'] 'love' for *The New Yorker* as anything other than a compensatory fantasy meant to gloss over or to deny the realities of producer-consumer relationships within the modern culture industry? Can we ever see Mr. Shawn's 'love' for the magazines and its readers as more than a calculated strategy to increase reader loyalty by flattering his audience's craving for cultural distinction?" (254). My own sense is that "calculated strategy" goes too far. Those of us who work in institutions—and who love our work—regularly live the tension between idealistic goals and institutional demands.

20. Numerous sources describe the split between the business and editorial sides of the magazine, see, most notably, Kramer; Kunkel. See also Travis's discussion, including text of memos by Ross underscoring the fundamental principles of this division (257). While Ross felt that it

was "readers from the outside" who might notice any transgressions, it is likely that readers "read" or consumed the magazine differently, selectively taking in both content and ads. Mary Corey's study is the most sustained analysis of the advertising content of the *New Yorker*.

21. Katharine White to Patricia Maxwell, August 7, 1974, Katharine Sergeant White Papers, Special Collections Department, Bryn Mawr College Library, box 7, folder 7.

22. New York Public Library, Manuscripts and Archives Division, *New Yorker* Records (1924–1984), box 17, Lois Long folder, April 21, 1934.

23. New York Public Library, Manuscripts and Archives Division, *New Yorker* Records (1924–1984), box 3, folder 13, March 1, 1927.

24. New York Public Library, Manuscripts and Archives Division, *New Yorker* Records (1924–1984), box 9, Lois Long folder, 1931.

25. Ibid.

26. Likely *Mademoiselle* too, although Long doesn't specifically mention this publication. See New York Public Library, Manuscripts and Archives Division, *New Yorker* Records (1924–1984), box 394, folder 16, letter of July 28, 1943.

27. Grant's essay "Confession of a Feminist," was published in the *American Mercury* in 1943.

28. The question of women's contributions to the *New Yorker* lingers: *MobyLives* editor and publisher Dennis Loy Johnson, a short story writer and graduate of the Iowa Fiction Workshop, directs a new barb at the staid, embattled *New Yorker*. Surveying the magazine's contents for 2002, he discovers that "the overwhelming majority of *The New Yorker* magazine's writers are men," and in the extreme, "there have even been issues of *The New Yorker* this year where the magazine's table of contents featured no women at all, or where the only contribution by a woman was a single poem" (D. Johnson). The *New Yorker* responded by recalling the long history of women's presence on the magazine. What's clear from this (and from the *New Yorker*'s response to *MobyLives*) is that the *New Yorker*'s "'womanly' influences" is written into and out of the magazine's history, as needed to sustain its reputation.

Conclusion: Lady Editors, Katharine White, and the Embodiment of Style

1. For academic treatment of fashion, see Crane; F. Davis; as well as the relatively new journal *Fashion Theory: The Journal of Dress, Body, & Culture*.

2. See Entwistle, "Fashioning the Career Woman."

3. Linda Davis details the "brand" of editorial letters that Katharine White "invented"— highly personal, "with its mixture of business and news about Katharine's private life" (108).

4. Katharine White to Brendan Gill, Katharine Sergeant White Papers, Special Collections Department, Bryn Mawr College Library, January 17, 1972. Brendan Gill had supplied a manuscript copy of an obituary on John O'Hara, to be published in the *Century Yearbook*.

5. Roger Angell's essay "Dry Martini" is one of the best essay portraits drawn of the cocktail shaker lifestyle, certainly more pleasurable and sophisticated than our own fast-food, transfat culture, but with disturbing physical and mental health implications nonetheless.

6. University of Illinois Library, Maxwell Collection, box 013–009a, E. B. White to Bill Maxwell, August 12, 1977.

7. Ibid.

8. Ibid.

9. Ibid.

10. Quotes found in her notes on her edition of Dorothy Parker's *After Such Pleasures*, which she donated to Bryn Mawr Library.

11. E. B. White to James Tanis, August 31, 1977, Katharine Sergeant White Papers, Special Collections Department, Bryn Mawr College Library, box 31, folder 1–6.

12. Frank Sullivan to Katharine White, October 25, 1957, Katharine Sergeant White Papers, Special Collections Department, Bryn Mawr College Library, box 12, folder 3.

13. E. B. White to James Tanis, August 31, 1977, Katharine Sergeant White Papers, Special Collections Department, Bryn Mawr College Library, box 31, folder 1–6.

14. Katharine White to James Tanis, July 21, 1975, Katharine Sergeant White Papers, Special Collections Department, Bryn Mawr College Library, box 31, folder 1–6.

Afterword: Katharine White's Bequest, or Ruminations on an Archive

1. Katharine White to Jean Stafford, at that time Mrs. A. J. Liebling, August 20, 1968, Katharine Sergeant White Papers, Special Collections Department, Bryn Mawr College Library, box 11, folder 1–8. The volume, *Onward and Upward in the Garden*, was published posthumously in 1979 by Farrar, Strauss, Giroux and reviewed sentimentally.

2. Katharine White to Katherine McBride, office of the president, April 3, 1970, Katharine Sergeant White Papers, Special Collections Department, Bryn Mawr College Library, box 30, folder 9.

3. Katharine White to Jean Stafford, at that time Mrs. A. J. Liebling, August 20, 1968, Katharine Sergeant White Papers, Special Collections Department, Bryn Mawr College Library, box 11, folder 1–8.

4. Katharine White to Nadine Gordimer, January 21, 1957, Katharine Sergeant White Papers, Special Collections Department, Bryn Mawr College Library, box 4, folder 17–18.

5. Elsewhere, Katharine insisted on the monetary value her work added to the collection. In a letter to President Harris Wofford, Bryn Mawr College, received August 3, 1974, she writes "I was sorry to see that in the report to the Class of 1914 about it reunion they had included an estimated value of the collection. The value is more than that, actually, because it was an appraisal of everything not written by me and I suppose what few letters of mine are in there, and my comments, add a little more to the value" (Katharine Sergeant White Papers, Special Collections Department, Bryn Mawr College Library, box 31, folder 9).

6. Katharine White to Janet Agnew (librarian at Bryn Mawr College), May 23, 1959, Katharine Sergeant White Papers, Special Collections Department, Bryn Mawr College Library, box 30, folder 1.

7. Ibid.

8. Katharine White to James Tanis, February 23, 1974, Katharine Sergeant White Papers, Special Collections Department, Bryn Mawr College Library, box 31, folder 1–6. Characteristically White corrects what may be perceived as a slight against her alma mater: "Of course we were allowed to write essays on American writers if we cared to. Winifred Goodale won the Essay Prize in my class for her essay on Emerson. Nonetheless I am grateful for what I got out of majoring in English at Bryn Mawr."

9. Katharine White to James Tanis, April 20, 1974, Katharine Sergeant White Papers, Special Collections Department, Bryn Mawr College Library, box 31, folder 1–6.

10. Ibid.

11. Katharine White to Brendan Gill, January 17, 1972, Katharine Sergeant White Papers, Special Collections Department, Bryn Mawr College Library, box 4, folder 15.

12. Katharine White likely to James Tanis, April 20, 1971, Katharine Sergeant White Papers, Special Collections Department, Bryn Mawr College Library, box 31, folder 1–6. Katharine finally was not comfortable criticizing Shawn: "Possibly, in fairness to Bill Shawn, it should be said that he has been just too overworked to bother with this side matter. Unlike Ross, he tends not to delegate work but to try to do it all himself and it's a marvel how much he does do. Ross, for instance, delighted in editing 'The Talk of the Town' but he left the rest of the manuscript editing, with certain exceptions like Rebecca West, entirely to others."

13. Katharine White to Brendan Gill, January 17, 1972, Katharine Sergeant White Papers, Special Collections Department, Bryn Mawr College Library, box 4, folder 15,

14. Katharine White to James Tanis, April 20, 1974, Katharine Sergeant White Papers, Special Collections Department, Bryn Mawr College Library, box 31, folder 1–6.

15. Ibid.

16. Katharine White to James Tanis, July 31, 1972, Katharine Ser-

geant White Papers, Special Collections Department, Bryn Mawr College Library, box 31, folder 1–6.

17. Katharine White to George Healey, August 17, 1964, Katharine Sergeant White Papers, Special Collections Department, Bryn Mawr College Library, box 29, folder 9.

18. Katharine White to Katherine McBride, April 3, 1970, Katharine Sergeant White Papers, Special Collections Department, Bryn Mawr College Library, box 30, folder 9.

19. Katharine White to Brendan Gill, January 17, 1972, Katharine Sergeant White Papers, Special Collections Department, Bryn Mawr College Library, box 4, folder 15.

20. Ibid.

21. Katharine White to James Tanis, April 20, 1973, Katharine Sergeant White Papers, Special Collections Department, Bryn Mawr College Library, box 31, folder 1–6.

22. E. B. White to Katherine McBride, April 1, 1970, Katharine Sergeant White Papers, Special Collections Department, Bryn Mawr College Library, box 30, folder 9.

23. Katharine White to Katherine McBride, April 3, 1970, Katharine Sergeant White Papers, Bryn Mawr College Library, box 30, folder 9.

24. E. B. White to James Tanis, April 16, 1970, Katharine Sergeant White Papers, Special Collections Department, Bryn Mawr College Library, box 31, folder 1–6.

25. Katharine White to James Tanis, May 1, 1970, Katharine Sergeant White Papers, Special Collections Department, Bryn Mawr College Library, box 31, folder 1–6.

26. Katharine White to James Tanis, August 18, 1972, Katharine Sergeant White Papers, Special Collections Department, Bryn Mawr College Library, box 31, folder 1–6.

27. Katharine White to James Tanis, May 26, 1975, Katharine Sergeant White Papers, Special Collections Department, Bryn Mawr College Library, box 31, folder 1–6.

28. Ibid.

29. Katharine White to Josephine Gibbs, April 30, 1973, Katharine Sergeant White Papers, Special Collections Department, Bryn Mawr College Library, box 31, folder 1–6.

30. Katharine White to Brendan Gill, January 17, 1972, Katharine Sergeant White Papers, Special Collections Department, Bryn Mawr College Library, box 4, folder 15.

31. Katharine White to Katherine McBride, April 3, 1970, Katharine Sergeant White Papers, Special Collections Department, Bryn Mawr College Library, box 30, folder 9.

32. University of Illinois Library, Maxwell Collection, box 013–009a, E. B. White to Bill Maxwell, June 7, 1979.

33. Katharine White to James Tanis, May 26, 1975, Katharine Sergeant White Papers, Special Collections Department, Bryn Mawr College Library, box 31, folder 1–6.

34. Ibid.

35. Ibid.

36. The magazine had stopped Gill from using the signature Eustace Tilley or typeface on his cover and had compelled him to get releases from contributors. Katharine White lamented that the contributors signed before they saw the entire the book. Had they known what was in it, she implies, they would not have granted their permission.

37. University of Illinois Library, Maxwell Collection, box 013–009a, E. B. White to Bill Maxwell, June 7, 1979.

38. Ibid.

39. Archives are still thinner in the case of African American women's magazines and other less widely circulated and shorter-lived publications. Noliwe M. Rooks describes her experience tracking archives for the early twentieth-century *Woman's Voice*:

> Though *Woman's Voice* was published for fifteen years, initially I could find no copies of the publication, or indeed, mention of its existence outside of the Walker Archives. None of the bibliographies generally counted on to list periodical holdings by research libraries mentioned it. No one on the staff at the Library of Congress had ever heard of it, nor could the staff find any citations for it in their holdings. None of the scholarly works covering the African American press and its history in the United States noted its existence. No newspapers or periodicals published in Philadelphia or on the East Coast reviewed it. . . . I will save you the details of the my search except to say that when African American women's magazines from the nineteenth century through the 1950s are mentioned, it is rare to find a list of libraries in possession of the materials. One is more likely to find . . . notes or asides saying that the magazines themselves are either lost, missing or of such minor importance that their absence is negligible. (2–3)

40. See Rowlands; Tippins; and Clarke.

41. See Subramanian; Snow; and Tippins.

WORKS CITED

Adams, Katherine H. *A Group of Their Own: College Writing Courses and American Women Writers, 1880–1940.* Albany: SUNY, 2001.

———. *Progressive Politics and the Training of America's Persuaders.* Mahwah, NJ: Erlbaum, 1999.

Adler, Renata. *Gone: The Last Days of The New Yorker.* New York: Simon and Schuster, 2001.

Alexander, Paul. *Rough Magic: A Biography of Sylvia Plath.* New York: Viking, 1991.

Alpern, Sara. *Freda Kirchwey: A Woman of the Nation.* Cambridge: Harvard University Press, 1987.

Angell, Roger. "Andy." *NewYorker.com,* February 14, 2005. http://www .newyorker.com/archive/2005/02/14/050214fa_fact.

———. "Dry Martini." *New Yorker,* August 19, 2002.

Atwood, Margaret. "Nostalgia: A Stitch in Time." *Vogue,* December 2002.

Bashford, Alison, and Carolyn Strange. "Public Pedagogy: Sex Education and Mass Communication in the Mid-Twentieth Century." *Journal of the History of Sexuality* 13, no. 1 (2004): 71–99.

Baxandall, Rosalyn, and Linda Perlman Gordon. *America's Working Women: A Documentary History, 1600 to Present.* Rev. ed. New York: W. W. Norton, 1995.

Berg, A. Scott. *Max Perkins: Editor of Genius.* 1978. New York: Berkley Trade, 2008.

Biele, Joelle, ed. *Elizabeth Bishop and The New Yorker: The Complete Correspondence.* New York: Farrar, Straus and Giroux, 2011.

Bloom, Jonathan. "V. S. Pritchett's Ministering Angell." *Sewanee Review* 112, no. 2 (2004): 212–39.

Bok, Edward. *The Americanization of Edward Bok: The Autobiography of a Dutch Boy Fifty Years After.* New York: Charles Scribner's Sons, 1920.

Bolonik, Kera. "How Low Can They Go." *Salon.com,* December 10, 2001. http://www.salon.com/life/style/2001/12/10/women_s_mags.

Bolton, Isabel [Mary Britton Miller]. "Ruth and Irma." *New Yorker,* July 26, 1947.

Brandon, Henry. "A Conversation with James Thurber: 'Everybody Is Getting Very Serious.'" *New Republic*, May 26, 1958.

Brandt, Deborah. *Literacy in American Lives*. Cambridge: Cambridge University Press, 2001.

———. "Remembering Writing, Remembering Reading." *CCC* 45, no. 4 (1994): 459–79.

Brookner, Anita. "Days of Elegance." *Spectator*, January 16, 1999.

Brownmiller, Susan. *In Our Time: Memoir of a Revolution*. New York: Delta/Random House, 1999.

———. "In Our Time." *Susanbrownmiller.com*. http://www.susanbrownmiller.com/susanbrownmiller/html/in_our_time.html.

Buckley, Tom. "At *New Yorker*, Fete With a Difference." *New York Times*, February 22, 1975.

Burroway, Janet. "I Didn't Know Sylvia Plath." *Embalming Mom: Essays in Life*. Iowa City: University of Iowa Press, 2002.

Caserio, Robert L. "Queer Passions, Queer Citizenship: Some Novels about the State of the American Nation, 1946–1954." *Modern Fiction Studies* 43, no. 1 (1997): 170–205.

Chase, Edna Woolman, and Ilka Chase. *Always in Vogue*. New York: Doubleday, 1954.

Chauncey, George. *Gay New York: Gender, Urban Culture, and the Making of the Gay Male World 1890–1940*. New York: Basic Books, 1994.

Clark, Mavis. "Miss Eleanor Gould '38, Grammarian Extraordinaire, Holds the Line at *The New Yorker*." *Oberlin Alumni Magazine*. http://www.oberlin.edu/alummag/oampast/oam_spring98/gould.html.

Clark, Suzanne. *Sentimental Modernism: Women Writers and the Revolution of the Word*. Bloomington: Indiana University Press, 1991.

Clarke, Gerald. *Capote: A Biography*. New York: Simon and Schuster, 1988.

Coontz, Stephanie. *The Way We Never Were: American Families and the Nostalgia Trap*. 1992. New York: Basic, 2000.

Corey, Mary. *The World Through a Monocle: The New Yorker at Midcentury*. Cambridge: Harvard University Press, 1999.

Crane, Diana. *Fashion and Its Social Agendas*. Chicago: University of Chicago Press, 2001.

Damon-Moore, Helen. *Magazines for the Millions: Gender and Commerce in the Ladies' Home Journal and the Saturday Evening Post*. Albany: SUNY, 1994.

Davis, Fred. *Fashion, Culture, and Identity*. Chicago: University of Chicago Press, 1994.

Davis, Linda H. *Onward and Upward: A Biography of Katharine S. White*. New York: Harper and Row, 1987.

Dayton, Dorothy. "Marriage or Career?" *Mademoiselle*, July 1935.

Dougherty, Philip H. "*The New Yorker* Loses Ground." *New York Times*, March 26, 1975.

Douglas, George H. *The Smart Magazines: 50 Years of Literary Revelry and*

High Jinks at Vanity Fair, The New Yorker, Life, Esquire, and The Smart Set. New York: Archon, 1991.

Editors of Vogue. Vogue's Book of Etiquette: Present-Day Customs of Social Intercourse with the Rules for Their Correct Observance. New York: Condé Nast Publications, 1924.

Eldred, Janet Carey. "Modern Fidelity." Sentimental Attachments: Essays, Creative Nonfiction, and Other Experiments in Composition. Portsmouth: Heinemann, 2005. 49–68.

Eldred, Janet Carey, and Peter Mortensen. Imagining Rhetoric: Composing Women of the Early United States. Pittsburgh: University of Pittsburgh Press, 2002.

———. "Reading Literacy Narratives." College English 54, no. 5 (1992): 512–39.

Entwistle, Joanne. The Fashioned Body: Fashion, Dress, and Modern Social Theory. Cambridge: Polity Press, 2000.

———. "Fashioning the Career Woman: Power Dressing as a Strategy of Consumption." All the World and Her Husband: Women and Consumption in the Twentieth Century. Eds. Margaret Andrews and Mary Talbot. London: Cassell, 2000. 224–38.

Felski, Rita. Literature after Feminism. Chicago: University of Chicago Press, 2003.

Fenwick, Millicent. Vogue's Book of Etiquette: A Complete Guide to Traditional Forms and Modern Usage. New York: Simon and Schuster, 1948.

Ford, Corey. The Time of Laughter. New York: Little, Brown, 1967.

Friedan, Betty. The Feminine Mystique. New York: Norton, 1963.

Gere, Anne Ruggles. Intimate Practices: Literacy and Cultural Work in U.S. Women's Clubs, 1880–1920. Urbana: University of Illinois Press, 1997.

———. "Kitchen Tables and Rented Rooms: The Extracurriculum of Composition." CCC 45, no. 4 (1994): 75–92.

Gill, Brendan. Here at The New Yorker. 1975. New York: De Capo Press, 1997.

Gill, Sally. "And Now a Word About Sponsors: Advertising and Ethos in the Age of the Global Village." Rhetoric, the Polis, and the Global Village. Eds. C. Jan Swearigen and Dave Pruett. Mahweh: Psychology Press, 1999. 199–208.

Gough-Yates, Anna. Understanding Women's Magazines: Publishing, Markets, and Readerships. London: Routledge, 2003.

Gould, Bruce, and Beatrice Blackmar Gould. American Story. New York: Harper and Row, 1968.

Graff, Gerald, and Michael Warner. "Introduction." The Origins of Literary Studies in America: A Documentary Anthology. New York: Routledge, 1989. 1–14.

Grant, Jane. Ross, The New Yorker, and Me. New York: Reynal, 1968.

Grumbach, Doris. Extra Innings: A Memoir. New York: W. W. Norton and Company, 1993.

Hammer, Langdon. "Plath's Lives: Poetry, Professionalism, and the Culture of School." *Representations* 75 (Summer 2001): 61–88.

Harris, Sharon M., and Ellen Gruber Garvey, eds. *Blue Pencils & Hidden Hands: Women Editing Periodicals, 1830–1910.* Boston: Northeastern University Press, 2004.

Henry, Susan. "Gambling on a Magazine and a Marriage: Jane Grant, Harold Ross, and *The New Yorker.*" *Journalism History* 30, no. 2 (2004): 54–65.

———. "We Must Not Forget That We Are Dealing with a Woman." *Journalism History* 33, no. 3 (2007): 151–62.

Hess, John L. "Katherine White, Ex-Fiction Editor of *The New Yorker*, Is Dead at 84." *New York Times*, July 22, 1977.

Hobbs, Catherine. "Introduction." *Nineteenth-Century Women Learn to Write.* Charlottesville: University Press of Virginia, 1995. 1–33.

Hutchens, John K. Review of *The New Yorker. New York Herald Tribune Book Review* 2 June 1963: 1, 8.

Hyde, Michael J. *The Ethos of Rhetoric.* Foreword by Calvin O. Schrag. Columbia: University of South Carolina Press, 2004.

I. B. "The Genius for Banality." *Nation* 111, no. 2895 (December 29, 1920): 783–84.

Jarratt, Susan C., and Nedra Reynolds. "The Splitting Image: Contemporary Feminisms and the Ethics of Ethos." *Ethos: New Essays in Rhetorical and Cultural Theory.* Eds. James S. Baumlin and Tita French Baumlin. Dallas: Southern Methodist University Press, 1994.

Josephy, Helen. "I Don't Want to Play the Harp." *Mademoiselle*, April 1935–April 1937.

Johnson, Dennis Loy. "The Talk of the Rest of the Town." *MobyLives.* http://www.mobylives.com/NYer_survey.html.

Johnson, Nan. *Gender and Rhetorical Space in American Life, 1866–1910.* Carbondale: Southern Illinois University Press, 2002.

Kendall, Connie. "A Case Study in Metaphor: How K-12 Teachers Resist the Discourse of Crisis." Rhetoric Society of America Biennial Conference. Westin, Seattle. 25 May 2008. Roundtable.

Kessler-Harris, Alice. *In Pursuit of Equity: Women, Men, and the Quest for Economic Citizenship in Twentieth-Century America.* New York: Oxford University Press, 2001.

Klinkenborg, Verlyn. "The Point of Miss Gould's Pencil." *New York Times*, February 16, 2005. http://query.nytimes.com/gst/fullpage.html?res=9F06EED6123AF935A25751C0A9639C8B63.

Krabbendam, Hans. *The Model Man: A Life of Edward William Bok, 1863–1930.* Amsterdam: Rodopi, 2001.

Kramer, Dale. *Ross and The New Yorker.* New York: Doubleday, 1951.

Kreyling, Michael. *Author and Agent: Eudora Welty and Diarmuid Russell.* 1991. New York: Noonday, 1992.

Krim, Seymour. "Who's Afraid of The New Yorker Now?" Village Voice, November 8, 1962.

Kunkel, Thomas. Genius in Disguise. New York: Random House, 1997.

———. Letters from the Editor: The New Yorker's Harold Ross. New York: Modern Library, 2000.

"Ladies and Syphilis." Time, July 19, 1937.

Lady Editor: Careers for Women in Publishing. Coauthored by Marjorie Schuler, Ruth Adams Knight, and Muriel Fuller. New York: E. P. Dutton, 1941.

Lee, Harper. To Kill a Mockingbird. Philadelphia: J. B. Lipincott and Co., 1960.

LeFevre, Karen Burke. Invention as a Social Act. Carbondale: Southern Illinois University Press, 1987.

Lehmann-Haupt, Christopher. "A Swarm of Affectionate Bees." New York Times, February 10, 1975.

Leonard, John. "Fifty Years and All Grown Up." Review of Here at the New Yorker, by Brendan Gill. New York Times Book Review, February 16, 1975.

Long, Lois. "And in New York——." New Yorker, May 29, 1937.

Mademoiselle Prize Stories: Twenty-Five Years 1951–1975. New York: M. Evans and Company, Inc., 1976.

Marek, Jayne. Women Editing Modernism: "Little" Magazines and Literary History. Lexington: University of Kentucky Press, 1996.

Mastrangelo, Lisa. "Learning from the Past: Rhetoric, Composition, and Debate at Mount Holyoke College." Rhetoric Review 18, no. 1 (1999): 46–64.

Mattingly, Carol. Appropriate[ing] Dress: Women's Rhetorical Style in Nineteenth-Century America. Carbondale: Southern Illinois University Press, 2002.

Mayes, Herbert Raymond. The Magazine Maze: A Prejudiced Perspective. New York: Doubleday, 1980.

McCracken, Ellen. Decoding Women's Magazines: From Mademoiselle to Ms. New York: Palgrave Macmillan, 1992.

McDonald, Gail. Learning to Be Modern: Pound, Eliot, and the American University. New York: Oxford University Press, 1993.

Michaels, Lisa. Review of New York Mosaic. Salon, October 23, 1997. http://www.salon.com/books/sneaks/1997/10/23review.html.

Mehta, Ved. Remembering Mr. Shawn's New Yorker: The Invisible Art of Editing. New York: Overlook, 1998.

Merrick, Beverly G. "Jane Grant, The New Yorker, and Ross: A Lucy Stoner Practices Her Own Style of Journalism." The Serials Librarian 37, no. 2 (1999): 59–88.

Meyers, D. G. The Elephants Teach: Creative Writing Since 1880. New York: Prentice Hall, 1995.

Meyerowitz, Joanne, ed. *Not June Cleaver: Women and Gender in Postwar America, 1945–1960*. Philadelphia: Temple University Press, 1994.

Mortensen, Peter. "Reading Material." *Written Communication* 18, no. 4 (2001): 395–440.

Moskowitz, Eva. "'It's Good to Blow Your Top': Women's Magazines and the Discourse of Discontent, 1945–1965." *Journal of Women's History* 8, no. 3 (1996): 66–97.

"Mother Danforth's Story." *Time*, March 28, 1949. http://www.time.com/ time/magazine/article/0,9171,799967,00.html

Nafisi, Azar. *Reading Lolita in Tehran*. New York: Random House, 2003.

National Register of Historic Places. "Barbizon Hotel for Women." *Places Where Women Made History: A National Register of Historic Places Travel Itinerary*. http://www.cr.nps.gov/nr/travel/pwwmh/ny25.htm.

Nast, Condé. "Class Publications." *Merchants' and Manufacturers' Journal*, 1913.

Nerney, Brian James. "Katharine S. White, 'New Yorker' Editor: Her Influence on 'The New Yorker' and on American Life." Diss. University of Minnesota, 1982.

Okker, Patricia. *Our Sister Editors: Sarah J. Hale and the Tradition of Nineteenth-Century America*. Athens: University of Georgia Press, 1995.

Palmer, Gretta. "Marriage Is a Career." *Mademoiselle*, May 1938.

Patton, Frances Gray. *Good Morning, Miss Dove*. New York: Dodd and Mead, 1954.

———. "As Man to Man." *New Yorker*, June 21, 1958.

Plimpton, George A., and Frank H. Crowther. "E. B. White, The Art of the Essay No. 1." *Paris Review* 48 (Fall 1969): 65–88.

Poore, Charles. "Books of the Times." *New York Times*, October 28, 1954.

Radway, Janice A. *A Feeling for Books: The Book-of-the-Month Club, Literary Taste, and Middle-Class Desire*. Chapel Hill: University of North Carolina Press, 1997.

Rayner, William P. *Wise Women: Singular Lives That Shaped Our Century*. New York: St. Martin's, 1983.

Remnick, David. "Postscript: Miss Gould." *New Yorker*, February 28, 2005. http://www.newyorker.com/archive/2005/02/28/050228ta_ talk_remnick.

Reneham, Edward J., Jr. "Why Robber Barons Self-Publish." *MobyLives*. July 23, 2005. http://www.mobylives.com/Renehan.html.

Review of *Lady Editor*. *Journal of Home Economics* 33, no. 10 (December 1941): 746–47.

Reynolds, Tom. "Selling College Literacy: The Mass-Market Magazine as Early 20th Century Literacy Sponsor." *American Periodicals* 15, no. 2 (2005): 163–77.

Robbins, Sarah. *Managing Motherhood, Mothering America: Women's Narratives on Reading and Writing in the Nineteenth Century*. Pittsburgh: University of Pittsburgh Press, 2004.

Roethke, Theodore. *Words for the Wind: The Collected Verse of Theodore Roethke*. Bloomington: Indiana University Press, 1961.

Rooks, Noliwe M. *Ladies' Pages: African American Women's Magazines and the Culture That Made Them*. New Brunswick: Rutgers University Press, 2004.

Rowlands, Penelope. *A Dash of Daring: Carmel Snow and Her Life in Fashion, Art, and Letters*. New York: Atria, 2005.

Royster, Jacqueline Jones. "Sarah's Story: Making a Place for Historical Ethnography in Rhetorical Studies." *Rhetoric, the Polis, and the Global Village*. Eds. C. Jan Swearingen and Dave Pruett. Mahwah: Psychology Press, 1999. 39–52.

Rowley, Hazel. "The Shadow of the White Woman: Richard Wright and the Book-of-the-Month Club." *Partisan Review* 66, no. 4 (1999): 625–34.

Rubin, Joan Shelley. *The Making of Middlebrow Culture*. Chapel Hill: University of North Carolina Press, 1992.

Sanders, Jack, and Hersam Acorn Newspapers. "Betsy Talbot Blackwell: Magazine Refashioner." *Notable Ridgefielders: A Who's Who of People Who Made News in 20th Century Ridgefield*. http://jackfsanders.tripod.com/A-F.htm.

Scanlon, Jennifer. *Inarticulate Longings: The* Ladies' Home Journal, *Gender, and the Promises of Consumer Culture*. New York: Routledge, 1999.

Scott, Janny. "On the Trail of Missing Antecedents (and Meaning)." *New York Times*, February 4, 1998. http://www.nytimes.com/1998/02/04/arts/on-the-trail-of-missing-antecedents-and-meaning.html.

Scribner, Sylvia. "Literacy in Three Metaphors." *American Journal of Education* 93, no. 1 (1984): 6–21.

Seebohm, Caroline. *The Man Who Was Vogue: The Life and Times of Condé Nast*. New York: Viking, 1982.

Shipman, George. "Introduction." *Jane Grant, 'The New Yorker,' and the Oregon Legacy of a Twentieth-Century Feminist*. University of Oregon Libraries Special Collections. http://libweb.uoregon.edu/ec/exhibits/janegrant/

Snow, Carmel, with Mary Louise Aswell. *The World of Carmel Snow*. New York: McGraw-Hill, 1962.

Steinberg, Salme Harju. *Reformer in the Marketplace: Edward W. Bok and* The Ladies' Home Journal. Baton Rouge: Louisiana State University Press, 1979.

Strunk, William, Jr., and E. B. White. *The Elements of Style*. 4th ed. New York: Longman, 1999.

Subramanian, Alexandra. *Katherine Anne Porter and Her Publishers*. Diss. College of William and Mary, 2001.

Thomas, M. Carey. "The Curriculum of the Women's College." *Journal of the Association of Collegiate Alumnae* 10 (May 1917): 585–91.

Thurber, James. *The Years with Ross*. 1962. New York: Harper Perennial Modern Classics, 2000.

Tippins, Sherrill. *February House: The Story of W. H. Auden, Carson McCull-ers, Jane and Paul Bowles, Benjamin Britten, and Gypsy Rose Lee, Under One Roof in Brooklyn*. New York: Mariner, 2006.

Travis, Trysh. "What We Talk About When We Talk About *The New Yorker*." *Book History* 3 (2000): 253–85.

Townsend, R. D. Review of *The Americanization of Edward Bok*. *Outlook* 126 (September–December 1920): 514–15.

Vidal, Gore. *The Last Empire: Essays 1992–2000*. New York: Vintage, 2002.

Wade, Betsy. "Eleanor Gould Packard, 87, Editor Who Oversaw the *New Yorker*'s Prose, Dies." *New York Times*, February 15, 2005. http://www.nytimes.com/2005/02/15/business/media/15gould.html.

White, E. B. *Poems and Sketches of E. B. White*. New York: Harper and Row, 1981.

Wilson, Edmund. Review of *Do I Wake or Sleep*. *New Yorker*, October 26, 1946.

Winship, Janice. *Inside Women's Magazines*. London: Pandora, 1987.

Witchel, Alex. "After 'The Bell Jar,' Life Went On." *New York Times*, June 22, 2003.

Wolfe, Tom. *Hooking Up*. New York: Farrar, Straus and Giroux (Picador), 2000.

Yagoda, Ben. *About Town: The New Yorker and the World It Made*. New York: Scribner and De Capo, 2000.

Young, Edward. *Conjectures on Original Composition*. 1759. Leeds: Scholar Press, 1966.

Young, Morris. *Minor Re/Visions: Asian American Literacy Narratives as a Rhetoric of Citizenship*. Carbondale: Southern Illinois University Press, 2004.

INDEX